CONSTRUCTING PUBLIC OPINION

*How Political Elites Do What They Like
and Why We Seem to Go Along with It*

Justin Lewis

COLUMBIA UNIVERSITY PRESS

NEW YORK

Columbia University Press
Publishers Since 1893
New York   Chichester, West Sussex

Copyright © 2001 Columbia University Press

Library of Congress Cataloging-in-Publication Data

Lewis, Justin, 1958–
    Constructing public opinion : how political elites do what they like and why we
    seem to go along with it / Justin Lewis.
        p. cm.
    Includes bibliographical references and index.
    ISBN 0–231–11766–3 (cloth) — ISBN 0–231–11767–1 (paper)
        1. Public opinion   2. Public opinion—United States   3. Mass media and public
    opinion—United States   4. Political psychology—United States   I. Title.

HM1236 .L48 2001
303.3'8—dc21

                                                                                    00–063924

Casebound editions of Columbia University Press books are printed on permanent and
durable acid-free paper.
Printed in the United States of America
c 10 9 8 7 6 5 4 3 2 1
p 10 9 8 7 6 5 4 3 2 1

CONTENTS

ACKNOWLEDGMENTS

Earlier versions of chapters three and eight of this book were published in *Critical Studies in Mass Communication* and the *International Journal of Cultural Studies*. My thanks to those journals for allowing me to float sections of these pieces in the public domain.

A more personal thanks to Michael Morgan, who was a coconspirator on three of the surveys described in the second half of the book. Much of the data analysis used in chapters seven and eight are developments from this collaborative work. I am also grateful to Michael in a broader sense for helping to inspire a project in which quantitative data can be used for the analysis of hegemony, and whereby power and social relations become the context for interpretation rather than merely an empirical by-product.

In the same vein, I am grateful to Sut Jhally and Andy Ruddock, who also collaborated on some of these surveys, and who shared a sense that cultural studies and quantitative data were not necessarily incompatible. Thanks also to Kirsten Zirkel for her work on the 1992 student survey, and to Mike Hinkley for his help in coding the TV coverage of polls discussed in chapter three.

I am indebted to Lisa Henderson, who gave me the benefit of her perspicacious and critical insight in reviewing the manuscript. Thanks also to Ann Miller, my editor at Columbia University Press, to Godwin Chu for his help on the manuscript, and to my anonymous reviewers, whoever they may be. Any flaws in this book are entirely their fault and have absolutely nothing to do with me.

INTRODUCTION

Let me begin with a confession. As an academic, I have spent a great deal of time and energy exploring what people think and why. Although I have used quantitative surveys periodically during the past fifteen years, I have always found qualitative forms of research more illuminating. Opinion surveys, it seemed to me, were like the faces plastered on the side of advertising billboards—obvious and yet enigmatic, loud without depth. The expression on each face was a tiny moment in someone's life, chosen by someone else as a form of demonstration or display. If the three-dimensional complexity of social life could never be captured entirely, it was, I have always felt, much more likely to reveal itself in interactions—in looser conversations whose parameters were not so rigidly imposed by researchers.

And yet—and this is the confession—I have always been an ardent consumer of polls. For all my suspicion of them as a form of inquiry or social description, there was always a lingering sense of their importance. My efforts to turn that lingering sense into something more tangible gradually became a preoccupation, a development of my interest in audiences and media and political power rather than a tangential diversion. Hence this book is an attempt to understand what polls are in a social and cultural sense, what they signify about ideology, and how they might be used to question rather than validate the many inequities of our age.

This book is about the construction of public opinion, in two different senses. Part one deals with how public opinion is constructed through the technology of polling and by the news media that report and interpret polls. Part one is therefore concerned with how public opinion is *represented*. Part two looks at the roles played by the media and by political elites in shaping public opinion—as it is signified through polls. My main concern here is to explore the poll as a form of approbation (or lack thereof) for elite political agendas—and to therefore look at significant questions of consent and resistance to those ideologies pursued by political and economic elites.

Part one begins by retracing some of the arguments about the merits and flaws of surveys as a form of social science. Within the academy, polls and surveys are either revered as objective tools that bring science into the social or despised as crude and manipulative technologies that tell us little about the way people actually experience the world. Chapter one considers polls as expressions that mark this intellectual divide and their significance beyond that division. My argument is that the quantitative forms of inquiry that polls embody are important and necessary, but that their significance can be understood only if we appreciate the limits and the constructed nature of survey and polling technologies. Polls may not produce objective, scientific knowledge, but they produce *something*—and we need to consider what that something might tell us. Or to put it another way, polls are significant precisely *because* they are ideological rather than "scientific" instruments. They therefore tell us something about contemporary ideologies.

Chapter two develops this point, arguing that the notion of public opinion has always involved including some people and excluding others, and that despite the claim that polls represent everyone, the "public opinions" they construct exclude a range of ideas or populations. They are, in this sense, ideological formations with particular inferences. They can therefore be considered not merely as a tool of social science but *as a cultural form*.

Whatever we think of them, surveys are an increasingly significant form of representation in our culture. But, as with other cultural forms, we need to assess not so much their authenticity but their significance. Television, for example, is not an authentic representation of the world, but because television supplies images and frameworks that inform social life, those representations *matter* a great deal. Opinion polls may be a less ubiquitous technology, but they are deeply implicated in the structure of contemporary politics. My point is not that politics is now poll-driven—politicians are as likely to ignore polls as they are to use them—but simply that polls play a significant role in constructing an understanding of what people think and what they want.

The construction of public opinion therefore involves an analysis of the way public opinion is signified. This takes place through two different mediums: survey technology and media technology. These two moments in the representation of hearts and minds are both creative (the opinion pollster and the reporter who covers the results of polls are both authors of various kinds, even while they claim to be mere messengers) as well as constraining. This does not mean, however, that these two moments are equivalent.

Chapter three explores the ways in which media representations *limit* the meaning of public opinion polls, so that the range of public opinions appears to be in tune with the probusiness, center-right spectrum of political elites. My argument here is that for all their adherence to elite concerns, opinion surveys paint a much more progressive, left-leaning picture of popular opinion than we would imagine from dominant media representations. It is the media rather than pollsters that sustain the impression that most people are in sync with a governing class that excludes the political left—an image of a moderate-to-conservative America that forms part of conventional wisdom at home and abroad. Public opinion is thereby molded—as a form of representation—in ways that render it compatible with the views of the powerful, and chapter three explores in detail some of the mechanisms by which this takes place.

Part two deals with the construction of public opinion in its second sense: the ways in which media shape responses to survey questionnaires. Chapter four thus begins by reviewing the evidence on media influence from a variety of research traditions. In order to make sense of this research, I argue that we need to distinguish between different forms of influence. This, in turn, requires us to understand the very different manifestations of what might be loosely called "public opinion" rather than search for an authentic space in which public opinions are formed or expressed. Thus, for example, agenda-setting research may tell us very little about the way in which people talk about politics, but it tells us a great deal about what informs certain kinds of responses to public opinion questionnaires. In short, since there are many spaces in which public opinion can be defined and articulated, the nature of media influence will depend upon where we look for it.

Chapter four then proceeds to lay out the central framework for the analyses that follow. Overall, research suggests that media influence is widespread but not absolute or inexorable. This requires us to understand the precise forms that media influence takes, the moments of presence and absence that contribute to the complexity of ideological formations. My argument is that the media's ability to encourage certain ways of responding to public opinion polls is most clearly identifiable in *specific discursive moments*. While these moments are limited, they are nonetheless instrumental in maintaining a degree of public acquiescence to the procorporate, center-right hegemony in U.S. politics. Precisely *how* this happens is the subject of the rest of the book.

Chapter five takes a brief step back to develop the framework established in chapter four, arguing that if we are to explore media influence, a narrow focus on public opinions is epistemologically untenable. While we may be able to analytically distinguish opinions from other forms of discourse, this distinction collapses when we try to explore how and why people understand the world in particular ways. In short, the world of opinion is formed from interconnections of knowledge, beliefs, and assumptions. In this context, media influence is unlikely to involve an overt transfer of opinions from media discourse to public expression. Instead, we have a much more complex picture in which the media create, develop, or sustain clusters of information—a context in which some opinions are more plausible than others.

The relationship between media representations and public opinion polls is complicated by a kind of discursive misfit. In short, the bulk of media content is descriptive rather than *overtly* evaluative or propagandist, while polls tend to focus less on the way people describe the world and more on their value judgments, or "opinions." These are different levels of discourse, and one does not translate simply into the other. If the general drift of media coverage describes the world in ways that make some value judgments more plausible than others, opinion polls merely offer clues to some of the consequences of these descriptions. They don't tell us *why* some opinions seem more appealing than others. Or, to put it another way, they tell us very little about the discursive structures on which opinions depend.

Chapter five then explores the relationship between knowledge and opinion, and, in so doing, considers the issue of the "uninformed" or "misinformed" citizen. I argue against two dominant models of understanding political knowledge or ignorance: the notion that more knowledge is necessarily good, and the rather different thesis that accepts low levels of knowledge but argues that most people are nonetheless able to think rationally. Both notions fail to confront the *ideological* nature of information. Whether we have more or less of it, information is neither neutral nor necessarily benign, and if we are to understand the nature of contemporary ideologies—and the opinions that spring from them—we must understand what people learn from the media in its broadest sense.

Chapter six proceeds to look at what surveys can tell us about that more descriptive realm. This draws upon not only polling data but a body of survey work conducted by myself and with colleagues over the past eight years, sur-

veys that explore popular assumptions about society and the ideological outcomes of those assumptions. What emerges from this analysis is a series of
powerful but limited hegemonic processes. While the media—particularly the
news media—convey the world in ways that tend to favor the interests of those
with power (notably, government and business elites), there is evidence of a
failure (sometimes widespread, sometimes intermittent) to achieve popular
consent for what used to be called "dominant ideologies." And yet, the informational structure of media coverage does have, in political terms, a profound
influence on popular opinion at *certain strategic moments*. What this ideological process amounts to is less government by consent than government
through occasions of acquiescence. Thus, for example, the broad thrust of the
neoliberal economic policies pursued by the U.S. and other governments since
the early 1980s have generally *not* been embraced by poll respondents.
Similarly, there is only tepid support for the form of procorporate, highly interventionist foreign policy that guides most U.S. administrations. In both cases,
support for these policies in public opinion polls is demonstrable in only limited moments under particular discursive conditions, and it is in creating or
sustaining these conditions that media influence is most profound.

Two important instances of this process are examined in the last two chapters. Chapter seven looks at the limited but important ways in which ideological support for (or, in this case, lack of resistance to) the U.S. military industrial complex is sustained in the absence of a global enemy. Again, a comprehensive reading of public opinion polls suggests that military spending is routinely
regarded by most people as a much lower priority than areas like education or
the environment. I argue that support for continued high levels of spending in
the post–cold war era exists only as far as most people tend to underestimate the
size of the military budget, and, more insidiously, in the form of support for
strategic interventions that appear to demonstrate we live in a dangerous world.
These interventions are predicated on narratives that highlight certain facts and
exclude others. Indeed, the success of U.S. leaders in so doing suggests that one
of the most effective ways to generate indirect political support for military
spending is by fighting wars against a select group of "dangerous dictators."

Chapter eight considers the more general question of ideological support
for a system of governance that *does not* reflect public opinion. The chapter
begins with the premise that the political economy of the electoral and legislative processes in the United States pushes government to reflect the views of
those with wealth and power—notably, the business sector. While these interests are not without nuance, the general direction of this pressure is to push
government to the right. Thus we see that on a whole range of issues public

opinion appears to be more progressive than the officials elected to represent it. How can such a lack of ideological syncronicity be sustained? The answer involves a very particular form of hegemony, one that often fails to win consent for many aspects of a procorporate ideological program but that engenders just enough support for what Tony Bennett refers to as the political rationale of the system as a whole (Bennett 1995), thereby sustaining the system without too much pressure for democratic reform. The media's role in this process is pivotal, and in this chapter I outline the nature of a media framework in which the views of political elites are represented as being in broad alignment with the views of the people.

My approach, throughout, is interdisciplinary, drawing from work in sociology, political science, mass communications, and cultural studies, although it is only in the last two of these that I can claim any kind of expertise. Like many such efforts, it runs the risk of irritating those who approach some of the questions raised here from within specific disciplines. Political scientists, for example, may see this book as an audacious—and at times, disrespectful—intrusion into well-laid-out territory, while those within cultural studies may find it skips rather too lightly through some complex epistemological questions. At the very least (although this book was not written with this intent) the arguments pursued here offer opportunities for some to peer into different worlds, even if they don't much care for what they see.

The main purpose of this book, however, is not to build interdisciplinary bridges but to address some fundamental and practical political questions in ways that implicate certain strategies for building a popular left-wing politics. Some may see this motivation as suspect for a work of scholarship; I take the opposite view. This is not only because none of us stands outside ideology. It is because, for me, to be driven by a serious political commitment requires using forms of analysis that apply to the world as it is, not the world as we would like it to be. Restricting oneself to evidence that is theoretically convenient only diminishes the political utility of a piece of work. In brief, I hope those on the left will find this book useful. This is not to say that the analysis offered here might not be just as useful for those on the right, but I am confident that they are too preoccupied with running the world to pay any attention to the likes of me.

Throughout the book, I refer to myriad polls and polling trends gathered from a range of sources. This has been facilitated by the considerable amount of data now available online. I have found two Web sites particularly useful in this regard: the National Election Studies site at the University of Michigan and the Pew Research Center site. They are splendid resources—just so long as we do not expect them to interpret themselves.

CONSTRUCTING PUBLIC OPINION

PART ONE

THE REPRESENTATION OF PUBLIC OPINION

CHAPTER 1

WHY NUMBERS MATTER AND WHY WE SHOULD BE SUSPICIOUS OF THEM

In Norton Juster's *The Phantom Tollbooth*, there are two competing kingdoms: Dictionopolis, the kingdom of words, and Digitopolis, the kingdom of numbers. The two kingdoms are divided by a philosophical squabble. Words, according to King Azaz of Dictionopolis, are indisputably more important than numbers. Numbers, argues the Mathemagician of Digitopolis, are measurably more significant than words. The dispute is, of course, irresolvable: a fact that only feeds the intransigence of the two positions.

If this argument has not exactly been replicated in the weightier tomes of academic writing, there are moments when it is possible to catch a whiff of a similar kind of territorial obduracy. Opinion polls—and quantitative surveys in general—are mechanisms for turning words into numbers. For some, this mechanism is one of the fundamental tools of social science, the apotheosis of an enlightenment project in which hypotheses about social structures can be measured, evaluated, proved, or invalidated. It is a mechanism that allows, as Melvin DeFleur puts it, "the accepted epistemology for research" to be "defined by the rules of natural science" (DeFleur 1998, 92). For the statistically well-equipped, Herbert Kritzer points out, "data are fun" (Kritzer 1996, 26). Indeed, Kritzer ingeniously borrows Roland Barthes's exposition of free-floating literary criticism (Barthes 1975) to write about "the pleasures of the statistical text"—one that is a creature of context and interpretation, both confirming and revealing.

For others, the process of reducing words to numbers is like sucking the life out of language, a remorseless exercise in Gradgrindery whose limited world-view masquerades as objectivity and universal truth. The pollster is like Juster's Mathemagician, transforming the complexities of social life into numbers on a page, into a form where they can be manipulated. As Andrew Ruddock puts it, those who reject a quantitative approach see surveys as "blunt objects bludgeoning heterogeneity out of audiences and rendering them amenable to the control of politicians and marketing executives" (Ruddock 1998, 116).

There are many fault lines that divide academics in the social sciences and the humanities, but the use of quantitative surveys as a way of probing what, how, and why people think is perhaps one of the most pervasive. Those who embrace the technology of surveys find themselves exasperated by social scientists who make claims without recourse to systematic forms of evidence. For social scientists like DeFleur, the quantitative survey is the only apparatus that allows us to progress. "The milestones of the future," he writes, "will be products of carefully conducted scientific research, as opposed to qualitative writings or ideological criticism" (DeFleur 1998, 94). Others reject these forms of quantification, arguing that you do not understand something as complex as language by turning into something neat and quantifiable, or by turning complex human beings into what Ien Ang calls "taxonomic collectives" (Ang 1991). In the corridors of academe, the two camps can be singularly less polite, adopting monikers for one another that display anything from mockery to withering contempt.

The opinion survey, in other words, is a contested object, one that is both revered and reviled. It is either the quintessential scientific tool of a democratic age or the discarded machinery of a bygone intellectual era. This is partly because, as Susan Herbst points out, while the act of quantification is regarded by some as a scientific process, it is also a symbolic one (Herbst 1993a). Changing words into numbers is, in short, a semiotic act. It takes soft, rambling, shambling views of the world and turns them into hard figures and percentages. In so doing, what was once meandering and imprecise is pushed into a world governed by a series of inarguable mathematical truths. Humanity becomes science. And in a culture where science is often elevated above the petty squabbles of history and ideology, this gives the pollster a degree of power and authority. The argument about the use of quantitative surveys is, in this sense, an argument about the use—or abuse—of power.

If the use of quantitative surveys is a symbolic bid for authority, the public opinion poll is especially fraught with notions of power. Its subject, after all, is the theoretical basis for political legitimacy in a modern democracy. In a system in which politicians are supposed to be the public's representatives, the power to define and interpret public opinion is paramount. The debate about public opinion polls is therefore an issue of political legitimacy, a matter of conferring upon representatives the right to govern in the public's name. The long-term stakes could scarcely be higher.

For many on the nonquantitative side of the academic divide, the opinion poll is derided as the epitome of empiricist social science, a clumsy old technology that cranks and creaks its way toward untenable, simple-minded conclusions. Dismissals are usually made in the short-hand language of social theory: quantitative survey work is described as being mired in functionalist, empiricist, and positivist views of the world. In plainer language, there are two broad thrusts to the criticism of polling and quantitative surveys: the failure of pollsters to see the "big picture" and the crudity of the method—criticisms I shall elaborate on shortly.

The purpose of this chapter is not to come down on one side or the other or to offer some form of compromise. My argument—and the premise of this book—is that the process of enumeration is an important (and in many instances, inevitable) part of any study of culture and society, but that enumerative forms—such as the opinion survey—have specific limits and operate in ideological contexts that give meaning to those limits. To interpret poll responses therefore requires an understanding of the constrained, ideological conditions in which they are produced.

The Value of Numbers

Although few academics would admit it, the nature of the divide between those who rely on numbers and those who don't often becomes territorial, where membership on one side or the other is often less a matter of rigorous analysis than a product of simpler preferences. As Kritzer writes: "The debates that surround methodological choices are important, but they often are specious. Most analysts make their broad methodological choices based on what they like doing" (Kritzer 1996, 25). Regardless of the origin of one's position, both sides have often focused more on the egregious aspects of the other rather than on their more careful or incisive moments. If polling has its limits, so too do some of its critics—many of whom feel that the opinion poll literature is so full of erroneous assumptions that it is of little interest.

My own background, for example, is influenced by cultural studies, which, like other fields of poststructuralist inquiry, has always maintained a strong suspicion of quantitative research. When empirical work has been done, less intrusive, more qualitative methods—such as the focus group interview or more ethnographic forms of inquiry—are invariably preferred (e.g., Morley 1980, 1986, 1992; Radway 1984; Ang 1985; Hodge and Tripp 1986; Corner, Richardson, and Fenton 1990; Lewis 1991; Press 1991; Jhally and Lewis 1992; Heide 1995; Tulloch and Jenkins 1995; McKinley 1997). Qualitative research imposes frameworks and categories upon its subjects, but it waits longer before doing so, allowing people more time to speak in their own way. Rather than turning words into numbers, words are turned into other words. In this qualitative milieu, quantitative surveys of thought and opinion have been out of fashion for so long that they have, for many, been consigned to a methodological junkyard. The technology lies abandoned, out of sight and out of mind.

For those who are used to dealing in words rather than numbers, the very notion of reducing one to the other is to lose the infinite complexity of language. If qualitative methods are, like polls, a kind of intervention into the social world rather than an innocent means of reflection, they nevertheless retain something of that world's discursive form.

While a preference for qualitative form is often well conceived and fruitful, the lingering suspicion of numerical data has, I think, degenerated into habit. It is as if the argument with these methodologies was so comprehensively settled that one can be spared the time and effort of any further thought on the subject. But more than this, survey-generated statistics are neglected partly because of how they have traditionally been used, partly because of *what they have come to signify*. Favored by empiricists and positivists—people who believe an objective world will simply reveal itself in columns and percentages—the honest toil of number-crunching is interpreted as a signifier of empiricism itself, dismissed with little more than the patronizing wave of a hand.

The symbolic power of numbers to connote science and scientific rigor is inverted on this critical terrain: numbers are seen to symbolize a narrow, controlling view of the world, an arrogant, anal-retentive, and characteristically male approach to social science. Thus the term "number cruncher," with its connotations of empty-headed manual labor, becomes a pejorative term. Since many of the characterizations in the disputes between practitioners of quantitative and qualitative methods are symbolic, it is worth noting the class-bound snobbery in this dismissal—one that connotes a stand by an educated class against philistine incursion.

More importantly, we have to acknowledge that the moment we begin the process of sorting and categorizing qualitative data, we are treading, ever so lightly, into the world of numbers. This is necessarily so. As Andrew Ruddock writes, "The very notion of culture depends on the relative coherence of meaning within a given society," and that while understanding difference is integral to any sophisticated analysis of media and audiences, "so too is the recognition that the possibilities for difference are not boundless" (Ruddock 1998, 122) or chaotic.

Qualitative audience research, for example, is full of inferences about the wider applicability of particular cases. It suggests how certain people understand TV programs, films, or other cultural forms—not always or absolutely or to the nearest percentage point, but in the general run of things. And if a critical reading of a text is written as cultural (rather than purely literary) criticism, it implies a quantitative presence of that reading in contemporary culture. We may not be able to enumerate it, but in describing its presence we assume that it is, in some measure, significant or quantifiable. We assume that it counts.

It is difficult to discuss political power without, at some point, implicating majorities within civil society. We might prefer to gloss over the nitty gritty, arithmetic aspects of these implications, but they still lurk, operational but unspoken, beneath the tentative conclusions of qualitative research. Underlying discussions of resistance, dominance, or the significance of media are enumerative questions of space and place. As Stromer-Galley and Schiappa argue, a great deal of the work that has gone on within the more qualitative traditions of textual or rhetorical criticism has made implicit claims about the way media texts are understood—what they call "audience conjectures." The fact that "only a handful provided evidence for such claims" (Stromer-Galley and Schiappa 1998, 34) may grant them a degree of poetic license, but it does not free them from evidentiary burdens, which, in turn, forces them to consider quantities as well as qualities.

If quantitative surveys (particularly those carried out by the television and marketing industries) tend to reduce citizens or television viewers to crude typologies, or else forget that the production of social science is itself a discursive enterprise, it is partly a function of design, partly of interpretation. The general technology of data production does not automatically prescribe or determine the meaning of the data. And although the act of counting is not theoretically innocent—we must categorize before we can count—it implies a process integral to social science. Most forms of social science are dependent upon categories and typicalities. Educational levels, race, income, sexuality, or gender may be constructions, but it is difficult to talk about society or history without them (Christians and Carey 1989).

Similarly, to the argument that "public opinion" itself is partly a construction of the person who defines and describes it, one might respond with: so what? All forms of social categorization—such as race or class—can be seen as constructions. This does not mean that those constructions do not refer to real practices and real objects—or even that those constructions are not meaningful in people's lives. What is important is how those constructions are used and how they relate to people and practices.

It is also apparent that many of those in qualitative fields are unaware of the volume of critical work by those closer to quantitative traditions. Contributions to the critical history of polling have come from various disciplines and perspectives; from political science, mass communications, sociology, and cultural studies—in short, from those who use quantitative methods to those who regard machines for turning words into numbers as inherently flawed. The overview that follows reflects this range of critical thinking. It is not, however, offered as the precursor to a rejection of the use of surveys but rather as a means for establishing the specific and limited ways in which those surveys might be useful.

THE LIMITS OF NUMBERS:
A CRITICAL HISTORY OF POLLING

Early opinion research—in the 1930s and 1940s—took place in an age of mass production and mass entertainment: everything, it seemed—from the sensibilities of art to the practicalities of science—had become almost infinitely reproducible. New philosophical and sociological conceptions were required to make sense of an emerging era of mechanized uniformity at a time when fascism and Stalinism raised troubling questions about the politics of propaganda and mass culture. These doubts were manifested in films like *Modern Times* and in the work of the Frankfurt School (e.g., Adorno and Horkheimer 1979; Benjamin 1985), Walter Lippmann (Lippmann 1922, 1925), and others.

The opinion survey was an appropriate tool with which to begin to make sense of the emergence of a mass society informed and entertained by mass media. In the early research on mass culture, public opinion was therefore conceived *as part of a social process*, a way to chart the meaning of an emerging mass culture and the power of mass media. James Beniger describes how the first issue of the journal *Public Opinion Quarterly* (published in January 1937) promoted the idea of using polling technology to examine the relationship between mass communication and mass opinion within the more general conception of a mass society (Beniger 1987).

The problems with the "mass culture" and early media effects traditions have been elaborated elsewhere (see, for example, Morley 1980; Radway 1986). Suffice it to say that early research in this field was methodologically limited (Lewis 1991), partly because it had a narrow conception of *how* media might be influential. Research in this tradition focused, for example, on overtly propagandist forms and on easily observable changes in behavior rather than more subtle or long-term shifts in views of the world; as a consequence, its findings were limited and inconclusive. According to Beniger, the comparative failure of the "mass society" and "effects" models to advance an understanding of the relationship between mass society and mass opinion meant that "sociologists and political scientists lost interest" and hence "the study of mass communication separated from that of public opinion" (Beniger 1987, 50).

Subsequently, the development of the representative survey method allowed a slippage to occur, so that public opinion came to be understood *as no more than* the aggregation of responses to survey questions. Once this slippage became institutionalized, public opinion tended to be portrayed as an empirical "fact" to be measured by polling rather than as a manifestation of social processes, like mass media consumption.

In this context, we might say that for all the flaws of the early mass communication approaches, they nonetheless involved a conception in which public opinion was seen—however crudely—*as part of a social process*. Public opinion was conceived, at least potentially, as a construction that may or may not be a product of ideological apparatuses (such as the media).

Once freed from the specters of "mass communication" and "mass society," public opinion research became something of an end in itself, a subdiscipline of political science. The dominant notion of public opinion polls that replaced the mass society conception was pseudoscientific and straightforwardly empiricist: *public opinion simply existed as an independent entity* to be gathered by neutral and objective experts. The socially constructed nature of public opinion surveys was implicitly denied by this empiricist model. Public opinion was simply *out there*, a set of facts to be collected and analyzed.

The move toward the study of public opinion in isolation—as a fact of political life—is in many ways an understandable one. If we see public opinion as a social construction—a product of a complex interplay of personal circumstances and ideological influences (such as the education system and the media)—it becomes a more difficult object to deal with. As a social construction, public opinion seems less authentic and, by definition, less independent.

Indeed, it is not immediately clear what we are measuring. Are we measuring the way people think, or the power of certain institutions to influence how we think? Does public opinion, in itself, mean anything at all, or is it merely the consequence of the larger forces that surround it?

The best known early challenge to this new science was published in 1948, when Herbert Blumer argued persuasively that polls do not so much represent public opinion as manufacture it. Public opinion, he argued, was something more than a column of percentages derived from precoded questionnaires. The instrument of measurement was thus being mistaken for the thing itself (Blumer 1948). Later, Habermas argued that these kinds of surveys were not an expression of democratic will but a substitute for it, since they curtailed the discursive conditions necessary for the development of ideas in the public realm (Habermas, 1974, 1989).

What Blumer and Habermas were objecting to, in different ways, was more than the problem of what is lost when words are turned into numbers. The machinery of polling was denying not only its own existence but the *nature of the process*. Even if one accepts polling as a scientific (rather than an ideological) process—like the use of heat to change water into steam—its purpose is to turn one thing into another. Once public opinion is defined as the raw material for opinion polls, the various techniques used for turning words into numbers disappear, so that the columns and percentages emerge as if they are unmediated expressions of public attitudes and desires.

The spread of poststructuralism in European universities broadened the gulf between sectors of the academy and the pollster. In the late 1970s, the French sociologist Pierre Bourdieu—who, unlike some of his contemporaries, uses quantitative data in his own research—issued one of the more comprehensive dismissals. "Public opinion," Bourdieu argued, "does not exist"—not, at least, in the pseudoscientific form of the opinion survey (Bourdieu 1979). So, for example, people who had no clearly identifiable opinion about an issue might nonetheless proffer one in response to a specific survey question. The survey is, in this sense, constructing public opinion rather than measuring it. Following Bourdieu, poststructuralist critics have seen polls as the mythic constructions of a modernist age, the products of a series of epistemological and methodological procedures whose factual appearance signifies a smug rationality.

While much has been written about issues and problems in the statistical and methodological machinery of opinion polling (see, for example, Asher 1998), these tend to be directed toward the perfection of a fairly traditional, "scientific" model of polling (see, for example, Traugott and Lavrakas, 1996).

Indeed, it could be argued that such work reifies the notion of the opinion poll as a rational, transparent technology. The more serious critiques, I would argue, are precisely those that acknowledge the discursive nature of the process, that turning words into numbers is not only a transformation but one that makes assumptions about the world of words. In this chapter I shall focus on three substantive critiques: the way in which polling engages with public discourse rather than simply channeling it; the limits of looking at "opinion" as a discrete category; and the question of who we might see as the "author" of public opinion research.

OPINION POLLS MANUFACTURE RATHER THAN RECORD RESPONSES

While polling advocates admire the precision of methodological tools like precoded survey questionnaires and statistical forms of verification, critics see them as blunt instruments, incapable of the sensitive exploration required to look at something as complex as public opinion. The precoded questionnaire is so tightly scripted that the pollster has defined public opinion before he or she has begun. Public opinion is, in this sense, seen largely as a product of the pollster's rather limited imagination.

It is well known in the opinion poll literature that disparity in responses can be generated by something as basic as question wording or by apparently innocuous information given by the interviewer (see Schuman and Presser 1981). As John Zaller writes, "Entirely trivial changes in questionnaire construction can easily produce 5 to 10 percentage point shifts in aggregate opinion, and occasionally double that" (Zaller 1992, 29). The questionnaire itself can also provide a framework that inclines respondents in different directions. Sussman (1986), for example, found that African American respondents were more likely to give negative evaluations of President Reagan if they were told they were taking part in a survey of black American attitudes—thereby triggering a specific discursive context (Reagan's treatment of the black community) in which Reagan was less likely to appear favorable. There are, however, two ways of interpreting this observation: we can see it either as a technical problem or, more profoundly, as an inevitable part of the process.

If we see question wording as merely a methodological problem, this implies that problems of bias might be overcome by the use of "neutral" or objective forms of questioning. And yet, while it may be possible to distinguish between more or less explicit forms of bias in question wording, to posit the notion of a neutral question or questionnaire is to deny the inherently intrusive nature of opinion polling. What do we conclude from Sussman's findings, for example? Is it more or less objective to remind respondents of their racial identity? There can never be a definitive answer to this, because, as William Gamson (1992) points out, opinions are always constructed in contexts, and part of that context in the opinion survey will be the survey itself.

So, for example, when the Boston polling agency Marttila and Kiley did a survey for the Anti-Defamation League in February 1991 (during the Gulf war), they asked two questions in order to gauge public attitudes toward the establishment of a Palestinian state. The first of these was phrased simply thus:

Do you favor or oppose giving the Palestinians a homeland of their own in the West Bank?

Asked in this way, the response was fairly decisive: 58 percent of the sample supported a Palestinian homeland, with only 20 percent opposed. A few questions later, the survey then asked the same question in a more specific informational context.

Many people feel that if the West Bank were under Palestinian control, Iraq or other enemies might be able to use it as a base for attacking Israel. With this in mind, which of these opinions about a Palestinian homeland is closer to yours:

The Palestinians should have a homeland on the West Bank, even if the risk to Israel's security cannot be completely eliminated, or The Palestinians should not be allowed to have a West Bank homeland because the risk to Israel's security can never be completely eliminated.

This form of questioning successfully transformed public opinion on the issue: 44 percent now supported a Palestinian homeland, and 41 percent opposed it. Public opinion had thus, apparently at least, shifted from being 3 to 1 in favor of a proposition to being almost evenly divided.

It could be argued that by introducing information on one side of the issue, the second question is biased in a way that the first is not. But this would miss a more general point: the shift occurs because opinions are not fixed and independently secured. In a certain context, the first question might be seen as structured to prefer a positive response: to say no without seeming unreasonable requires access to a very specific political discourse that most people are unable to easily reproduce. Indeed, since the pollster's clients are a campaigning group on one side of this issue, the questions are less intended to "measure" public opinion than to inform a discursive strategy to influence it. Both questions are therefore structured interventions into public discourse rather than independent verifications of it.

As Murray Edelman has pointed out, this is even the case with the use of phrases that appear neither evocative nor adjectival. Even an apparently innocuous phrase like "foreign policy," he argues, "excludes from crucial attention the ways in which domestic policy influences the outbreak and nature of war" (Edelman 1995b, 110). Similarly, the phrase "national defense" suggests a military designed to defend the nation rather than a military budget which, in the United States, is premised upon the defense of a pseudoempire (in the form of client or compliant states). People who think it is important to defend the United States from attack may be less enthusiastic about paying for a military budget based upon an ability to fight two simultaneous wars *outside* the U.S.— a distinction that is obscured by the term "national defense" (a point that will taken up again in chapter seven).

In later chapters, I discuss how some of the words that are commonly used in public opinion surveys become loaded with a particular set of ideological inferences—words like "welfare," "government," or "liberal." Indeed, part of the purpose of this book is to explore the ideological nature of contemporary political language, and to consider some of its origins. The words "welfare," "government," or "liberal" have all been implicated in specific ideological campaigns in which they become associated with other words—like "idleness," "waste," "inefficiency," or "excess"—so that they tend to signify within a cluster of negative terms. As Roland Barthes made clear, language is connotative and suggestive rather than neutral and flat, and even the apparently denotative language of opinion surveys is full of connotations (Barthes 1974). Moreover, Barthes would have argued, the *appearance* of denotation (language that is literal rather than evocative) in public opinion polls enhances their ideological power. Slippery metaphors come dressed up as facts.

Pierre Bourdieu argues that even if we pursue the ideal of "objective questioning," this is such a contrived form of discourse that it is difficult for people to recognize or situate themselves in relation to it. The idea of conversing using the carefully weighted interrogative of polling questionnaires is faintly comical—who has ever asked someone in the course of a conversation—"which of the following issues do you consider to be the most important?" In this sense, it is precisely the attempt at precision in surveys that makes them such an idiosyncratic form of discourse. "In other words," argues Bourdieu, "the opinion poll would be closer to reality if it totally violated the rules of objectivity and gave people the means to situate themselves as they really do in real practice"

(Bourdieu 1979, 127–8). It is as if opinion surveys purport to represent the public by speaking to them in another language.

This is not to devalue opinion surveys, it is simply to acknowledge that they are, in some form or other, a type of engagement with someone's world. The nature of the engagement will influence the nature of the response—this is the way language works. My own view of the questions in the Marttila and Kiley poll is to see them in the context of a discursive climate in which Arab groups in general and Palestinians in particular are portrayed in negative stereotypical terms (as inexplicably anti-Western or as terrorists—see, for example, Shaheen 1984). The initial positive response to a Palestinian homeland suggests that even if these stereotypes are present in people's minds, in most cases this does not constitute a powerful enough reason to oppose the Palestinian cause. Only when these stereotypes are articulated with a specific rationale can they be said to mobilize opinion—and even then in only 41 percent of cases. This suggests that a general discourse in support of a people's right to self-determination is powerfully entrenched, so much so that a great deal of ideological work is required to override it (a discussion explored further in chapter six).

The realization that polls actively engage with public opinion has caused some public opinion scholars to abandon the idea that polls are, in any simple sense, a reflection of independently constructed, rationally formed views (see, for example, Taylor and Fiske 1978; Zaller 1992). As Bourdieu points out, there is no neatly structured empirical world of opinions that the opinion poll then records. The opinion poll's function—for better or for worse—*is to structure opinions into forms measurable against elite political discourse.* Thus Wilson and Hodges (1991) have—following Bourdieu—questioned the traditional notion that opinions are fixed, discretely formed entities that we pluck from our mental files upon solicitation. In this vein, John Zaller has suggested that we abandon "the notion that individuals typically possess preformed attitudes that they simply reveal when asked to do so" (1992, 54)—to which we might add that even if we do have preformed attitudes, we tend not to reveal them simply.

The point here is not that polls are nothing but fabrications of a pollster's imagination, but that any form of investigation into the social world—from Freudian psychoanalysis to focus group responses to television programs—is also an intervention. While the responses we get may be limited or constrained, this does not make them meaningless or without value. We do, however, need to understand the limits and constraints of the information being generated.

Collapsing the Separation Between Knowledge and Opinion

Plato's distinction between *doxa* (opinion) and *episteme* (knowledge) sees the two realms as properties of two quite distinct practices. Knowledge comes from philosophy, while opinions are the more transitory expressions of everyday social life. In the social world where opinions are developed and constructed, the two are interwoven. Nonetheless, a distinction between knowledge and opinion is both meaningful and useful. Knowledge, or assumption, is verifiable in a way that opinion is not. This is *not* to invoke notions of universal or eternal truth, merely to assert that it is possible to use systems of truth and falsity to classify statements of knowledge. Opinions, on the other hand, are generally classified in political or moral terms.

But, while the two realms are distinct, they are not mutually exclusive. Statements of fact do exist independently of a political or moral realm, and opinions are informed by what we believe to be certain facts. Scientific claims may be evaluated by systems of truth/falsity, but they are also given value by political and economic conditions (i.e., those that serve governmental, institutional, or commercial interests). Indeed, facts themselves come inscribed within complex evaluative contexts in which statements of knowledge and opinion intermingle. In a useful example, Kuklinski and Quirk point out that the amount of money spent by the U.S. government on welfare may be verifiable, but it is difficult to articulate in a way that does not inflect certain meanings. Put in simply dollar terms—and hence measured in billions—the U.S. welfare budget may sound almost inconceivably large. Put as a percentage of the overall federal budget, however, it may sound fairly small and insignificant (Kuklinski and Quirk 1997). While the figures are verifiable facts, the moment we express them we enter into a discursive world full of inflection and meaning.

This fairly simple point about knowledge, value, and context is consistently obscured—not least by the ideology of serious news journalism that strenuously differentiates between facts and opinions (facts on the front page, opinions in the editorials). And yet the practice of political journalism—with its philosophical ideal of "objectivity"—simultaneously undermines this distinction, premised as it is upon the presentation of "both sides" of an issue with *little recourse to independent forms of verification.* Thus environmentalists present one set of facts, and corporate interests present another set of facts. The assiduous journalist records both *precisely because* he or she cannot make an easy distinction between fact and opinion. Indeed, journalists who systematically attempt to verify facts—to say which set of facts is more accurate, for example—runs the risk of being accused of abandoning their objectivity. Indeed, when journalists are asked to evaluate competing claims, they invariably fudge the issue by referring to instances of truth and veracity on both sides—a relativist cop-out of the most facile and predictable kind.

Journalism thus proclaims, with Platonic authority, to be in the business of *episteme*, while advancing a method that suggests no confidence in the existence of an independently factual realm. It could be argued that the popularity of opinion polls in news journalism occurs because they embody this contradiction. By turning words into numbers, they also take the world of opinion—the fickle *doxa* of the masses—and turn it into verifiable facts. This conceals three important points. First, as I have argued, it implies that opinion polling is an act of stenography—a recording of public statements—rather than a process of interpretation. Second, it focuses our attention on the *outcome* of social processes that construct opinion (including the act of polling) rather than the social processes themselves (thus the news media often talk about themselves, but rarely seriously consider their own role in the construction of public opinion). Third, by asking people about their opinions but not about their assumptions, it conceals the role information systems play in opinion formation.

By replicating—but never exploring—this distinction between knowledge and opinion, a great deal of public opinion research thereby conceals as much as it reveals. More recent research, however, has begun to question the relationship between knowledge of an issue and attitudes toward it. As Delli Carpini and Keeter (1992, 1996), point out, responses to polls depend upon an (unequal) distribution of knowledge, and their meaning—or lack thereof—is thus conditional. We need to understand what people know, in short, to make sense of what they think. This is not simply a call for more research, it signals an important move away from the long-standing empiricist distinction between knowledge and opinion—one encapsulated in Cohen's well-known maxim for agenda-setting research: the media "may not be successful in telling people what to think, but it is stunningly successful in telling [people] what to think about" (Cohen 1963, 13.). Indeed, more recent work in agenda-setting research has also begun to reconsider the split between knowledge and opinion as two independent categories (McCombs, Danielian, and Wanta 1995).

I take up the relationship between knowledge and opinion in the second half of the book. Suffice it to say, at this point, that there is an increasing realization among some of those working within the opinion or quantitative survey traditions that if we are to make sense of the opinions represented in polls, we need to explore the discursive conditions—the knowledge, assumptions, and forms of articulation—that make them possible and give them their meaning.

POLLING AND AUTHORSHIP

While dabbling in various notions of social construction, opinion research often operates in a social vacuum, looking at public opinion as an almost pregiven category (albeit one that may be "tainted" by such things as media influence) rather than something shaped and buffeted by a range of social forces. So, for example, when U.S. pollsters recorded high levels of public support for the bombing of Iraq in 1991 and 1998, such support was often presented as a straightforward instance of a functional democracy, a moment when the people and their representatives were in happy accord. Such conclusions are simplistic: support for the bombing of Iraq is not a spontaneous and independent public response but the product of various institutional forces. In this instance, public opinion cannot be understood without looking at the character of the agencies that influence and define it—by looking at, for example, the way the news media framed the issue and, in turn, by the pressures on the news media to construct a favorable view of the bombing.

The conventional view of opinion research is that it is a neutral technology. The poll is generally represented as a way to give the public a voice. The public, like the subject of a ghost-written autobiography, is granted a form of second-hand authorship. Pollsters merely use their expertise to express the public mind.

But if pollsters are ghostwriting, then their shadowy hands are opaque rather than transparent, so much so that we can observe a number of discernable features. As Siune and Kline (1975) point out, the manufacturers of polls are likely to be close, in a general ideological sense, to media professionals and political leaders. More recently, Salmon and Glasser (1995) have developed Habermas's approach to public opinion by characterizing polls as a form of consent (or lack thereof) in response to questions framed by elites rather than the representation of more substantive or discursive processes. Others have moved along a similar trajectory: following Foucault (1977), the mechanics of quantitative surveys are regarded as less an object of study than an exercise of power and control. So, for example, Ien Ang argues that the TV ratings system is less for finding out what people think about television than for defining audiences in the narrow terms of commercial television (Ang 1991). The ratings system does not tell us whether people are moved, inspired, enlightened, amused, or engaged by television programs; commercial television companies need to know little about their viewers other than whether they are watching. If the viability or significance of a television program is measured only in ratings, commercial television can claim to be giving people what they want without ever really asking them.

Lisbeth Lipari develops this point when she argues that polls often tell us more about the assumptions of the questioner than the respondent (Lipari 1996). If polls can be said to be authored, then the author might best be identified as the pollster rather than the public. In most opinion surveys, it is the questioner who establishes the framework and sets the parameters for each response: most of the ideological work has therefore been done before a single question is put. The respondent is merely asked to inhabit the questioner's world for a few fleeting moments and push various buttons (Democrat/Republican, Economy/Crime/Healthcare, Yes/No, etc.).

Yet, unlike some forms of cultural production, such as film or literature, any notion of authorship in mainstream polling is deeply suppressed. The technology of polling and the people who design and program that technology are seen as technocrats rather than cultural producers. Polls are, in this sense, like the news in which they appear: legitimacy is often seen as dependent upon transparency. The discourse of public opinion is thus constructed from a particular set of perspectives, while the process of polling is hidden behind the data it produces.

If polls are carried out in the public's name, members of the public are reluctant to make any proprietary claims. Thus, although media and polling professionals are comfortable identifying the public as the object being represented, members of the public often feel very little identification. Indeed, Susan Herbst's work reveals the poignant irony that people themselves feel alienated from — rather than represented by — the official discourse of "public opinion" (Herbst 1993b). Thus the most frequent popular criticism of polls is a matter of sampling, the idea that "they don't ask people like me." This is, on one level, an unfair criticism — questions of sampling and statistical representation are taken very seriously in the polling industry and often dealt with in refined and sometimes complex ways. The complaint is therefore a symptom of another problem: while pollsters may be scrupulous in representing a wide range of people in a statistical sense, they fail to do so *discursively*. In other words, they pay attention to people's race, income, or educational level but not to the diverse ways in which people talk about the world. As a consequence, members of the public respond to polls as if they represented someone else's opinion. And, inasmuch as polls are created and designed by people whose view of the world may be fairly different from the respondents', they are quite right to do so.

I take up the question of authorship in the next chapter, arguing that once we begin to look at polls as a cultural form, the question of authorship is brought to the surface rather than being submerged beneath the technocratic language of quantitative methods.

Beyond the Boundaries

Neither reformist nor more comprehensive critiques of polling—as an undemocratic, overzealous, technological determinism—have prevented the multiplication of cross-tabulations, or the assumption that public opinion is no more or less than the aggregates recorded by opinion polls. Among mainstream pollsters and those who commission them, scholarly suspicions—from the technical to the profound—have been almost completely disregarded. Polls of the crudest kind are now so ubiquitous that contemporary politics is almost unimaginable without them. Polls drive both political campaigns and the media coverage of those campaigns. In a spiral of imperfect circles, a distant public comments upon a discursive world shaped by the remorseless repackaging and representation of itself.

The ubiquity of the opinion poll is not without its consequences: polls create the impression of public participation while circumscribing the limited nature of that participation. This book offers neither a dismissal nor an embrace. For all its flaws, the opinion survey is now an accepted part of public life, a technology as routine and robust as the television set. If we look at polling as we might look at television—as a cultural form, a technology filled with form and content—what role does it play in contemporary society? And if we change its form and content, what might it tell us?

While we can take the position that "the public" is a socially constructed category (Ang 1991; Herbst 1998), as all categories are, this does not mean such a category isn't worth retaining. The technology of polling is not neutral, but neither is it ideologically fixed. There are, in short, many ways of signifying the "public": the issue is how one inscribes the public within political discourses. *How, in other words, is public opinion articulated with forms of political power?*

At the beginning of this chapter, I quoted Melvin DeFleur, a forthright advocate of quantitative methods. In his critique of nonquantitative forms of research, he contrasts the scientific methods of quantitative researchers with the methods of those engaging in ideological critiques, which he sees as possibly of interest but invariably speculative. While it is valid to criticize research that makes claims without the use of reliable forms of evidence—without evidence, after all, all claims to understand the social world are equal—his use of the science/ideology dichotomy is entirely at odds with my own approach (and, ironically, consistent with some forms of the Marxist criticism that he belittles). Public opinion polls are, like most scientific technologies, also ideological instruments, and the rest of this book is about how they work, how they are used, and what they might tell us about ideology and media power.

CHAPTER 2

WHO'S IN AND WHO'S OUT:
PUBLIC OPINION POLLS AS A CULTURAL FORM

Writing about the history of public opinion, Carroll Glynn, Susan Herbst, Garrett O'Keefe, and Robert Shapiro reflect on the point that "*Who* is a member of the public is always shifting, depending upon historical context and the agendas of those measuring public opinion" (Glynn et al. 1999, 56). Their remark is made in the context of the prehistory of opinion polling, but it might equally be extended to contemporary scientific polling techniques. In this chapter I consider issues of inclusion and exclusion as a preface to the more general argument that we understand opinion polls as cultural rather than scientific objects. In this way, questions of methodology and accuracy give way to questions of representation and political ideology.

INCLUSION AND EXCLUSION:
PUBLIC RELATIONS AND TRANSFORMATIONS

The history of public opinion is part of a broader history of political power. In ancient Greece, political power was not contingent upon public opinion in the way we now understand it. However, both "publics" and the idea of "opinion" were not only relevant conceptual categories but political and philosophical issues. Groups of citizens would assemble, debate issues, and be addressed by performers and politicians. The arts of rhetoric and oration—skills with little relevance in many of the feudal societies that followed—developed in this context. This classical tradition might be said to inform contemporary notions of citizen participation, in which people come together to debate and discuss issues of the day—an ideal of rational citizenship that stems partly from Aristotle, who regarded the "joint pronouncement" of the public as a greater source of wisdom than the views of discrete individuals. The public realm, in the Aristotelian sense, had an organic quality: the coming together of separate ideas which, through the process of rational discussion or consideration, emerged as something greater than the sum of its parts (Aristotle 1962).

Plato's work offers a well-known counterpoint to this view: Plato saw the citizenry as wayward and malleable, and his conception of *episteme*—or universal knowledge—was quite separate from mere *doxa*—opinion. The former was the property of philosophers, the latter, the untrained caprice of the populace. But both Aristotle and Plato had conceptions of the public realm that were informed by a social structure in which an active citizenry had the means to express itself. Both conceptions were also limited by the nature of that realm: as a category, "the public" left out a majority of the population. Women, slaves, foreigners, laborers, merchants, and farmers were implicitly or explicitly excluded from active participation in civic life. While this exclusion is also embedded in the power structures of ancient Greek society, it suggests something about the notion of the public that is fundamental to its genealogy as a term. This is especially so in the more democratic Aristotelian sense, where matters of *inclusion* and *exclusion* are critical to political power.

In Europe, the notion of citizenship, like a great many other notions, seemed to disappear in the dark ages between the classical period and the Renaissance. This was, in part, because the dominant forms of political power made them irrelevant. Ancient Greece and Rome had more sophisticated conceptions of citizenry and the public sphere than medieval Europe, where institutional hierarchies and religious doctrine addressed people more as subjects—to feudal law and to religious discipline—than as citizens. Public gatherings were often acts of bearing witness to the exercise of legal or religious discipline, which was open to public display but not—in any meaningful way—public debate (Foucault 1977).

The Renaissance softened the rigidity of these political and economic structures. The emerging class of merchants and traders could not be easily subsumed within the old order, while the invention of the printing press in the sixteenth century created new possibilities for the construction of publics and the dissemination of opinion (Eisenstein 1979; Habermas 1989). During the seventeenth century collective forms of expression evolved from riots and parades in the first half into more overtly political forms—notably the petition—in the second. Susan Herbst writes:

> As early as 1640, English citizens petitioned Parliament on a variety of topics from the abuses of monopolies to the importance of peace . . . citizens who signed a petition would often form an unruly mob, marching toward Parliament with their grievances in hand.   (Herbst 1993a, 52)

While these forms of collective expression were often suppressed, they were also, at times, indulged—in some instances, as a matter of political necessity (Thompson 1968). Although sometimes tolerated, these instances of public opinion were not, at this juncture, generally endowed with political legitimacy. To do so would be to threaten a power structure still based largely on the hegemony of a landowning aristocracy. It was in the interest of the ruling classes to regard popular opinion more in Plato's sense than Aristotle's. But the gradual shifts in political power brought about by the emergence of capitalism required new forms of political legitimation, and public opinion became a more contested notion.

During the eighteenth century, the public was not a concept of universal citizenship. The public was partly constructed as a platform for the rising middle classes to challenge the legitimacy of a crumbling feudal order. The emerging bourgeoisie sought a more rational form of politics, one that might replace the more arbitrary edicts of monarchs. Following John Locke, David Hume argued for a notion of governance based on the idea that "the governors have nothing to support them but opinion. It is, therefore, on opinion only that government is founded" (Hume 1963, 29). These sentiments, within the ideology of the enlightenment, thereby linked the notion of public opinion to a rational form of discourse, one that might thereby have the power to oppose traditional governmental hierarchies (Peters 1995). Discussions of public affairs in the genteel salons and in the less exclusive coffee houses and colonial taverns, and the increasing availability of information and ideas in published forms, facilitated the creation of what Jürgen Habermas has called the "public sphere," an arena in which rising middle-class prosperity could challenge governmental authority—and, in time, become enmeshed within it.

The concept of the "public" was therefore less a signifier of democracy than a shift in power toward an educated, property-owning middle class, one which—as opposed to the common people who could be collectively identified and dismissed as "the mob"—defined who the public were. Nevertheless, once political, economic, and discursive space for a powerful citizenry had been opened up, other, more inclusive notions became more difficult to resist. The rise of artisan and working-class movements in the eighteenth and nineteenth centuries—along with the dramatic spectacle of the French Revolution— forced a broadening of the term. It was further solidified by the development of public spaces (such as parks and museums) in the more urban landscape of the ninteenth century.

Once "public opinion" could no longer be contained in the polite gentility of the salons, it was necessarily viewed with ambivalence. Some of this ambivalence was fairly sophisticated—in *Democracy in America*, for example, Alexis de Tocqueville saw public opinion both in its potentially egalitarian sense but also as a burden upon individual liberty (Tocqueville 1969). The framers of the U.S. Constitution were similarly divided between a notion of the public as the keepers of liberty and the less sanguine view that the public was, as John Adams put it, "no keepers at all. They can neither act, judge, think, or will" (Adams 1971, 7). The birth of American democracy was therefore, at best, a circumspect, tentative step toward an embrace of more inclusive notions of public opinion, with a voting franchise of white male property owners that excluded more than 80 percent of the population.

Whether in the Unites States or Europe, evaluations of public opinion were implicitly contained in the limits of voting privileges, which couched public opinion (whether responsible or irresponsible) in class terms. While the views of polite society were often seen as an appropriate sanction on behavior, poorer sections of the public, in particular, were often seen as unruly and unsophisticated purveyors of subversive doctrines. Some, like John Stuart Mill or Rousseau, saw class differences in political acumen as a function of education—and hence changeable—while others believed in less malleable hierarchies. In the context of British debates about extending the electoral franchise in the early 1830s, Whig Thomas Macaulay suggested: "The higher and middling orders are the natural representatives of the human race. Their interests may be opposed, in some things, to that of their proper contemporaries, but it is identical with that of the innumerable generations which are to follow" (quoted in Thompson 1968, 905). The notion of public representation, Macaulay argued, was inextricably linked to class distinction—one partly based on education.

If this period saw notions of public opinion that echoed some of the distinctions found in Plato and Aristotle, the concept of public opinion that emerged in the eighteenth and nineteenth centuries was also identifiably different. While classical publics were often unified by time and space—in other words, by assembly—the modern public "bases social solidarity on participation in discourse rather than locality" (Peters 1995, 9). Although the development of urban public spaces is consistent with classical notions of public assembly, the growth of the popular press in the nineteenth century allowed for a more dispersed public: thus the press not only "made things public," it made publics. Newspapers and periodicals gave a dispersed group of citizens access to a discourse about public life. Publicity or publication, in this sense, was an act of making public, of opening up the affairs of state to citizens who had no other way of knowing.

As the use of elections as a basis for representative government developed, political power was, in one form or another, contingent upon public opinion. Issues of exclusion and inclusion became concrete areas of political struggle, notably on grounds of gender, class, and race. The right to vote was, in a basic sense, the right to be included in the public sphere.

Although historians of public opinion sometimes see voting and opinion polls as separate—related but distinct moments—electoral polls provided the philosophical and technological conditions for opinion polling. Elections, after all, are simply attempts to quantify public opinion—to turn words into numbers as the basis for a rational system of government (a point I will return to later). As Susan Herbst writes, "Some of the early public opinion surveys were attempts to reconstruct electoral polls. These efforts were generally rhetorical and technologically crude. The fiercely partisan press in nineteenth century America would use straw polls to further the claims of the candidate they were supporting" (Herbst 1993b). Although this way of representing the public was seen as a form of political advocacy rather than a science, its emphasis on counting made the development of more sophisticated forms of enumeration inevitable. By the twentieth century, the needs of advertisers and other institutions to paint faces on the enigma of a mass, urban society became more pressing.

The extension of the political franchise toward a more encompassing notion of the public allowed polling to be overtly linked to a discourse about democracy. James Bryce, a nineteenth-century theorist of American democracy, provided the pollsters of the twentieth century with a laudable rationale: the opinion of the common man was, and should be, as valid as the opinion of those in positions of power—the two, in true democratic spirit, are of equal weight. Thus he called for a means by which "the will of the majority of citizens" might "become ascertainable at all times . . . without the need of passing through a body of representatives, possibly without the need of voting machinery at all" (Bryce 1895, 258). George Gallup, for one, embraced Bryce's idea and, unlike Bryce, was able to realize it. But although Gallup's polls bypassed "the need for voting machinery" in the most literal sense, the polling technology he developed was merely a sophisticated version of the same device. If techniques of sampling gave the process a magical quality—the ability to reduce the labor of counting by over a thousandfold—the procedure of asking people to vote for a series of pregiven ideological choices was essentially the same.

Beginning in the 1920s, Gallup became an advocate of the poll as a more scientific and democratic expression of public will than pressure groups and other vocal minorities (Gallup 1966). Although this argument has become somewhat jaded, it is, as Sidney Verba argues, an important one—particularly in a system in which the economic power of big business is linked with the cultural power of public relations (Verba 1996). If the pioneers of modern polling were technocratic, they were also motivated by Bryce's egalitarian spirit (Salmon and Glasser 1995), and during the twentieth century, the notion of public opinion *appears* to finally become an inclusive category: one in which the techniques of sampling guarantee participation by every section of the population.

And yet this inclusion was also a form of exclusion. One could argue, as James Carey does, that the "decline and dismissal of the public sphere, paradoxically, corresponded to the emergence of public opinion and the apparatus of the polling industry" (Carey, 1992, 11). There are undoubtedly ways in which the shift to more technocratic and, in theory, democratic notions of the public was less radical a break from the Enlightenment commitment to a rational, educated class than it might have initially appeared. It is possible to identify in contemporary models of public opinion polling at least four traces of the class-bound constraints of the eighteenth-century conception.

It is notable, first of all, that the development of a modern concept of public opinion has almost inverted classical notions of assembly. It is not just that assembly is more difficult in mass societies, but the notion of public opinion has been used to delegitimate assembly by large groups of citizens in pursuit of a cause—whether to condemn popular protests and riots in the eighteenth and nineteenth centuries or to marginalize demonstrations or strikes in the late twentieth. Assembly, because of its unruly or "irrational" form, or, in more recent times, because of its "unrepresentative" nature, is often conceived *in opposition to public opinion*—or more specifically, in the contemporary era, in opposition to public opinion *polls*. Thus it was possible for President Nixon, in a time memorable for its large public assemblies, to appeal to the "silent majority." The modern definition of public opinion thereby tends to *exclude* those moments when members of the public gather to express a collective opinion (Herbst 1993b).

Second, the creation of a scientific apparatus with which to record public opinion creates a significant gap between the public and their opinions. Stuart

Hall, in his analysis of the development of the popular press in Britain, comments on the way in which a press *by* the working class was replaced with one merely *for* the working class (Hall 1986). In the same way, the development of polling allowed a professional/managerial class to construct a technological apparatus with which to create—and, to some extent, control—a more scientific notion of the public (see Ehrenreich and Ehrenreich 1979). The public did not express itself, but was subject to a rational order dictated by the scientific procedures of measurement, evaluation, and precision. As Salmon and Glasser (1995) point out, like other forms of consumer culture, the public's role is limited to that of consumption—we buy this idea or that candidate—without any meaningful input into the choices made available. It is worth observing that for mass society critics like Walter Lippmann, this is an eminently desirable development—a way for educated experts to mold a generally uninformed and hedonistic mass public (Lippmann 1922, 1925).

Despite the undoubted efforts of pollsters, this makes the "public" in public opinion polls a less inclusive category than its sampling techniques imply. As Lisbeth Lipari has shown, the way in which questions are phrased can implicate a public sphere in which certain categories of people are excluded. Thus questions about welfare or the rights of immigrants tend to assume that the respondent is *not* an immigrant or a welfare recipient (Lipari 1996). Immigrants and welfare recipients are thereby signified as a "problem" *for* the public rather than a *part of* the public. So it is that even in the environment of a theoretically universal franchise, the question of who or what is included in the representation of public opinion is a critical political question.

Third, the close relationship between opinion polls and electoral polls has created subtle, cultural forms of exclusion. As Delli Carpini and Keeter (1996) and Nie, Junn, and Stehlik-Barry (1996) argue, electoral politics is an arena that requires specific forms of cultural competence: those closer—culturally and economically—to ruling elites and the discourses that define politics are better placed to use the system for their own benefit and to understand its terms of reference. Those without this form of what Bourdieu (1984) has termed "cultural capital"—those who, whether because of race, income, or education, are farther from the world of political and media elites—are much more likely to feel alienated from the system. As a consequence, the voting population is wealthier and more privileged than the nonvoting population (Hellinger and Judd 1991). In countries like Australia, compulsory voting minimizes these inequalities, while systems of proportional representation tend to offer a wider range of choices for a greater diversity of interests. In the United States, by contrast, those who feel they have enough at stake in the system to vote are generally a minority in congressional elections and barely a majority in presidential elections.

Although they are rarely understood in these terms, opinion polls—particularly in countries with a socially skewed voting population—are often *more* representative of the public as a whole than elections. Indeed, if we applied the basic sampling criteria that govern opinion polling to elections—using a sample made up of an entirely self-selected group—they would have to be dismissed as unscientific and, almost by definition, unrepresentative. This point is generally lost because it is often the *voting public*—rather than the *general public*—that polls attempt to replicate. Since pollsters will regularly be required to predict the outcome of elections, they are obliged to construct samples based on likely voters rather than the electorate. If the second category is—at least in theory—an inclusive, universal one, the first is decidedly not. Polling will, in these instances, replicate the class-bound, cultural bias of the system as a whole.

Fourth, as Pierre Bourdieu points out, even those polls that draw their sample from the electorate, rather than likely voters, may still favor more educated, privileged respondents. Since pollsters tend to construct questions from the perspective of political and media elites (Siune and Kline 1975), the political competence required to *produce* an opinion in response to a pollster's question is unequally distributed in the population—the further one is from a familiarity with elite political discourse, the more responses are likely to be arbitrary or unsure. Since those with more income and formal education are less likely to say "don't know" or to nominate choices at random, their responses will play a greater role in determining the overall statistical aggregate (Bourdieu 1979, 126). So, for example, those who are more comfortable professing an opinion about support for free trade agreements will also tend to be from a social group that stands to benefit more from such agreements.

If we judge contemporary public opinion polling in terms of widespread claims of democratic inclusion, these four forms of exclusion are serious problems—particularly as they all tend to exclude precisely those people who *are least likely to be heard in other ways.*

I mentioned that Salmon and Glasser describe opinion polls as part of consumer culture, as a way of registering consumer preferences in the marketplace of ideas (Salmon and Glasser 1995). Because they are measuring polls against more democratic notions of the public sphere, their analysis lays bare the limitations of this consumerist model. But if we extend this notion, and begin to study opinion polls as a part of a representational culture—comparing them not to a scientific ideal but to other forms of representation—polls might be seen as one of the *more* democratic forms of representation in the cultural mainstream. The news, for example, is a form of representation which, like polls, is based on the actions and discourses of elites, and yet public access to the production of news is far more limited. Either way, the presence of polls in the cultural mainstream is such that we can no longer restrict discussions of polls to debates about methodology or the nature of the public realm.

The Polling Arts

I suggested in the previous chapter that many critical scholars have tended to deride or ignore opinion polls, seeing the accumulating multitude of narrowly defined responses as a ceaseless barrage of flimsy information. At best, public opinion polls are condemned as a persistently poor method for capturing the character of public discourse.

And yet the very persistence of polls indicates that these dismissals might be a little too rarefied. We might, instead, interpret the abundance of polls as one of the many cultural forms that implicitly or explicitly purport to represent the public. Polls are *part* of popular culture, as carefully scripted as media messages like TV programs or advertising billboards. We do not ignore the significance of television or advertising simply because its representations are ideologically loaded. On the contrary, the study of media and culture begins with the assumption that these cultural forms reveal aspects of ideology and culture. They are produced in the context of political, economic, and cultural power structures, and they tell us something about those structures. They may not reflect the world they signify, but they do relate to it, as well as to the shifting battleground of meaning in which the popular is configured. Indeed, it is partly *because* polls are taken seriously as a form of representation that we should not dismiss them.

As a cultural form, opinion polls provide partial, shorthand clues to the world they signify, even as we lose whole dimensions and many details. Polls do not so much stand for "the public" as signify it within a carefully structured frame. To understand those significations we need to contextualize them: the answer to a pollster's question has no absolute truth but is dependent upon a set of ideas that give it a more specific, particular meaning. An individual on the doorstep or on the telephone may give an uncertain or tepid response, but that response signifies, within a social realm full of ideological connections, a place where ideas are repeated and shared.

Although people are allowed to respond only within the tightly scripted narratives of precoded questionnaires, and although these responses are limited by the carefully sculpted moments in which they are uttered, they are neither arbitrary nor meaningless. In a well-known discussion of "mass culture," Raymond Williams argued that the public "includes us, but yet is not us. . . . There are in fact no masses, there are only ways of seeing people as masses" (Williams 1963, 289). As Williams demonstrated in his own work, this understanding does not prevent us from using fragments of discourse to chart the "structures of feeling" that allow us to describe a culture. What matters, in this regard, is that we acknowledge the conditions of production. Thus we read a novel, a speech, a newspaper, a film, an advertisement, or an opinion poll as representations or accounts constrained by ideology and style.

We may read Charles Dickens as social commentary, but we do so in the context of the moral and aesthetic structures of *Bleak House* or *Hard Times*, a context enriched by all the other available accounts of Victorian England. An opinion poll is a rather less complex and less imaginatively crafted exercise in social description: it speaks from the narrow confines of elite conceptions of public affairs (thus "crime" is usually on the list of issues for government to address, while inequality of wealth is not), and in a staccato voice that jumps from one gnomic expression of noisy terms ("the economy," "freedom," "government") to the next. The opinion poll is partly an attempt to suppress the ambiguities and contradictions of public discourse—to produce rational knowledge about a rational public, neatly displayed in the apparent purity of arithmetic terms (Edelman 1995b). As such, it is a kind of fiction. But like most fiction, it bears a relation to the world it tries to represent.

In Murray Edelman's book *From Art to Politics*, he describes the way in which texts traditionally classified as news rather than art actually function through intertextuality—a news video clip will work within an interpretative frame that draws upon a slew of cultural forms. He writes:

> If twelve members of a Simi Valley jury could see a videotape of the merciless beating of Rodney King in 1992 and conclude unanimously that King, not the police, was "in control of the situation from start to finish," then the stories the defense lawyers told them must obviously have led them to see precisely the opposite of what most viewers of the videotape saw. The defense, in turn, benefited from hundreds of novels and movies that depict the police as protectors of social order against the violence of criminals. It relied as well upon oral and written stories portraying blacks as violent and criminal.
>
> (Edelman 1995a, 2)

The news clip, in other words, makes sense in terms of the array of "models, scenarios, narratives, and images" (ibid., 1) that people refer to when they interpret it. The news clip or the opinion poll is, in this sense, part of this artistic panoply: its technological or scientific status does not make it any less a form of cultural production than a piece of sculpture.

Reading polls critically has often been seen as an act of rejection, of focusing on what surveys do not or cannot tell us. What I shall attempt here is another kind of critical reading, to begin to think about opinion surveys as a cultural form, and hence to ask what polls, in their circumscribed, confined way, suggest about the state of public discourse and the broad politics of inclusion and exclusion.

Opinion polls tend to allow little space for maneuver: in intent, they are self-consciously "closed" rather than "open" texts (Barthes 1974). Indeed, part of the pollster's job is to minimize ambiguity: to try to word questions in ways that permit only one interpretation and to categorize (usually in advance) a range of responses whose meaning is clear and uncontestable. Polls are, in various ways, tightly structured texts overtly encoded with preferred meanings (Hall 1980; Morley 1992)—preferred in the sense that they encourage but do not guarantee semantic possibilities.

As Stuart Hall has suggested, the processes whereby cultural forms are encoded and decoded do "not operate in a unilinear way" (Hall 1994, 254). Thus the production of cultural forms is not the beginning of those forms but a moment in a circuit. The production of polls is based upon interpretations of the world based, in turn, upon these and other cultural forms in an imperfect cycle of reproduction (imperfect because subject to change). Or, to put it another way, we just keep polling along. Opinion polls are produced in the context of the encoding and decoding of previous polls. They are also powerfully informed by the landscape of the media and the elite discourses in which they will be interpreted. What complicates the poll as a cultural form, then, is that it is constructed in a number of different encoding/decoding moments.

Once it has been commissioned and designed, the poll is first decoded by respondents to the questionnaire. In a broad, social context, the poll acts as a way of verifying the preferred meanings of social and political issues or events (Siune and Kline 1975; Salmon and Glasser 1995)—or, in Hall's terms, "a moment in the reproduction of hegemony" (Hall 1994, 260). So, for example, if the dominant media frame for the coverage of welfare is to see many welfare recipients as pampered and irresponsible, the poll can solidify this preferred meaning by asking respondents whether the welfare system should be reformed to discourage indolence or abuse. An affirmative response implies—or, at least is interpreted as implying—acceptance of the dominant frame. However, in a complex world defined partly by struggles over the meaning of popular representations—whether news items or pictures of women on advertising bill-boards—there is always a degree of uncertainty. In short, respondents may not reproduce this preferred meaning in response to a pollster's question. Polls are, in a Gramscian sense, ideological devices that require a degree of consent (Gramsci 1971). In other words, they not only depend upon a degree of acqui-escence, the less overtly manipulative surveys allow space for the refusal of con-stent.

This space is limited, of course, as Salmon and Glasser put it:

> Public opinion in the arena of the market place confers consent, of course, but it is consent of the kind that is characteristically weak, uncritical and ten-tative. Existing as it does through the polls that measure it and which give it its public appearance, public opinion in the tradition of Gallup conceives consent as a sign of allegiance; the public is allowed to respond by acclama-tion—or by withholding acclamation—but the public is not expected to respond substantively and discursively.   (Salmon and Glasser 1995, 446)

We cannot raise a different issue or question the logic of the questionnaire, we can merely say "No." At times, we cannot even do that. For example, in a poll conducted during the massive build-up of U.S. troops in the Persian Gulf in November 1990, Gallup asked this question:

All in all, which of these courses of action do you agree with?

The U.S. should keep troops, planes, and ships in and around Saudi Arabia as long as it is necessary to prevent Iraq from invading Saudi Arabia, but without initiating a war.

The U.S. should initiate a war against Iraq in order to drive Iraq out of Kuwait and bring the situation to a close.   (from Meuller 1994, 218)

In this instance, the question forces us to reproduce one of the two options promoted by political elites. The importance of using significant military force to defend Saudi Arabia is taken for granted—our only options are whether to escalate this involvement or not. We cannot give a response that questions the expense of a military operation to defend a rigid theocracy with the largest mil-itary budget in the region—particularly by a government responsible for arm-ing Iraq in its war with Iran—or that questions the need for such deterrence (invading tiny Kuwait is one thing, invading Saudi Arabia, quite another). Our only means of refusal is to offer an incoherent "don't know" (to be fair to Gallup, in later polls the option of withdrawing troops from Saudi Arabia was included).

Responses are limited not only by the structure of the questions but by the information available to us to question dominant versions of events. As I argue in chapter seven, the information available to most people about events in the Persian Gulf makes it difficult to avoid consenting to elite opinion. Nevertheless, like other cultural forms, polls are imperfect expressions of dominant frameworks of thinking: for all their ideological limits, they can also allow a great deal to seep through that does not easily "fit" those dominant frameworks (it is worth noting, for example, that despite the strenuous efforts of the Bush administration and other sections of elite opinion, only 28 percent of respondents favored initiating a war with Iraq when this question was put).

The construction of meaning does not only occur in the space between question design and public response. The results of the poll are then interpreted and written up, a second moment of encoding in which pollsters will record and interpret responses. The audience for this moment of the polling text is very different but also fairly select. In the case of those polls conducted for public consumption, it will generally take the form of a polling firm's report or press release designed for editors or reporters. If they are deemed to be sufficiently newsworthy, these texts are then decoded and reencoded, once more, into media texts. This is, I shall argue in the next chapter, a decisive stage in the dominant representation of public opinion and the meaning of polls. It is also at this point that the opinion poll becomes most culturally and politically significant in the construction of—or resistance to—consent. If a majority of respondents is interpreted as favoring cutbacks in welfare, this can enter the dominant frame in which the issue is interpreted. If responses cannot be interpreted in this way, they will either be excluded from the dominant frame or force the dominant frame to shift. Furthermore, by this stage, the technology of polling often disappears altogether, and the results of polls are simply reported, in their most rhetorically powerful form, as unmediated public opinion.

THE INFLUENCE OF POLLS

Much has been written about the significance of this cultural form, about the power of polls to influence both public and elite opinion. Summing up the research on the influence of polls, Michael Traugott and Paul Lavrakas argue that there is "no longer any need to question the 'power of the polls' or the news they generate" (1995, 257). Perhaps the best known work in this area comes from Elizabeth Noelle-Neumann, who has presented persuasive evidence that polls can act to solidify the preferred meaning of events by creating a "spiral of silence," in which opposition to a dominant idea or view is diminished by polls that may intimidate or encourage people into tacit acceptance of a majority view (Noelle-Neumann 1993). This has a number of well-known manifestations, such as the "bandwagon effect" of shifting support toward political candidates whose poll numbers portray them as popular and successful. Although aspects of the "spiral of silence" thesis are contested (see, for example, Schoenbach and Becker 1995), the research nonetheless suggests that while it may not be a universally applicable principle (people may, for example, be unaware of polling trends), there do seem to be moments and instances when the results of polls do enter into and become a part of public discourse. And because polls claim to speak for the public, they are difficult texts to oppose or negotiate with: if we disagree with the 80 percent in the poll who favor one position over another, our response is still structured by the poll's overall premise, which defines us as a minority voice.

Overall, the influence of opinion polls on public opinion itself is generally a question of reinforcement—polls validate and strengthen dominant media frames, which may, in turn, influence public opinion. Perhaps the most dramatic example of the insertion of polls into media and elite discourse occurs during "moral panics" when polls powerfully inform the interplay between the media and elites during an apparent moment of social crises. This will involve the ritual vilification of what Stan Cohen calls "folk devils"—a group held culpable for the breakdown of social order (Cohen 1972). In *Policing the Crisis*, Hall, Critcher, Jefferson, Clarke, and Roberts describe how the rapid escalation of concern about "muggings" in Britain in the 1970s developed into a full-scale crisis. Suddenly, it seemed, "muggers" were everywhere—the subject of front page stories and statements of concern by politicians and judges. What makes the mugging crisis notable is that it was completely disproportionate to any changes in the official discourse of crime statistics. The process the authors document involves a three-way spiral in which media coverage, elite response, and opinion polls reinforce one another to such an extent that the state is apparently forced to respond—in this case in the form of police operations and judicial sentencing (Hall et al. 1978).

A similar process occurred with the "drug crisis" in the United States in the 1980s. Polls indicating rapidly growing public concern about drugs in the middle to late 1980s were an intrinsic part of an upward spiral of media coverage and institutional response, each one playing off the other in complete disregard of fairly stable statistics on drug use (Reeves and Campbell 1994). If the drug "crisis" diminished by the end of the 1980s after President Bush ordered the invasion of Panama in a dramatic escalation of the "war on drugs," its residual effects on police operations and more draconian sentencing have had profound and lasting effects on the prison population and on depopulated communities. In these instances, polls play a significant role in the escalation of the "moral panic" and the legitimation of a more punitive state.

What is notable about the moral panic phenomenon is that the influence of polls on public opinion is significant only if it is an intrinsic part of media and elite discourse. The same can be said of the "spiral of silence" or bandwagon effects. Polls have no direct route into public consciousness; their significance depends entirely upon their insertion into media frames and elite discourses. This is no small matter: the codes that sanction admission of polling data into elite discourse lead to notable patterns of inclusion and exclusion (I shall elaborate on this in the next chapter). The influence of polls is therefore bound up with their impact on media and political elites.

In this vein, Schoenbach and Becker argue that, in general, the public response to "media content that implicitly indicates public opinion" is "less significant than the responses of the political and governmental elite, who either feel the content is an indicant of already formed public opinion or an indicant of public opinion about to be formed as a result of the influence of the media themselves" (Schoenbach and Becker 1995, 337). And yet the effect of polls on political elites is complex—not least because those elites are very much a part of the encoding process that informs the construction and content of polling questionnaires and the way they are interpreted.

Barry Sussman's account of politicians and the polls suggests that the degree to which politicians follow public opinion polls is often overstated: political leaders routinely ignore the results of polls that do not inform their own political goals (Sussman 1988). Even if we accept polls as transparent reflections of public opinion, there are, as Benjamin Page puts it, significant gaps between elite and mass opinion (Page 1996). As Helliger and Judd have written: when public opinion does not fit with their interests, elites "have a significant capacity to ignore it" (Helliger and Judd 1991, 248). This is an important point; unless polling majorities become part of media or public discourse, there is generally little pressure for well-entrenched elites to represent public opinion. Occasions when the gap between public opinion polls and elite opinion becomes a significant theme of media coverage are fairly rare (Monroe 1975; Traugott and Lavrakas 1995). When this does happen, it is usually indicative of a split in elite opinion—and even in these cases political elites can elude the issue of democratic representation by appealing to a discourse of principled leadership, a discourse in which the failure to heed public opinion can be represented as a virtue. In Britain, Tony Blair's Labour Government has sometimes been content to place itself conspicuously to the right of opinion polls on social policy issues in order to demonstrate its "toughness." This was also notably evident during the impeachment of President Clinton, which proceeded in spite of polls that consistently reported clear majorities against impeachment and generally high presidential approval ratings. Voicing his support of the Republican campaign to oust Clinton, the widely syndicated conservative columnist George Will wrote:

> By leaning against the wind of opinion regarding impeachment, the reflective Republicans are exercising leadership. This is perilous in a democratic age because leadership suggests, if not a defect, at least an insufficiency on the part of the people. Although people clamor for leadership, when it occurs they are apt to regard it as an act of lèse-majesté.
>
> (from the *Daily Hampshire Gazette*, December 21, 1998)

At times Will's language suggests an almost Platonic contempt for the "clamoring" masses — desiring leadership but insufficiently reflective to appreciate its wisdom. It is a rhetorical position perhaps most forcefully expressed by Margaret Thatcher's declaration that she was a "conviction" rather than a "consensus" politician. Nonetheless, Will is careful to inscribe the Republican position within a general democratic frame. The people, he states, *want* principled leadership, and he concludes by arguing that the ousting of President Clinton would be in the public interest.

Since public opinion is generally signified in an Aristotelian rather than Platonic sense, the discourses that place elites above the whims of public opinion carry certain risks and therefore tend to be used parsimoniously. Political and media elites prefer, in general, to be seen as being in accord with public opinion, and polls play a powerful role in legitimating and enforcing elite policy agendas. They do so, however, only in the context of the opinion poll as a cultural form. If opinion poll findings do not enter into media frames, they are generally regarded as politically irrelevant. The significance of polls, like the significance of other cultural forms, is therefore a question of *how they are encoded into media and popular culture.*

Polls are most often invoked in disputes *between* elites rather than between elites and the public at large (Page and Shapiro 1992; Zaller 1992; Page 1996). Polls are used to reinforce one side's political position — to allow political leaders to speak in the public's name and thereby to shift the media frame in their favor. Polls will, for example, be instrumental in informing calculations about which positions might be sacrificed in negotiations between parties. For this reason, there is no doubt that politicians and political operatives often pay close attention to polls, but this is less a response to democratic or populist impulses than a desire to use poll data as a strategic or rhetorical tool. A line from a memo by a staff member in the Reagan White House makes this point fairly clearly: "It may be useful to have some survey research," the staff member wrote, "to back up our judgments and opinions about the policy options facing the president. To make this happen, I understand you will need to raise the issue with Jim Baker, the coordinator of White House survey research" (Heith 1998, 172). In other words, polls are used to *sell* policy positions rather than *construct* them. One political operative in Susan Herbst's study of the way polls are understood or interpreted put it even more bluntly: polls, he suggested, are "used by us when it's to our advantage and kind of discounted when they're not" (Herbst 1998, 48).

President Clinton's signing of the Welfare Reform Act took place in a political context powerfully inflected by opinion polls that were almost universally interpreted as being favorable to welfare reform. This is not to say that Clinton was unsympathetic to welfare reform, but that the Republican Party's ability to push its version of the issue was enhanced by its ability to claim a popular mandate. Similarly, the Republican willingness to bow to pressure from President Clinton and congressional Democrats and vote for a modest increase in the minimum wage in October 1995 was informed by poll numbers indicating large majorities in favor of such a measure. Glynn et al. argue that these are democratic moments in our political culture (Glynn, Herbst, O'Keefe, and Shapiro 1999 234). But it is important to stress that in both cases polls were not instances of spontaneous public pressure in the light of current events: polls on welfare and the minimum wage have, over several decades, indicated similar and fairly consistent majorities for reforming welfare and increasing the minimum wage (Page and Shapiro 1992). Polls became influential in these cases because *they were strategically invoked in elite—and consequently media—discourses.*

The significance of polls as a cultural form is therefore bound up with the practices that govern their representation. In this case, the very specific form of inclusion and exclusion used in reporting them to the public—which responses are inserted into media discourse and which are not—is a critical political question.

SIGNIFYING THE PUBLIC

Sidney Verba argues that, for all its flaws, the public opinion poll is a more egalitarian and democratic form of public representation than citizen participation

(Verba 1996). While citizen participation may involve grassroots organizations that operate in opposition to dominant power structures, the *influence* of pressure groups will largely be a function of access to resources. Since these resources are distributed unequally, those pressure groups with access to funding will be significantly more effective than those with more meager means at their disposal. Thus it is, for example, that while the oft-mentioned "special interests" in U.S. politics are often associated with broad-based citizen groups, the most powerful lobbyists in Washington are much more likely to be from big business (Hellinger and Judd 1991; Harrigan 1993).

The power of corporate pressure groups to affect legislation makes the efforts of more grassroots citizens' groups look inconsequential. So, for example, the various pressure groups advocating on behalf of children's television — arguing for a less commercial, more educational model of children's entertainment — have been fairly ineffective. The National Association of Broadcasters (the commercial industry's interest and lobby group), on the other hand, has been consistently successful in shaping broadcasting regulation. The 1996 Telecommunications Act, which further extended the Reagan administration's efforts to relieve the industry from regulatory "burdens," was — quite literally — underwritten by the broadcast industry. As Eddie Fritts, the president of the National Association of Broadcasters, revealed to the broadcast industry press, "We spent several millions of dollars to pass the [Telecommunications Act of 1996]" (Huntemann 1999). This is scarcely a trivial point.

Opinion polls, argues Verba, can offer a useful counterpoint to this use of economic power:

> Poll results on gun control may not have overridden the power of the NRA, but they have been useful as a counterfoil. Legislators may still fear the concentrated resources the NRA may bring to bear, but polls showing that the public at large (and even gun owners) disagrees with the NRA gives some ammunition — perhaps the wrong word here — to the other side. Similarly, polls have shown that half the Cuban Americans in the United States disagree with the position of the National Cuban American Foundation, which believes we ought to isolate Cuba, or that many fundamentalist Christians do not support the agenda of the religious right.   (Verba 1996, 5–6)

Verba's argument is an important one. There is undoubtedly a romantic tinge to some of the criticism of opinion polls in which citizen activism is celebrated as a more authentic form of democratic response without seriously considering, as Verba does, the political economy of pressure group politics. Verba's enthusiasm for polls is also considerably more circumspect than Ross Perot's vision of a poll-driven electronic town hall. He acknowledges the limitations of sample surveys and the power of those who design and commission them. As he points out, the ability to commission a poll also requires access to considerable resources: less, perhaps, than the money required to make a television program but enough to put polls well beyond the reach of most grassroots organizations—particularly if the survey is to be conducted by one of the more well-established (and hence, in publicity terms, credible) polling companies, and if it is to include a large enough sample for journalists to take it seriously. This second point, it should be noted, is often more an issue of perception than scientific scruple—although surveys of 1,000 are certainly preferable, it is quite possible for a survey of 300 to produce results that are statistically representative (if less precisely so). Since grassroots organizations are generally regarded as less authoritative than elite sources, a small sample is likely to compound journalistic skepticism.

In the world of large corporate budgets, the resources required to conduct survey research are regarded as far less onerous, and the corporate world has sometimes been adept at commissioning polls and inserting them into mainstream media discourse. Jon Kronsnik provides an illustrative example in his analysis of the *New York Times* coverage of a poll conducted by the well-known firm Louis Harris Associates for Aetna Life and Casualty. The poll's purpose was to convey the impression that Americans favored changes in the civil justice system—changes that would be directly beneficial to Aetna. This was achieved by a fairly straightforward distortion of emphasis: respondents were asked whether they regarded certain changes as acceptable—a distinctly tepid form of approbation, particularly on an issue most respondents had probably given little thought to. This acceptance was then interpreted in Aetna Life and Casualty's press release as outright "support" for "a number of specific reforms to improve the nation's civil justice system." Not only did the *New York Times* cover the poll, but it amplified Aetna's somewhat misleading terms, claiming that the poll not only indicated "broad public support for changes in the civil justice system," but suggested public "demand for reform" (Krosnik 1989). The journey from a passive acceptance to an active demand is a considerable one, and Krosnik's study is an insightful investigation of the use of polling technology to carefully manufacture public opinion for specific political goals. This is a luxury that few grassroots organizations can afford.

Krosnik's study raises another important issue: while Verba's argument about polls may apply to the broad mass of opinion survey data, it does not fully address the opinion poll *as a cultural form*. Although Verba acknowledges that *access* to the production of polls—their publication, presentation, and distribution—is unequal, the overall drift of his argument runs the risk of overstating the significance of polling data and underestimating the significance of the media frames used to report—or ignore—that data. Verba uses the example of AFDC recipients who, because of their lack of education and resources, will be poorly represented by effective citizen advocacy, but who might be located through a survey. This is an important point—particularly for those well endowed enough to think about strategic forms of intervention in the debates about welfare. It remains to be seen, however, whether the forms of exclusion and inclusion in the media representation of polls would permit such a poll to inform mainstream media discourse.

In order to understand opinion polls as a cultural form, we need to make a distinction between the results of opinion surveys—what we might call, in all its voluminous and contradictory glory, the *opinion data text*—and the more public realm of opinion data in media discourse. This distinction is central to the path this book is following: namely, to explore the ways in which political power influences how the public is represented. The technology of polling, by itself, facilitates a degree of control, but the *popular significance* of that control is contingent upon the ways in which polls are inscribed (or excluded) in media discourses.

As Verba's argument suggests, any serious examination of the politics of polling and public expression must consider the political economy in which such things take place. A cultural product—whether an opinion poll or a TV show—is not reducible to economic structures, but it does operate in a set of economic conditions which shape or constrain forms of representation. While the world of commercial television is too complex and too contested to be understood as a simple reflection of the economic interests of the corporate world that produces it, there are nonetheless powerful ways in which those economic interests influence a range of probabilities. Thus, for example, the need to raise advertising revenue in an unregulated climate of profit maximization means that for every hour of commercial television, at least one-quarter of that time will be spent celebrating the joys of consumption.

The world of survey production is vast. In mass societies, survey technology is central to the corporate or governmental apparatuses of organization, surveillance (or, as we might put it in this context, "surveylance"), and control (Foucault 1977; Herbst 1993a, 1993b)—whether as a means to construct or institute government policy or to explore and shape consumer behavior. In the United States, several million people are called upon each year to answer questions about themselves, their circumstances, or their attitudes. Government agencies alone—such as the Department of Labor, the National Center for

Health Statistics, and the Department of Justice—account for over a million survey interviews a year. The corporate world—whose existence is partly contingent on its ability to measure and control desire—is even more assiduous in its surveillance. AT&T's Telephone Service Attitude Measurement program, for example involved more than five million interviews annually, while agencies like the AC Nielson company (which measure program ratings) are billion-dollar enterprises whose function is to transform public preferences into commodities to be bought and sold on the open market (Miller 1995).

Although public opinion polls as most people understand them—those polls whose purpose is to represent popular opinion about politics and society in the public sphere—amount to a fairly modest enterprise among this volume of quantification, their significance as a cultural form makes them the most visible of the survey genres. The production of public opinion polls can be divided into four broad—though not mutually exclusive—categories:

1. Independent companies or organizations such as Gallup, Roper, and the Pew Research Center, which produce polls partly as matter of public record, but whose revenue is derived from market research or foundation support

2. Private polling companies like MOR and the Wirthlin Group, which conduct polling for clients—such as the U.S. Republican Party—and whose work may or may not be released for public consumption, depending on the wishes of the client

3. In-house polling agencies for news corporations—either full in-house operations like CBS and the *New York Times* or services for the *Washington Post* and ABC (which do in-house design but subcontract out for sampling and field work)

4. Academic institutions, notably the National Opinion Research Center (NORC) at the University of Chicago or the Institute for Social Research at the University of Michigan

Of these, the more well-known independent agencies like Gallup, while their work is regularly used by the news media, are no longer as synonymous with public opinion polling as they once were. As part of a crowded field they have, in relative terms, seen their influence decline. Conversely, as polling has become increasingly understood as a way to enter, control, or influence public debate, private polling has become increasingly commonplace. But in terms of the construction of *a discourse about public opinion,* the producer/commissioner of polls whose growth has been most conspicuous is undoubtedly the news media.

The news media's use and commissioning of polls has grown precipitously since the 1970s. In 1976, major U.S. media organizations conducted a (mean)

average of four polls annually. By 1988 the number had risen to thirty-two, with all media outlets—large and small—increasingly likely to commission their own polls. In the four election years between 1980 and 1992, the *New York Times* published 697 stories based on its own polls, 30 percent running on the front page (Ladd and Benson 1992). In 1995 and 1996, one-third of the cover stories in *Time, Newsweek,* and *U.S. News and World Report* involved the use of polls (Asher 1998), while all the television network news operations have become accustomed to including the results of their own polls as stories in their own right. This is by no means an American preoccupation: the growth of polls for media use has been as global as other technologies. Even in France, where the publication of polls before elections is restricted, the annual number of opinion surveys conducted for the national press doubled during the 1980s to an average of two a day (714 a year) by the last year of the decade (Brule and Giacometti 1990).

At the level of political economy, the technology of polling is intertwined with the manufacture of news. This is exacerbated by the tendency of the larger media to favor their own polls, thereby giving their own research an advantage in the manufacture of news. The growth of private polling companies, meanwhile, has tended to favor those groups or companies with the resources to commission and produce polls. The political economy of polling is nevertheless complicated by the production and publication of polls that are not necessarily the product of commercial interests and which are less clearly designed for media use. In the United States, for example, there are around sixty academic survey organizations, some of which—like NORC at the University of Chicago and the Institute for Social Research at the University of Michigan—are fairly well-endowed, robust institutions producing a wealth of data. These academic pollsters play a significant role in broadening the range of publicly available *opinion data text* (particularly as their research is increasingly accessible online), but they play a much smaller part in the media construction of public opinion. In this sense, while the production of polls is closely linked to news production, there is, even in an institutional sense, a gap between the opinion data text as a whole and the more select, powerful manifestations of public opinion in the media.

This gap informs the distinction between those polls that are given prominence in the reporting of public opinion—and which thereby contribute to the conventional wisdom espoused by political and media elites—and those that do not. In the first instance we have a mass of complex data, much of which, like discarded film footage or videotape, is strictly the domain of industry analysts, archivists, and academics. In the second instance we have an intermingling of discourses—the language of polls and the language about polls—that creates dominant conceptions about the nature of public opinion.

The fact that the political economy of polling is bound up with news production—or with attempts to influence news production—provides us with a context for understanding the process, but it also leaves a number of things unexplained. Thus it is, for example, that even those polls commissioned or favored by the news media will be reported selectively and even, in some cases, ignored. The broad mass of unused opinion data can thus include parts of the media's own polls, suggesting that even within an organization there may sometimes be a divergence of professional ideologies between news pollsters and news editors.

During the first two years of the Reagan presidency, for example, the press continually repeated the assumption that Ronald Reagan was an extremely popular president. Although this was an assertion informed by a few highly selective nuggets of polling data, it was flatly contradicted by a series of comparative polls—including the media's own—that suggested Reagan was one of the *least* popular presidents in the postwar era. As King and Schudson argue, this was possible because the dominant frame in which Reagan was interpreted—as an amiable, personable figure—made polls that contradicted this frame irrelevant (King and Schudson 1995). To this day, there remains a gulf between two "public opinion" discourses about the former president, one version suggesting a leader beloved, the other suggesting widespread dissatisfaction. It is significant, in this respect, that it is the former that has generally proved more enduring (see chapter six), suggesting that what Robert Parry (1992) has called the dominant media's "conventional wisdom" is more than capable of overriding polling data in the definition of public opinion.

CHAPTER 3

SUPPRESSING DISSENT: THE MEDIA
REPRESENTATION OF PUBLIC OPINION

If opinion polls themselves are often limited, they nonetheless reveal ideological possibilities. Amid a swath of contradictions, we can identify strong or majority support for ideas spanning a wide range of ideological positions, from left to right. Particularly notable in the United States and elsewhere is *the degree of support for a variety of political positions on the left*—from gun control to social justice issues. Majorities consistently support increased government spending in traditionally "liberal" areas such as healthcare, education, environmental protection, and even—when the word "welfare" is not used—programs for assisting the poor. This has been well documented in a number of comprehensive studies (such as Paletz and Entman 1981; Ferguson and Rogers 1986; Mayer 1992; and Page and Shapiro 1992). And yet the media's interpretative frameworks tend to suppress the leftist leanings of opinion poll responses, creating a picture of a moderate to conservative citizenry that matches a moderate to conservative political elite. In other words, if one looks at the broad mass of opinion data, we find a much broader range of political possibilities than we do from more mainstream media accounts. At the heart of this argument is the need to understand opinion polling and the media coverage of polls as related but distinct ideological processes with a potentially different set of political outcomes.

While a few writers—such as Murray Edelman, David Paletz, and Robert Entman—have referred to the downplaying of popular progressive ideas in media/elite discourse, it is remarkable how often this argument is negated or submerged. Critics of media and opinion polling often tend to lump the two processes together as the work of professional/managerial or political elites, while much of the work in political science attempts a kind of journalistic even-handedness, in which criticisms of the media's representations of polls are seen as either technical or ideologically neutral or dispersed (favoring "both sides" at various times). Outside these circles, while it may be accounted for in very different ways, the assumption is that majorities in the United States *do* generally favor positions from center to right—an assumption, I would suggest, that is one of the dominant political myths of our era.

In what follows, I shall examine the ideological processes that incorporate—or exclude—public opinion surveys in news production. What we find is that these ideologies tend to reinforce a political economy that favors the powerful and excludes popular opinion when it contradicts those powerful interests. This finding is compatible with the large body of evidence from a variety of perspectives that—whether through professional ideologies or structural pressures—links the news media to elite perspectives and frameworks. A comprehensive bibliography of this evidence would be several chapters long, but a range of examples and approaches might include Tuchman (1978); Gans (1979); Gitlin (1980); Glasgow Media Group (1980); Paletz and Entman (1981); Herman and Chomsky (1988); Edelman (1988, 1995b); Hertsgaard (1989); Kellner (1990); Lee and Solomon (1990); Brody (1991); Parry (1992); Zaller (1992); Naureckas and Jackson (1996); McChesney (1997); Croteau and Hoynes (1997); and Croteau (1998). Paletz and Entman (1981), in particular, have described how the media tend to portray public opinion as more conservative than the polls would suggest.

We can discern the overall drift of media coverage by looking at those occasions when press articles linked public opinion to particular ideological positions. A Lexis Nexis search indicated that, in the decade between June 1990 and June 2000, there were 3,607 articles in which U.S. newspapers used the terms "public opinion," "voters," or "electorate" in conjunction with (in this instance, within two words of) the ideological labels "conservative," "moderate" or "independent," or "liberal" or "progressive." If we break down these ideological associations, we see a striking pattern, as follows:

References to public opinion in conjunction with the phrases "moderate" or "independent":	2,149 or 60%
References to public opinion in conjunction with the phrase "conservative":	1,089 or 30%
References to public opinion in conjunction with the phrases "liberal" or "progressive":	369 or 10%

This indicates a significant bias toward an articulation of public opinion as "moderate" or, to a lesser extent, "conservative." The liberal or progressive aspects of public opinion, by contrast, receive comparatively little attention.

While these imbalances were most pronounced in regions where voters do tend to be more conservative (notably in media based in the Southeast, where references to "conservative" public opinion outnumbered references to "liberal" public opinion by over four to one), these patterns were also manifested in the most liberal voting regions of the United States. Thus, even in the Northeast— home of the much discussed "liberal media," as well as the most progressive groups of voters—the term "conservative" was linked to terms signifying public opinion nearly twice as often as the terms "liberal" or "progressive."

There are, of course, many ways in which these linkages can be articulated. The most common instances involve references that imply most people are conservative, moderate, or liberal; or they involve a focus with the part of the electorate that can be identified as such. Either way, these repetitions suggest a focus that would seem to exclude the progressive or liberal aspects of public or popular opinion. In order to explore this further, I look at two smaller samples of U.S. media coverage.

I begin with an analysis of 123 television news stories on ABC, CBS, and NBC news in 1996 and 1997, a sample gathered using a Lexis Nexis search based on TV news stories in which the word "poll" was used. This data set provides a general picture of some of the tendencies that characterize news coverage. I then try to identify the politically inflected professional ideologies that produce these tendencies, drawing upon a broader sample of news reports, including a batch of 392 stories in the U.S. print media and on National Public Radio in 1994 and 1995, tracking coverage of all the Times Mirror polls released in that period (the Times Mirror Center for the People and the Press has since become the Pew Research Center).

Public Opinion on Television News

On a purely technical level, academic public-opinion researchers are, on the whole, well aware of the gap between pollsters and journalists—a clash of professional ideologies that includes a litany of journalistic uses and abuses (see, for example, Traugott and Lavrakas 1996; Asher 1998). Brady and Orren describe what they see as the inherent mismatch between the ethos of survey research and the ethos of journalism—the one concerned with technology and precision, the other with speed and story lines. They proceed to count the ways in which they see polling data misinterpreted, whether in relation to the technicalities of sampling error, the quasi-technicalities of measurement errors (such as the phrasing or context of questions), or the rather more abstract category of "specification error," in which the theoretical assumptions behind a survey are flawed or insufficiently complex to describe the phenomenon being surveyed (Brady and Orren 1992).

This mismatch is more than a matter of careless reporting in the rush to meet a deadline. The reporting of polls is governed by a series of interweaving journalistic *assumptions* about public opinion and polling technology. These assumptions create a profound distance between public opinion as it appears in the opinion data text and public opinion as it is reported. This gap is partly reflected in research by Behr and Iyengar (1985), who found that while the media coverage of issues influenced public concern about them, levels of public concern *did not* appear to influence TV news coverage, which takes its lead from debates among political leaders rather than poll responses nominating issues of concern. But the distinction between the results of public opinion polls and media representations is not ideologically innocent. In the few instances when television news *is* systematically responsive to public opinion, the frame used to extrapolate "public opinion" overtly limits the meaning of those responses. This occurs in three ways:

- the meaning of poll responses is extrapolated in terms established by political elites or in ways that fit preexisting media agendas;
- the notion that political elites represent public opinion is symbolized by the predominance of "horse race" polling, in which the only option available is approval for one elite political figure of another;
- when television uses polls that do express identifiable political positions, those associated with the left are much more likely to be neutralized, "balanced," or contradicted in news coverage than those opinions associated with the right.

These first two points are fairly easy to establish. For example, when CBS used one of its polls to inform part of its coverage of the 1996 presidential election (an approach that, as Behr and Iyengar suggest, is not typical), it did so in a way that defined those issues *entirely* within an elite framework. Dan Rather described the feature as follows:

Now as part of our commitment to inform you, the public, about the presidential candidates' positions on substantive issues, tonight we begin four nights of "Where I Stand." CBS News has made time available for these segments, offering President Clinton and Bob Dole air time to tell you directly, first person, unedited, where each stands on four key issues. The four topics they'll address were selected by you, the public, as determined by a CBS News poll: education, taxes, Social Security-Medicare, and health care.

(*CBS Evening News*, October 21, 1996)

CBS's approach here might be seen by some as encapsulating the best democratic tradition: the public defines the issues, and the political candidates respond. And yet, not only do we have little idea what people meant by their choices of issues or why they chose them, their meaning is entirely circumscribed by political elites (in this case, Clinton and Dole). Popular support for policies within this agenda are discussed only if they fit within the narrow range of elite opinion espoused by two presidential candidates, neither of whom is on the left. Thus, for example, polls suggested that the public favored spending more on education than either Clinton or Dole, and polls show majorities or pluralities favoring a "single-payer" healthcare system, an option favored by neither candidate and therefore not on the agenda for discussion. In other words, even at its most democratic moments, the news media slots public opinion into an elite framework.

More typical was CBS's use of the same poll on the previous evening, in which democratic pretensions are reduced to flimsy, almost arbitrary references to polling data. In this instance, poll responses are taken out of any meaningful context to inform a conventional crime story:

Although government figures show crime in decline, many Americans are not convinced. A CBS News poll out last week found nearly 30 percent of voters listing crime and drugs as important campaign issues. And that's tonight's Campaign '96 cover story: crime and politics, as viewed by some residents of Richmond, Virginia.   (*CBS Evening News*, October 20, 1996)

As we learn on the next night's broadcast, these law and order issues were fairly low down the list of priorities in the CBS poll, and yet these responses are used to make it appear that CBS is responding to public demand. CBS's poll is thereby loosely interpreted to inform a preexisting news agenda.

The more general point suggested by these two examples is that public opinion polls are routinely used and interpreted *within the confines* of TV news frameworks—whether the tendency is to focus on violent crime or to allow political elites to define the political terrain. Of the 123 news items in the television news sample, nearly half (58) were either straightforward horse race polls about various domestic elections (25) or polls that involved the approval or disapproval of various politicians or their actions—notably Bill Clinton (in the light of the White House scandal), but also Bob Dole, Newt Gingrich, and Al Gore (33). Such a use of polling data helps to create the impression that the public is broadly in line with its political representatives and the media coverage thereof—a point I shall return to in the next section.

While the use of "horse race" polls is not ideologically innocent, a number of the poll responses reported could be placed more easily in a left/right ideological frame. Overall, the news items were allotted to one of the following categories:

Categories of Poll Responses Reported in Network News

TYPE OF POLL	NUMBER
1. Horse race polls	25
2. Approval/disapproval of politicians	33
3. Responses suggest support for right-wing positions	11
4. Responses suggest support for right-wing positions pushed to the left	1
5. Responses suggest support for left-wing positions	4
6. Responses suggest support for left-wing positions pushed to the right	12
7. Polls with no clear political meaning	37

Specifically, categories three, four, five, and six all refer to poll responses that might be generally seen as politically inflected. Thus, for example, a report of a poll showing majority support for more education spending signifies a left-leaning public, while a report of a poll indicating majority opposition to affirmative action signifies a right-leaning public. The notions "pushed to the right" or "pushed to the left" refer to instances in which a poll might, on its own, suggest a left/right tendency in public opinion, but where that suggestion is modified or pushed in the other political direction by a reporter's interpretation.

Although the numbers here are relatively small (twenty-eight news reports, around a quarter of the total), a distinctive pattern emerges—which, since it accords with the overall bias reported earlier, is worth dwelling upon. Of the twelve instances of poll-based reports signifying a right-leaning public (categories three and four), only one is tempered, balanced, or redefined, while of the sixteen instances in which poll responses signify a left-leaning public (categories five and six), fully three-quarters (12) are tempered, balanced, or redefined. In some cases, indeed, this involves associating left-leaning poll responses with right-leaning policies.

What makes this finding particularly notable is that among the eleven reports based on poll responses that appear—in terms of their interpretation and representation—to indicate support for positions on the political right or within a center-right axis, some involved ignoring contradictory polls, as in the following example:

> The most recent ABC News/*Washington Post* poll, which was finished only last night, finds that while 59 percent of those we asked liked the idea of a tax cut, even if it means cutting some federal programs, 58 percent said that balancing the federal budget is more important, and 53 percent said they would actually oppose a tax cut if it would make it harder to balance the budget. The debate continues.   (*ABC World News*, August 5, 1996)

The "debate" referred to here is firmly rooted in elite discourse, one that functions within the confines of the center-right spectrum of the body politic. The only choices offered are either tax cuts or balancing the budget—options generally pursued within the Republican Party and the conservative wing of the Democratic Party. Thus, even in a growing economy, increased spending for various social programs (such as education or healthcare) is discounted from the agenda. The mass of polling data that suggests support for increasing many forms of public spending is absent from this framework.

On other occasions, these reports feature topics that do regularly generate a predominantly right-wing response, as in the following instance, where public opinion is seen to support a hawkish foreign policy position:

> Then the question, how to get rid of Saddam Hussein? President Bush and others thought that Iraq would turn on Saddam after the devastating defeat in the Gulf war. But, of course, that's not happened. And in a recent NBC News/*Wall Street Journal* poll, fully 56 percent of the American public said it would support the idea of assassination. Could we do it? Should we? Here's NBC's Fred Francis.   (*NBC Nightly News*, December 19, 1997)

Other reports in this category included polls showing support for the death penalty, opposition to affirmative action, and support for the idea that Bill Clinton is a "liberal"—all notions challenged by the left.

The one occasion in which a poll response with a generally conservative connotation was pushed to the center or the left by its framing was in response to the sensitive issue of affirmative action—a notion that, depending on its framing, most white Americans do not support (see Jhally and Lewis 1992):

Americans support diversity in the workplace and on campus but oppose racial preferences to achieve it, according to a new CBS News poll. A slim majority, 51 percent, said affirmative action is not necessary.

(*CBS Evening News*, December 13, 1997)

The use of the word "slim" waters down the impact of this response, and the news item went on to modify it further, reporting that:

But the poll showed wide support for spending money on a variety of remedial and outreach programs to prepare minorities to enter college or the job market.

These programs included "Extra Effort to Consider Qualified Blacks for Admission," "Government Spending for Minority Job Programs," and "Outreach Programs to Hire Minority Workers." From a conservative perspective, this report might be seen as viewing public opposition to affirmative action through rose-tinted spectacles, and yet it was the *only* instance in the sample of such an inflection. We might also note that this is an area of policy in which elite opinion is also divided.

By contrast, of the sixteen poll responses that might, on their own, signify on the left side of the political spectrum, only a quarter were reported in contexts that retained this inflection. The four items placed in this category were an NBC News poll that "found that a majority of women say Hollywood has made little or no progress in how it portrays women beyond the old stereotypes"; an NBC poll that found that education was a "top priority" for most Americans; an ABC poll that found more people felt that teachers' unions were a positive rather than a negative influence; and a CBS poll that found most people saying that government "can have a positive effect" in people's lives. While none of these responses indicate unabashed support for positions on the left, their general inference signify discourses that are sympathetic to feminism, education spending, unions, and activist government.

More significant, in this respect, were the twelve occasions when polling data that might *potentially* be part of a left-leaning political discourse were placed in a context that nullified their progressive connotations or that pushed their meaning to the right. The neutralizing (or inversion) of potentially left-leaning poll responses occurred in various ways. On some occasions, they were presented in the context of right-wing policy options. So, for example, a CBS News poll that reported "education and what to do about our schools is the issue that is the number one concern of voters" *might* have linked this to polls showing consistent support for more public spending on education. Instead, the response was used to introduce a discussion of *privatization* of the public schools.

In a rather different example, an ABC report on the 1997 British election discussed a Gallup poll in which Labour's lead over the Conservatives was "dramatic" (47 to 33 percent). The ensuing item *might* have portrayed this as a shift to the left (Tony Blair's rather lukewarm support for social democracy notwithstanding), and yet the discussion that followed was steadfastly apolitical. The tone was set when political correspondent Simon Hoggart observed, "My feeling is that the British people have decided it's time to vote these rascals out and vote a whole new bunch of rascals in" (*Nightline*, April 30, 1997). On other occasions, left-leaning poll responses were countered by other poll responses—or interpretations of those responses—that neutralized or negated any notion that public opinion might be on the left. Thus a CBS News report (*CBS Evening News*, August 30, 1997) on public support for the right to higher education began:

> One big issue for anyone thinking about going to college these days is the cost. Eighty-six percent of those questioned in our CBS News poll believe every capable person has a right to receive a college education, even if he or she cannot afford it.

However, this support was modified by the subsequent statement:

> But just 48 percent believe the federal government has the financial responsibility to make sure every qualified person gets it.

The tone here suggests that most people believe that a college education is important, but that it is not up to the federal government to subsidize it. What is interesting about this example is the degree to which a progressive interpretation of the data is suppressed. Public financing to ensure universal access to higher education—regardless of ability to pay—appears to be supported by nearly half of those polled, figures that might easily be seen as placing public opinion well to the left of political elites (very few of whom feel such a "financial responsibility"). Instead, we are left with the impression that while people feel that higher education is generally a good thing, increased public financing has little support.

Similarly, CBS reported on a poll showing public support for the Teamsters Union in its dispute with the United Parcel Service (UPS) in the summer of 1997:

This is the first time in years the public has supported labor in a major strike. A CBS News poll shows when asked to choose between the union and the company, 52 percent favored the union, and the union did manage to deliver.

(*CBS Evening News*, August 19, 1997)

While progressives placed the Teamsters' victory and the public support for it in the context of a growing anticorporate sentiment, the CBS report adopted a framework in which union activity is regarded as marginal to the contemporary economy. As reporter Ray Brady concluded:

While this may get them good press, the unions are in no shape to really expand. They need to enroll 400,000 new workers a year just to stay even, they're losing that many members, and that alone is going to be an almost impossible job for the unions.

Again, while the numbers are small, the pattern that emerges here suggests that poll support for ideas on the left is suppressed in very particular ways—a point I will explore further shortly.

Among the remaining news items in the sample (the seventh category in the table), around one-third (21) could be categorized as facets of public opinion that are self-consciously placed outside the realm of electoral politics, for example: "In a recent CBS News poll, 80 percent of Americans say they consider pets real members of their families"; "85 percent of the parents surveyed said they have had a serious talk with their kids about drugs, but fewer than half the teens recalled such a talk"; "Happy Valentine's Day! A just released CBS News poll finds most married Americans are happy with their mate." This is not to say these polls have no political content or interpretation: the "Happy Valentine's Day" poll, for example, could be seen to work within a discourse that naturalizes the exclusion of gay couples from a discussion about love. These polls are categorized thus simply because they are not intended to convey a political meaning or to signify within a political realm.

Closely related to this category are sixteen news items in which poll responses are more self-consciously related to a conventional political realm but without any clear—or even vague—ideological frame with which to interpret them. Thus, for example, CBS reported:

Also today, NASA released this computer-enhanced view of the red sunset over the red planet. And while you enjoy this view as the sun sinks slowly over Mars, the latest CBS News poll out tonight indicates about six out of ten

Americans believe the money and effort for the Mars mission, and space exploration in general, are well worth it.

(*CBS Evening News*, July 15 , 1997)

If we ignore the rather smug complicity between NASA and network news that surrounds this use of polling data, the responses signify majority political support for a specific government program and a specific form of public spending. The space program tends to be low on the list of spending priorities for those on the left and fairly high for those on the right, so one could categorize this as a poll response more easily associated with the right than the left. While such a categorization would fit the general thrust of my argument, since this is one of the few areas of public spending for which support is difficult to categorize on a left/right ideological map, it was coded as ideologically ambiguous.

A rather different example concerns a news item about U.S.–Japan relations:

Three years ago, the ABC polling unit asked the question, "Do you think Japan's current economic strength poses a threat to the United States or not?" A majority, 55 percent, said yes; 40 percent said no. But in a new ABC poll those numbers are reversed: 40 percent see Japan as a threat, 56 percent do not.   (*Nightline*, April 10, 1996)

The question asked by ABC comes from a reactionary discourse in which an Asian country is identified as a "threat" simply because its "economic strength" might be seen to rival that of the United States. And yet, while this discourse *may* inform a racist ideology and/or support for defense spending (in the light of such threats), it also might be seen as antagonistic toward a U.S. policy—one supported and pursued by most political and economic elites—that emphasizes open markets and the free flow of capital. The meaning of these poll responses—or the trends they suggest—is therefore particularly ambiguous.

Overall, what impression might this pattern of coverage convey? The important comparison, I would argue, is between those polls that indicate public opinion operating within the terms of an elite center-right framework (categories one, two, three, and six), and those that indicate support for ideas to the left of that framework (categories four and five). The proportions here are fairly unambiguous, the former outnumbering the latter 81 to 5. It would appear, from this sample, that television's representation of public opinion clearly operates within the terms of the center-right axis of Washington politics, thereby ignoring the many manifestations of support for a left-leaning social democratic agenda that we find in the opinion data text as a whole.

The patterns suggested by these findings are summed up by Lance Bennett's argument that

> in matters of lifestyle and taste, the media keep the public in touch with its own pulse. In the electoral arena and on matters of presidential popularity the voice of the people is raised loud and often. From these expressions of popular sentiment one might receive the impression that popular democracy is alive and well. However, when it comes to many areas of serious policy considerations, the polls, while equally available, are barely whispered around the edges of the policy process, and are seldom drawn on centrally by the media in the coverage of emerging policies.   (Bennett 1989, 328)

Thus it is possible for polls to be very much symbolically present while polls that do not fit with what Bennett calls an assumption of "institutional superiority" are generally absent.

This bias might be seen as entirely predictable: the news media, after all, are part of corporate empires whose interests are generally in line with those of procorporate elites (Herman and Chomsky 1988; Schiller 1989; Kellner 1990; McChesney 1997). And yet the process by which the implied interests of the media's political economy are connected to a set of ideological practices is complex (Hall 1996; Slack 1996). In what follows, this analysis is developed by focusing on the how the media's *interpretative frameworks* tend to suppress polling data that might be articulated with a left-leaning politics. While press reports of polls tend to be more complex than the terse world of television news, the following points draw upon the sample of press reports and refer to the news media in general.

FRAMEWORKS OF INTERPRETATION

In his analysis of the media coverage of the Reagan administration's policy to destabilize the Sandinista government of Nicaragua, Lance Bennett demonstrates how public opposition to the Reagan policy was ignored in media accounts. Bennett found only 30 references to polls in a total of 2,312 articles on Nicaragua in the *New York Times*, and fully half of these references were attacks on the quality of popular thinking (i.e., the degree to which the public was ignorant or confused). Thus, in less than 1 percent of cases did the *New York Times* use public opinion to inform discussion of this issue. Bennett uses this data to make the point that popular opinion is generally regarded as inferior to institutionally powerful sources on such issues. While my own analysis is generally in line with Bennett's, it is important to add that even in foreign policy, public opinion becomes more "relevant" to media discussion (although perhaps, in Bennett's terms, no less "inferior") when it is generally *in support* of policies pursued by elites. During the Gulf war, for example, media outlets gave far more attention to the polls and to support for President Bush's handling of the war. A Lexis Nexis search (using the terms "Gulf" and "poll") suggests that the percentage of *New York Times* Gulf war articles referring to polls was around 5 percent, and despite available evidence of significant knowledge gaps (Lewis, Morgan, and Jhally 1991), none of these articles questioned the quality of these opinions. The question is therefore not how public opinion polls are excluded, but which frameworks were used to determine inclusion and exclusion.

DEMOCRACY AND COHERENCE

Individual polling questions tend to be written in ways that limit ambiguities in order to produce clarity and consistency of response. But if polling questions are attempts to close down meaning, the broad mass of polling data as a whole is a relatively open text, one full of contradictions and ambiguities. This is not to say that these contradictions and ambiguities cannot be resolved—attempts to do so, however, tend to remain within the purview of scholarly interpretation. So, for example, Samual Popkin (1991), Benjamin Page and Robert Shapiro (1992), and John Zaller (1992) have all attempted to make sense of the vagaries and contradictions in the polling data in ways that find a coherent rationality of response—much as the skilled literary critic might find a unified, well-constructed meaning in a richly ambiguous novel.

The subtleties of these scholarly readings are generally incompatible with the codes of news reporting, where contradictions are more likely to be suppressed than resolved. While journalism embraces a specific and limited notion of difference in interpretation (the "two sides" model of objectivity) in the semiotics of the newsroom, ambiguity in the apparently scientific discourse of public opinion is more unsettling to journalistic norms. When poll findings do suggest ambiguity, the attempt to solidify their meaning can occasionally lead to forms of closure that, when juxtaposed, seem almost arbitrary. On March 10, 1998, for example, the *Washington Post* reported that "Trust in Government Edges Up, Survey Finds," while the *New York Times* summarized the same data with the stylistically similar but starkly contrary headline: "Americans Take a Dim View of the Government, Survey Finds." What is significant here is that neither of the two leads its story with the headline "Ambiguities in Attitudes to Government, Survey Finds."

If these attempts to close down meaning can diverge, they are more likely to push poll findings in one direction. The desire for closing down the meaning of public opinion rests, to some extent, on the assumption that poll results must generally conform to notions of a rational public inside a functioning democracy—hence the invariable attempts by pundits and reporters to try to reduce the electoral or opinion polls to a single meaning (thus we might hear the question: "What were the voters saying in this election?"). To maintain faith in modern democracies, the meaning of polls—especially electoral polls—must be seen as compatible with the political consequences that follow them. To think otherwise involves a radical rethinking of what democracy is and how it might work. Salmon and Glasser put it well:

> The quantification of public opinion appeals to, and simultaneously affirms, journalists' faith in a free and enlightened electorate; it vivifies the political authority of the citizenry and underscores the viability of each individual, separate and sovereign, as the locus of democratic power. By recognizing the value of individual opinion and by granting everyone, at least statistically, an opportunity to be heard, public opinion polls foster what appears to be an entirely open and egalitarian form of democracy.
>
> (Salmon and Glasser 1995, 444)

Nonetheless, as Salmon and Glasser suggest, polls are not simply described; they come tightly wrapped in a discursive framework that purports to make sense of them. As a cultural form, the opinion poll text is squeezed, pushed, and molded into apparent coherence by an army of reporters, experts, and pundits—part of Walter Lippmann's professional, educated elite (Lippmann, 1922; 1925)—committed to the rationality of the process. All the more so as the political economy of polling becomes bound up with the political economy of news production (Brady and Orren 1992).

Voting is thereby imagined as a coherent expression of political ideology. And yet there is often only a weak connection between majority survey responses to a broad range of policy questions and the candidates whom majorities vote for. So, for example, Ronald Reagan was elected to a second term in 1984 at a time when more specific, policy-oriented polls were generally registering a shift to the left (Ferguson and Rogers 1986; Mayer 1992). General social survey polls in 1984 found that while around 60 percent of those polled favored spending more on social programs like education, environmental protection, healthcare, and assistance to the poor, the proportion wanting to spend more on defense dropped dramatically from the unusually high figure of 56 percent in 1980 to only 17 percent by 1984 (Niemi, Mueller, and Smith 1989)—a set of priorities completely at odds with that of both Reagan administrations.

The structure of a number of polling questionnaires tends to contain implicit assumptions about why people vote: we are asked to nominate the most important issues, and then to say which candidate or party is "better" on those issues. Voting in this ideal, rationalist model is the apotheosis of a series of structured political calculations. But for a person to vote in such a way is *to ignore the ways in which people are generally addressed*. The mainstream news media's reluctance to devote time and energy to policy positions means that most people simply do not have the information available to make specific policy-driven judgments about candidates (see, for example, Iyengar 1991; Delli Carpini and Keeter 1992, 1996; Morgan, Lewis, and Jhally 1992; Lewis and Morgan 1996; Kuklinski and Quirk 1997; Lewis, Morgan, and Jhally 1998). We are encouraged instead to make decisions based on the less tangible clusters of images and symbols that fill campaign pitches and television news reports.

If many journalists are aware that the act of voting is not always commensurate with a person's political or economic interests, such thoughts are generally abandoned in subsequent discussions. So, for example, whether it was proclaimed with satisfaction or reluctance, the Republican victory in congressional elections in November 1994 was widely interpreted as a clear mandate for a conservative program. The *Los Angeles Times*, for example, reported a Times Mirror poll thus:

> With an activist, Republican Congress poised at the reins, most Americans strongly support many of the GOP's top priorities, including crime control, welfare reform, and further deficit reduction, according to a Times Mirror poll released Wednesday.   (*L.A. Times*, August 12, 1994)

While this is, on one level, a perfectly accurate representation, the same poll also found majority support for increases in spending on decidedly "liberal" projects such as public education (64%) and AIDS research (55%), as well as only minority support for basic aspects of the Republican platform, such as increasing defense spending (31%) or cuts in capital gains taxes (27%). A majority also said that they had never heard of the "Contract with America" or did not know enough about its contents to be able to comment upon it.

This is not to imply that reporters deliberately suppress polling data that do not fit the rational ideal of a representative democracy. Nevertheless, the survey's political ambiguities are lost in the gap between the polling data and the *L.A. Times*'s representation of that data. The *L.A. Times*'s emphasis reflects the dominant culture's commitment to what Edelman (1995b) calls "a discourse of rationality," whereby rational voters make rational, ideological choices in a way that renders elections coherent democratic enterprises. As Edelman writes:

> The focus on rational choice serves quite often to justify actions that powerful groups or officials favor but of which much of the public disapproves. . . . Majorities have long favored gun control, abortion rights, a higher minimum wage, and many other specific objectives that legislatures and administrative bodies have often rejected. . . . The focus on rationality muddles discussion of goal priorities while helping to rationalize the specific actions of bureaucracies.
>
> (Edelman 1995b, 408–9)

Even in more spacious, less conventional media outlets, attempts to invalidate the 1994 Republican victory invariably clung to these notions of systematic rationality. So, for example, an article in *The New Yorker* by Alan Brinkley argued that the Republican mandate was flawed because: "Republican candidates won 51 percent of the popular vote in a year in which 39 percent of the eligible electorate went to the polls; their 'mandate' thus comes to slightly less than 22 percent of eligible voters" (*The New Yorker*, January 29, 1996). While the voters in the 1994 election were certainly somewhat richer and less ethnically diverse than the population as a whole, it is also true that rather more representative (if much smaller) polls also found majority support for the GOP (a Times Mirror poll, for example, reported 57 percent of the general population content with the sweeping Republican victory). What is interesting about Brinkley's claim is the *refusal to question* the notion that people might choose to vote for parties that reflect neither their economic interests nor many of their professed wishes.

Thus while poll findings at odds with the views of the new Republican majority were underreported, those that could be interpreted as reflecting it were given greater emphasis as a way to illustrate the new tough-minded mood. On September 25, 1994, the press reported on a poll that found, as the *Houston Chronicle* put it, that "the nation has grown more cynical, sour and mean-spirited," or, as *Newsday* declared, "an angry disenchantment is unsettling the public, turning Americans against government and each other." The evidence in the survey that justified such a claim was based on findings that

> attitudes hardened on issues potentially affecting taxes and job security. In 1987, for example, 71 percent said that the government should take care of people who can't take care of themselves. That fell to 57 percent this year.
>
> (*The Columbian*, September 25, 1994)

While this shift may be notable, the minority—less than one respondent in six—who apparently changed their minds thereby come to represent a general shift in the state of the public mind toward an ideology that, as the poll itself indicates, most people (57%) would actually appear to reject.

If the fragments of discourse suggested by opinion polls do add up to something tangible and binding, they do so in ways that consistently elude the moments the political culture has chosen to construct such unities—namely, general elections. In Britain, the election of four successive Conservative governments from 1979 to 1997 was generally assumed to be an endorsement of an economic policy of lower taxation and cuts in social spending, and yet in five surveys taken between 1983 and 1994, the proportion of people who felt the government should "reduce taxes and spend less on health, education and social benefits" fluctuated between only 3 percent and 9 percent, while in three of the surveys majorities (between 54% and 63%) actually favored *increasing* taxes to pay for more social spending (Taylor-Gooby 1995). These poll responses were thus consistently at odds with the "mandate" of responses to electoral polls.

Peter Miller (1995) points out that the logic of the opinion poll is not entirely the creation of pollsters but of modern democracies. If polls are seen as problematic expressions of public opinion, elections are, in many ways, even more so. In this context, I would argue, modern elections are not necessarily the ideologically metonymic or symbolic events they are assumed to be—they may signify very little beyond themselves. Rather, they are what Murray Edelman calls "political spectacles"—forms of ritual rather than legitimation. Elections thus "give people a chance to express discontents and enthusiams, to enjoy a sense of involvement" without actually conferring a great deal of power (Edelman 1964, 3). I return to this issue in chapter eight: suffice it to say, it is hardly surprising that the main criticism made of opinion surveys is one that *legitimates* rather than undermines electoral polls. This involves the oft-repeated complaint that polls are insufficiently accurate or representative of the voting population to be reliable in predicting elections. To be accurate, in this framework, is not to capture public discourse about politics, but to reflect as precisely as possible the electorate's highly ambiguous answer to an extremely limited question. Paradoxically, the degree of technical precision involved in making polls accurate measures of party or candidate support tends to obscure the *lack* of precision about the meaning of such polls.

In this interpretative framework, scrutiny is reserved only for questions of mathematical or technical detail. The question "Is the poll accurate?" is not directed at the philosophical or ideological assumptions that reduce the citizenry to a few percentages but to the poll's statistical reliability. Pollsters are taken to task only when a large sample (the voting public) does not quite replicate the preferences of a smaller one. So, for example, the failure of pollsters to accurately predict the results of the 1992 elections in Australia or the United Kingdom induced a bout of journalistic skepticism in both countries in which the underlying assumptions about public opinion remained intact, leaving the pollsters with an admonition to get it right next time. The assumption behind this admonition is an inversion of the logic of representative democracy: *the role of polls is to reflect—as perfectly as possible—the make-up of the governing body*, rather than it being the role of the governing body to represent public opinion (at least as it currently measured).

THE RELEVANCE OF PUBLIC OPINION

As I have suggested, journalism is deeply tied to a "top-down" political framework, in which the range of legitimate political discourses is defined by political elites. For this framework to maintain its coherence, public opinion must also be broadly defined in those terms: polls can then be seen as a vindication of dominant political discourses and of representative democracy in general. When majorities expressed in opinion surveys place the public well to the left of political elites—as they do in many areas of government spending, for example (Page and Shapiro 1992)—they tend to be dismissed as inconsequential (since they do not appear to explain election results). So, for example, if polls show majorities in favor of a universal healthcare system while the main political figures are not, this majority is regarded as merely tangential to the political process (Canham-Clyne 1996).

Or consider, for example, that during the 1990s, polls indicated that public support for—and faith in—big business and the corporate world diminished. This is not surprising in an era when executive pay raises have considerably outstripped average earnings and when job security has been replaced by corporate demands for flexibility in a global labor market. From a corporate perspective, there are some potentially sharp edges to this growing public suspicion, fragments that might easily be articulated within a left-wing populist discourse (advocating, for example, the regulation of corporate responsibility, the restriction of corporate power, and a clamp-down on tax exemptions). And yet the only indication of this anticorporate sentiment in the sample of 123 TV news reports was buried in an item about volunteerism, a context that deflects any discussion of government intervention or neglect:

In Philadelphia next Sunday, Presidents Clinton, Carter, Bush, Ford, and a host of other dignitaries will host a summit on volunteerism. The idea is to motivate Americans to become more involved in charitable and community causes. An NBC News/*Newsweek* magazine poll found that 60 percent already feel that volunteering is very important, and that 46 percent regularly donate their time to a cause. Eighty percent of those polled said corporations have a major responsibility to give back to their communities. Forty-five percent said giving back was just as important as making a profit.

(*NBC Nightly News*, April 21, 1997)

Needless to say, it is difficult to imagine most of those businesses involved in the summit prioritizing community service alongside profit-making, or being compelled to do so by government. Indeed, the promotion of private charity as a remedy for social problems is generally part of a right-wing discourse used to compensate for lack of governmental action (in this case, it provided a symbolic softening of the Welfare Reform Act President Clinton had signed the year before).

Similarly, a Times Mirror Poll reported on November 14, 1995, suggested the presence of both antigovernment and anticorporate sentiments (in the latter instance, only 4 percent of those surveyed said that corporations put their employees first, while an increasing percentage expressed an unfavorable view of business). While political elites repeatedly give voice to antigovernment sentiments (the dominant discourse of Republican politicians since Reagan, one often repeated in a kinder, gentler form by leading Democrats like Bill Clinton or Al Gore), the business funding base of both political parties makes American government far more procorporate than the American public (see, for example, Green, Herrnson, Powell, and Wilcox 1998). Of those media outlets covering the poll (the *Wisconsin State Journal*, the *Baltimore Sun*, the *Chicago Tribune*, the *Detroit News*, the *Atlanta Journal and Constitution*, the *Los Angeles Times*, the *Rocky Mountain News*, the *Tampa Tribune*, the *Phoenix Gazette*, the *Arizona Republic*, and National Public Radio), most led with the antigovernment views (as in "Jittery Americans Blame Congress"), while only one (the *L.A. Times*) even reported the anticorporate sentiments, and then only in the last line.

A procorporate slant is, at the very least, a convenient position for a corporate media to adopt. But the emphasis on antipathy to government in the reporting of these polls is also a response to the discursive world of Washington politics. The notion of "political viability" or "relevance" in the representation of public opinion thus privileges those poll findings that match the interests of political and corporate elites.

Another example of polls whose relevance is, in news terms, diminished by the limits of Washington's agenda is campaign finance reform. Polls on this issue generally place the public, who mostly favor it, to the left of political elites—who tend not to. This issue is fundamental to the structure of American politics, since the current system allows large sums of corporate money to dominate the selection and election of candidates (see chapter eight). Since serious campaign reform is fairly low on Washington's agenda, public support for campaign finance reform is, for network news, fairly irrelevant. While Republican attacks on presidential fundraising in 1997 made the issue temporarily newsworthy, most Republicans (and, by and large, conservative Democrats) had no intention of changing a system that favored business interests. During a discussion of the Republican attacks, *Nightline* used an ABC poll to both inform the discussion and appropriate it within the dominant frame.

Look at the latest ABC News poll. Do you favor campaign finance reform? Sixty-two percent said yes. Do you think it's likely to happen? Sixty-seven percent said no. In the meantime, President Clinton's approval rating . . .
(*Nightline*, July 10, 1997)

This cursory dismissal neatly encapsulates a journalistic code in which public support for issues outside elite agendas is rarely used to challenge those agendas; it simply becomes irrelevant to mainstream political discourse. As I suggested in the analysis of TV news coverage of polls, the use of elite frameworks in poll coverage is solidified by the well-known journalistic tendency to focus on the "horse race" aspects of political life (who is ahead, who is behind—see, for example, Diamond and Geller 1995; Jackson 1996), thereby vindicating a hierarchy of polling responses in which the choice of party or candidate becomes the ruling grammar of the discourse of public opinion (hence nearly half of the polls used on network news are about support for or approval of members of a political elite). Because the dominant narrative is based upon the shifting support for political parties or candidates signified by one set of polls, this obliges journalists to use *other* polling responses to explain those shifts.

So, for example, a Times Mirror poll reported on August 24, 1995, asked a number of specific policy questions and, in so doing, reported substantial support for a range of government programs, including Medicare, public housing programs, and the Environmental Protection Agency. While high levels of support for such programs has been a remarkably consistent feature of poll responses for some time, the popularity of many forms of government spending and intervention—so often out of fashion in Washington in recent years—

rarely receives much media attention. Of the eleven media outlets in the sample to cover the poll (CNN, the *Palm Beach Post*, the *L.A. Times*, the *International Herald Tribune*, the *Fresno Bee*, the *Dallas Morning News*, *Newsday*, National Public Radio, Reuters, the *Pheonix Gazette*, and the *Washington Post*), the responses indicating support for various government programs went unmentioned in all but two reports, and then only as a footnote to the main story.

Instead, *all eleven* focused on the growing support indicated for an independent presidential candidate (e.g.: "Unhappy Voters Back Independent," "Interest Rising for Independent Bid in '96," "Support for Third Party Rises in Poll")—a "horse race" story fueled by media speculation about a Colin Powell presidential candidacy. Of the two brief references to support for government programs, one was particularly interesting. At the end of an interview on National Public Radio, Times Mirror pollster Andrew Kohut stated:

> We asked people to rate themselves on a scale of how much they support cutting government versus maintaining government. They put themselves much closer to where *they think* Bill Clinton and Gore is than to Dole and Gingrich, and that's frustrating for many people, particularly on the left or independent Democrats who don't feel they have someone speaking to their concerns about the paring down of government.
>
> (*Morning Edition*, August 24, 1995; my emphasis.)

Kohut's statement is suggestive. First, he implies that his survey puts a majority of the public *to the left* of the Washington consensus that (as Bill Clinton put it) "the era of big government is over." Not only is this interpretation of the data absent from the press reports, but disenchantment with the political mainstream is *reappropriated within that mainstream* by the media's focus on a "horse race" discussion of independents in which the likely candidates—such as Colin Powell—are situated somewhere *between* Bill Clinton and a conservative Republican Party (rather than in the popular space to the left of Clinton obliquely identified by Kohut). The dominant discourse in which politics is reduced to the narrow range espoused by political elites is so powerful that it forces Kohut into a framework he must simultaneously undermine. People are thus closer to "where *they think*" Clinton and Gore are: they are thereby slotted into the political mainstream (in which Clinton and Gore represent the left), even while they support positions abandoned by those (such as Clinton and Gore) represented as the left side of that mainstream.

This process of reappropriation is not, I would argue, limited to the United States. As I have indicated, polls suggested a high degree of opposition among the British electorate to fundamental aspects of the Conservative Party's approach to taxation and spending during the 1980s and 1990s (Taylor-Gooby 1995), and yet this public opinion discourse was ignored by most journalists partly because it did little to explain a narrative in which the Conservative Party remained in power for eighteen years. The dominance of "horse race" polling becomes part of the hegemonic process, legitimating a limited range of options and thereby prescribing which discourses are politically relevant and which are not. Hegemony thus works less by imposing specific political discourses than by defining the discursive terrain.

THE SUPPRESSION OF DIFFERENCE

In contrast with other news values, the premise underlying the representation of public opinion tends to be an absence of conflict. While pollsters will often break down responses by region, gender, race, party, education, or income, these differences are routinely ignored in media representations. Any divergence of interests tends to get lost in the undifferentiated mush of statistical majorities. Conflicts that underpin and even define social life become mere hiccups. A careful reading of polling data in recent years would reveal that people separated by class, race, or gender tend to have different interests and often view the world differently, and yet these divisions sit uneasily within a framework that suppresses such an overtly political fracturing of "the public."

When polls *are* reported as expressions of conflict, it is often in response to a story in which divisions are already inscribed. Responses to the O. J. Simpson trial are a case in point: the racial conflicts embedded in the news story made differences between black and white responses relevant. Thus a report of a Times Mirror poll in the *Rocky Mountain News* (October 14, 1994) covered a number of issues but chose to disaggregate responses *only* when reporting on interest in the Simpson case. It is also worth noting that even while reporting that "Blacks were more than twice as likely to retain an intense interest in the case," the story began with a headline that masked this distinction: "Americans' Interest in O. J. Trial Fades, Poll Says."

Similarly, in April 1995, National Public Radio, discussing the findings of a recent poll, reported:

> Groups that approve of what the new Republicans in Congress are doing include whites, men, and people with money. Groups that disapprove include women, blacks, and people who earn less than $30,000.
>
> (*All Things Considered*, April 12, 1995)

They were, in so doing, tracing the outlines of a discourse in which clear social and political divisions are drawn. And yet, in the ensuing discussion between reporter and pollster, these divisions were repeatedly overridden by the discourse of homogeneity, in which uninamity of response was repeatedly evoked by use of the second- or third-person plural: "*We're* [the public] glad that the Republicans are in charge . . . ," "*many people* believe . . . ," "*the American people* don't seem to be feeling . . . ," "*many people* feel that . . ." (my emphasis).

In this discursive framework, the opinion poll—with its ability to reduce divisions to broad aggregates—is often the ideological glue that masks social division and creates the mythical notion of a common set of interests. This is tied to a broader political discourse in which *politics is reduced to a meritocracy* in which the public support the "better" candidate with the better policies (often the one who, from the same meritocratic lexicon, "wins" debates) rather than the candidate who best expresses particular interests (such as men/women, poor/rich people, etc). This is more than a process of reducing a complex political engagement to a couple of digits. The idea that politicians represent coalitions of different and conflicting interest groups is entirely absent from this formulation: candidates are, on some absolute and quantifiable scale, simply better or worse. In this context, not only do overall opinion poll frequencies fail to reveal a political response, but their articulation through "horse race" polling masks divisions beneath a sporting metaphor in which "the best man/woman (usually man) wins."

The "public" itself thus becomes a device that binds society's subgroups into one undifferentiated lump. The public becomes a coherent aggregate subject—the public mind who thinks and wants without contradiction and whose pluralities are, in the end, muffled by the search for monochromatic majorities. Typically, we read or hear statements such as: "*Americans consider* congressional leaders Newt Gingrich and Bob Dole more powerful than President Clinton, according to a poll released Wednesday" (Reuters, April 12, 1995; my emphasis). This statement is based on a poll in which Gingrich and Dole were seen as more powerful than Clinton by 57 percent to 35 percent and 55 percent to 36 percent, respectively. The slippage from "55 percent to 57 percent of Americans consider . . ." to "Americans consider" is more than mere shorthand in which minorities—in this case, substantial minorities—are apt to simply disappear: it is a philosophical presumption that one can speak of public opinion as an undivided, coherent being.

There are occasional exceptions to this—notably the discussion of "gender gaps" in party support or moments of racial conflict. In the TV news sample, the instances in which polls were not used to signify homogeneity were restricted to a brief discussion of the gender gap—which generally put women to the left of men—and the difference between black and white respondents in their support for affirmative action. In American politics, these exceptions are themselves revealing: thus it is that while race and gender are occasionally regarded as a basis for difference, other social divisions—the most obvious example being social class—are not. If class is discussed at all, it is invariably in the context of what Bourdieu has referred to as the myth of working-class conservatism (Bourdieu 1979), a notion that ignores the ways in which polls find working-class people consistently more radical and progressive on economic or structural issues than those higher up the social scale (a point I return to in chapter eight).

The typically consensual framework lends itself to an analysis in which public opinion can be unified around a series of generalities. It is an apparently egalitarian image that makes any introduction of questions of power and structural inequality difficult to formulate. This, in turn, facilitates attempts by elites to speak for "the nation" about other undifferentiated notions such as "the economy," masking the degree to which the interests of a corporate CEO or stockholder might be at odds with those of most working people (for the former, low unemployment is bad, for example, because it might raise the cost of labor, whereas for most people an increase in the cost of labor means a pay raise). As Benjamin Page writes:

> Ordinary citizens, at least when they are aware of what is at stake, tend to favor full employment, expansionist monetary policy, and low interest rates, whereas political, business, and media elites tend to prefer to fight inflation, even at the cost of severe budget cutting, tight money, economic slowdown, and high joblessness.   (Page 1996, 119)

Page illustrates the point by referencing the *Time* magazine issue of May 12, 1995, featuring a cover picture of a meat cleaver and enthusing about budget cutting while simultaneously reporting on a poll that showed large majorities opposed to cutting any major program other than defense—a finding glossed over by the article's stress on public willingness to "sacrifice" (Page 1996, 132).

Attempts to signify the unity of public opinion can be a struggle, as the following segment from ABC's *This Week with David Brinkley* (April 14, 1996) suggests. The discussion began with a report that "a new ABC poll found that 58 percent of employed Americans say they are working harder but earning less, and 42 percent think today's children will not be able to match their parents' standard of living."

In this instance, the poll responses reflect a feature of the growth in the U.S. economy since the late 1970s—namely, that while the wealthy have done extremely well, expectations of rising real wages and increased leisure time that were a hallmark of postwar growth have, for most middle- and lower-income Americans, been frustrated or reversed (Harrigan 1993). Although this point is discussed briefly by the show's commentators, rather than focus on class-based divisions between citizens, the author Robert Samuelson attempts to "put things in some perspective" by assuming a homogeneous public and discussing contradiction *within* a unitary "public mind":

> If you look at some of these polls, you find out that on some of these economic opinions, that we're actually much better today—that people think we're much better today than they have in years. Sixty-six percent of Americans, according to a Gallup poll, believe they'll be better off financially in a year than they are today, and that's the highest reading on that poll since it began in 1976. So the picture of universal gloom and doom, it seems to me, is not actually what most people are thinking.
>
> (This Week with David Brinkley, April 14, 1996)

In this instance, what might have been a discussion of class conflict within society becomes a kind of "inner conflict" *within the public mind*, thereby derailing any discussion of how perceptions of "the economy" depend upon who you are. This, in turn, preserves the ability of elites to define what the economy is and when it is "good" or "bad."

The unity of public opinion is also linked to the ideology of political elites by the use of misleading metonyms in descriptions of political allegiance. The most common manifestation of this is the tendency to use the "swing" voters in elections as symbols of the electorate en masse. If one in five voters switch from one party to another to precipitate a decisive shift in political representation, this group of "shifters" is crucial to the formation of aggregate majorities. The motives and predilections of this group are thereby assumed to represent the "public mind." The 80 percent who did not change their minds have little symbolic value and are consequently rarely discussed, giving us a syllogism that frames much of the media coverage of politics: *swing voters decide elections, therefore swing voters express the will of the electorate.*

This, in turn, creates a tendency to overestimate the popularity of those centrist political discourses likely to appeal to this (minority) group. In a familiar refrain, Cokie Roberts (political reporter for ABC news and National Public Radio and a reliable purveyor of the "conventional wisdom" of Washington journalists) stated that we often see candidates "moving to the center—where the voters are" (*Morning Edition*, June 14, 1999). Roberts's assumption contains a partial truth: *uncommitted* voters are more likely to to feel *attracted to the idea* of a centrist politics—and these voters are often regarded as pivotal in the creation of majorities. And yet the polling profile of nonaligned voters is often quite distinct (rather than being in an aggregate middle). The National Election Studies at the University of Michigan show that independent voters do not always fall between Democrats and Republicans—their ideological leanings are both complex and, in some senses, unusual. Roberts is nonetheless able to transpose a simplistic analysis of the views of uncommitted voters onto the entire electorate—swing voters become simply "the voters." The center becomes the whole.

It is also not entirely clear that moving to the center is the only—or indeed the most ideologically appealing—way of winning elections. Despite the journalistic approval that invariably greets such a move, running to the center is *not* a panacea for mobilizing public opinion. This point has been illuminated by Williams and Wollman, whose research found no evidence to support the conventional journalistic wisdom that the electorate favors moderate candidates. On the contrary, in their study of comparable performance, the more left-leaning Democratic candidates actually did better than their more "moderate" counterparts (Williams and Wollman 1996).

Similarly, 1996 elections in the United States installed a Democrat in the White House and Republican majorities in Congress. If this result depended on a degree of vote-splitting, the percentage who actually voted for both Clinton and Congressional Republicans was fairly small—the great majority voted straight Republican or Democrat tickets. According to the National Election Studies, only 13 percent voted for a Clinton presidency and a Republican Congress. The question repeatedly asked by journalists ignored this partisan consistency and instead pondered on "the message" that the electorate was sending by voting for a divided government—something that, in fact, the great majority *did not* vote for.

Many journalists are comfortable in the apparently centrist terrain between Republicans and Democrats—it coincides, after all, with a notion of objectivity in which the reporter is placed *in between* the two protagonists. For a commentator to claim that the voters are ideologically on the right or the left would be regarded as displaying a potential disregard for the norms of journalistic objectivity, and yet these norms allow Cokie Roberts and others to claim the center is "where the voters are" without any such qualms.

Moreover, the bias toward the middle ground—toward "moderation" rather than partisans or "extremists"—is *not* based on finding the middle ground among the broad mass of public opinion polls but is defined in terms of political elites. Thus a conservative Democrat or a liberal Republican may be to the right of public opinion on most economic issues, but they are the center-points of elite political and media discourse.

CLOSING THE PUBLIC MIND: PUSHING PUBLIC OPINION TO THE RIGHT

The representation of public opinion on TV news suppresses or ignores the left side of the broad opinion data text. Similarly, scattered among the 392 press and radio reports of Times Mirror polls in 1994/1995 were those showing majority support for a range of progressive positions that ran directly counter to the positions espoused by the Republican Congress elected in 1994, and sometimes to the left of a broader Washington consensus (e.g., support for raising the minimum wage, opposition to increasing spending on defense—and particularly to a "Star Wars" missile defense system—support for more federal spending on public education, support for stricter government regulation of environmental protection, support for more spending on government-run healthcare, support for increased gun control legislation, support for programs like the National Endowment for the Arts and the Corporation for Public Broadcasting, support for the United Nations, and a suspicion of corporate America). But in *none* of the 392 newspaper or radio reports were such attitudes straightforwardly articulated as support for anything farther to the left than Bill Clinton (the possible exception being Andrew Kohut's cryptic statement on National Public Radio, quoted previously).

The frameworks I have described bind public opinion closely to political elites, making such an articulation extremely difficult. Thus, even when disillusionment with the two main parties becomes newsworthy, it is reconnected to the political mainstream by tracking support for a "middle of the road" candidate like Colin Powell (or, on other occasions, like Ross Perot or Jesse Ventura).

In the chapters that follow, I discuss ways in which the media do or do not influence public opinion. What I want to stress at this stage is the way in which the media influence the *representation of public opinion*. This allows us to identify what Benjamin Page calls "elite-mass gaps" (Page 1996) in the distinction between one representation of public opinion—the opinion poll—and another—media coverage of public opinion polls. This gap is not arbitrary, but involves suppressing the progressive or social democratic tendencies expressed in opinion surveys and thereby pushing public opinion—*in its dominant cul-*

tural form—to the right. The range of popular opinions expressed in the opinion data text—from left to right—is calibrated to reflect the range of elite opinion—from center to right.

This happens, I have suggested, for a variety of reasons. The political economy of polling tends to favor the powerful—specifically those, including the corporate media, with the resources to use the technology—while a variety of ideological/professional frameworks push media professionals toward a selection and interpretation of polls that reflect the broad thrust of elite (rather than popular) opinion. This exclusion is not deliberate or malevolent, but the product of a series of economic and ideological/professional practices that make such an outcome probable. In this landscape, the construction of a view of the American public in Washington's image—as generally moderate or conservative (and certainly distrustful of positions on the left)—is a hegemonic exercise, one that works to exclude the more oppositional or left-leaning discourses present in the broad mass of polling data.

We should not underestimate the power of this representation. It has led many, including those on the left, to characterize recent history as a period in which a resurgent free market ideology has, on a global scale, built a consensus for the gradual dismantling of the welfare state. And yet the evidence for such a consensus is based on a highly selective reading of the opinion poll data. There is instead the *appearance* of consensus, one that a selective reading of opinion polls has helped manufacture. Right-wing parties (like the Republican Party or the British Conservative Party) or influential right-wing factions within parties (like the Democratic Leadership Council and Labour Party "modernizers") may have succeeded in "capturing public opinion," *but only in the narrow terms in which public opinion is usually defined and described.*

Thus, in the United States, we see simultaneously a decline in the willingness of people to embrace the term "liberal" and consistent support for a range of left-leaning liberal programs and positions. Both can be tied to poll responses, but it is the first that is generally signified as an expression of public opinion in media coverage. The more left-wing politician advocating a program of increased social spending and government intervention that matches poll responses is thus cast adrift from those responses so that he or she appears to be "out of touch" with public opinion. Liberal Democrats in Congress can thus be defined—in the words of political correspondent Dan Schorr on National Public Radio—as "extremists" (*Weekend Edition*, August 2, 1997).

We cannot, of course, underestimate the importance of appearance in an era tinged by postmodernism—election campaigns, after all, are dominated by such appearances. But the closure of public opinion around a center-right axis is a *political* rather than an *ideological* phenomenon, one that has little to do with the battle for hearts and minds—or, at least the battle to create certain tendencies in response to survey questionnaires—and a great deal to do with the way that public opinion is appropriated in the political system. Those within the dominant center-right political axis have, through the appropriation of media frameworks, succeeded in defining public opinion and manipulating its terms, but they have failed to move public opinion in even the limited terms of polling technologies.

So, for example, as Page and Shapiro point out: "questions about programs for 'the poor' . . . often get a remarkable thirty or forty percentage points more support than questions about 'welfare' that are asked at the same time" (Page and Shapiro 1992, 126). This is, for all practical purposes, an expression of contradictory feelings about welfare, although as Page and Shapiro argue, it implies that, for many, the word "welfare" establishes an operational distinction between the poor and the undeserving poor. In Australian slang, it is the difference between a "battler" (a poor person struggling against the odds) and a "bludger" (a shiftless recipient of government handouts).

The wish to—in contemporary political parlance—"end welfare as we know it" is thus contingent upon the *way* we know it. While there are undoubtedly complexities behind these figures (not least the racial inflections of stereotypically idle welfare recipients; see Gray 1995) they might just as easily signify a desire for fairness as suggest support for a radical curtailment of government assistance to the poor.

This discursive construction of welfare has been illuminated by Kuklinski and Quirk, whose research suggests that attitudes about welfare relate to a set of media stereotypes (who the welfare recipient is, how much they receive, the burden on the taxpayer, etc). When survey respondents were given certain facts about welfare programs—when, in one sense, welfare was redefined as a program for the poor—they were more likely to express support for welfare spending (Kuklinski and Quirk 1997).

The stigmatization of "welfare" can thus be seen as a piecemeal rhetorical device. It allows the right to sever the connection between welfare recipients and the deserving poor at the ideological level while more quietly connecting them at the political level. Programs for poor people—which are, according to polls, generally popular—are thereby reduced in the name of reforming what the polls suggest is an unpopular welfare system. Crucial to the success of this ideological project is the media's complicity in referring to poll responses to "welfare" and ignoring polls about "poor people."

In much the same way, attacks on government largesse (linked to notions of waste, bureaucracy, meddling, and indulgence) reflect an ideological project that neatly circumnavigates the popularity of most government spending (on education, healthcare, the environment, policing, and so forth). The attack on "big government"—one that comes from Democratic leaders like Bill Clinton and Al Gore as well as Republicans—can be linked to a well-established ideological frame in which individual freedom is pitched against a sea of faceless, interfering bureaucrats. Popular government programs can therefore be cut in the name of this abstract, populist discourse. Again, the success of such a project relies on reporting unsympathetic responses to government in general and neglecting support for government programs. The center-right's success in these endeavors is not to capture public opinion but the agencies that define it. Thus the unpopularity of welfare is reported, discussed, and allowed to adorn the conventional wisdom of media and political elites (Parry 1992). The popularity of programs for poor people is, in turn, a scrap of polling data that is discarded, unused and unintelligible in the dominant framework.

My central point here is that the distinction between different moments in the construction of public opinion is of enormous political significance, since it enables us to see how discourses *about* public opinion polls are as integral to the cultural form as the polling data itself. And if elites on the center-right have been rather patchy at influencing the latter, they have been singularly successful at shaping the former.

If public opinion, in its broader sense, is to be won or lost, it is necessary to understand not only how it is signified but the political cracks in that signification. What remains for the left, as Stuart Hall has argued in another context (Hall 1988), is not simply a question of highlighting the columns and percentages that are routinely ignored—of reading against the grain of media representations—but of using these discursive fragments to articulate a progressive politics. Or, to borrow Janice Radway's metaphor, of sewing ideological seams between the cluster of social democratic sentiments that polls tap into and a more general progressive vision (Radway 1986). This involves using polls as well as deconstructing them. Polls are, in this sense, an indication of the complexity of hegemony: they signify both dominance and the incorporation of resistance into dominant frameworks.

PART TWO

THE FORMATION OF PUBLIC OPINION

CHAPTER 4

GETTING THE RIGHT RESPONSE?
MEDIA INFLUENCE ON PUBLIC OPINION

I have, thus far, focused on an analysis of public opinion polls as a cultural form, on the politics of inclusion and exclusion involved in various representations of public opinion. The rest of the book retains this conception of public opinion but turns to the difficult question of the media's role in influencing the answers people give in response to opinion questionnaires. Or, to put it in the language of cultural theory, while the first part of this book looked at the construction of public opinion as a discourse, the second will look at the construction of public opinion as a series of ideological responses.

I begin this investigation by establishing two principles—first, following William Gamson (1992), that any evaluation of media influence on public opinion depends upon where public opinion is located and how it is defined; and second, that the lessons of a variety of approaches to media influence suggest both the hegemonic power of media and the limits of that power. The critical question for those interested in media or politics is to describe, as precisely as possible, the nature of this relationship. I then sketch the outline of an analysis that will be developed in subsequent chapters. My argument, in short, is that the media's ability to shape the way people respond to public opinion polls is most clearly identifiable in specific discursive moments—moments that are limited but nonetheless instrumental in maintaining a degree of public acquiescence to the corporate, center-right hegemony in U.S. politics.

LOCATING PUBLIC OPINION

Most news organizations claim—in their more pretentious, uncritical moments—to both represent and serve the public. The journalist addresses the politician on the public's behalf and reports the reply for public edification. As Bruce MacLaury, president of the Brookings Institution, declares: "Media polls—properly conducted, analyzed, and presented—can increase the independence and quality of news reporting and give the public a chance to help set the agenda of campaigns and define the meaning of elections" (quoted in Mann and Orren 1992, vii). The opinion poll—which, as I argued in the previous chapter, might equally well be used to undermine these claims—is a mechanism built to reinforce this high-minded mission, with the happy benefit of delivering public opinion in a form that can be packaged and sold as "news."

In this framework, the public is active, the media and political elites responsive. The rhetorical core of this framework is an unsullied view of democracy, in which a rational public expresses its interests in a quantifiable form. It is, perhaps, only to be expected that those in the news media should be coy about their own power (unless, of course, that power is being sold to advertisers). If the media's relationship with public opinion is seen as vague and indefinable, then calls for regulation or an admission of social responsibility can be resisted— often accompanied by apparently magnanimous tributes to the independence of the public mind. If the nineteenth-century press was self-consciously partisan (Herbst 1993a), most newspapers today like to claim they are above the fray. While they may indulge themselves in editorial endorsements, for a newspaper to claim that it has helped one side in an election is, within this framework, almost taboo. This is even true in Britain, where the press is generally less coy about its (mainly proconservative) allegiances. When the British daily, the *Sun*, crowed (in its self-parodying, pseudocockney vernacular) that it was "The Sun Wot Won It" the day after the Conservative Party was returned to power in 1992, it broke this taboo with such an egregious vulgarity that its claims were, regardless of their veracity, swiftly retracted.

As discussed in the previous chapter, there is now a substantial body of work from a wide variety of perspectives—from fields such as sociology, media studies, and political science—that suggests that the dominant media, and the news media in particular, tend to rely upon and overrepresent the discourses and interests of political and economic elites. Since contemporary media systems are generally owned by large and powerful businesses, it would be surprising if this were not so. Moreover, I suggested that the pressures of economic struc-

tures tend to be *exacerbated* rather than offset by professional/ideological practices that tie media representations to elite perspectives. This has meant that the
way in which public opinion polls are reported and interpreted tends to accentuate the degree to which they manifest support for elite (specifically, center-
right) perspectives and downplay the extent to which they do not. The media
thereby shape public opinion *as it is generally understood* without necessarily
influencing the way anyone thinks. But to what extent do media—or elites,
through media—influence or shape people's perceptions or the way they
respond to polls?

Although this question has been asked many times, it is by no means as
straightforward as it might seem. Media influence on public opinion is, in part,
contingent upon *how* public opinion is defined. In particular, if public opinion
is defined by the technology of polling, it may be possible to record apparently
significant forms of media influence. If, on the other hand, public opinion is
investigated using more qualitative forms of inquiry—such as small group
interviews—forms of media influence may appear to have a more incidental or
less profound impact on the nature of public conversation.

So, for example, when the U.S. media became more concerned with the size
of the budget deficit in the early 1990s, public opinion polls appeared to
respond in kind. In a classic case of agenda-setting, the more/less media coverage the subject received, the more/less polls recorded public concern about the
issue. If media coverage of the issue decreased, so did public concern, even while
the size of the budget deficit continued to increase (Zhu 1991). This would
appear to be a significant instance of media influence. It is, nevertheless, quite
plausible that despite evidence of decisive shifts in response to poll questions
about the relative importance of issues, there may have been little change in
people's more substantive political conversations or their basic political
assumptions. Indeed, as I suggested in chapter one, the use of a framework that
asks people to rank their "concern about issues" is a technocratic discourse that
has little relevance in day-to-day political conversations. Poll respondents who
are asked what is, in the normal run of things, such an unlikely question, may
therefore respond by shifting mental gears to the more abstract political terrain
of media and elite discourse about politics. Their response, like the question,
may be appropriate to the way they see the media world of politics, but it may
be less obviously situated in the context of their more practical concerns
(Lasorsa and Wanta 1990; Lewis 1991, 151–57).

This is not to say that the response to the survey questionnaire is less real
than a more open-ended conversation, but it may refer to *one form* of public
opinion rather than to another. It is as if people were led into a showroom of

expensive cars—none of which they could actually afford—and asked which one they liked best. The response, influenced by the not inconsiderable discourse of television car commercials, may be well considered and legitimate, while, at the same time, it may have little practical relevance to their everyday experience of cars.

William Gamson's work with a series of discussion groups attempted to more closely replicate everyday political conversations among peers. His analysis of these conversations indicates the complexity of the relationship between media frames and public discourse. On the one hand, the use of such frames among his discussion-group respondents can be related to their prominence in media discourse, and yet there are moments when public discussions, drawing from a range of experiential and other sources, can either elide or resist dominant media frames (Gamson 1992).

Advocates of qualitative surveys argue that open-ended, free-flowing discussions are more likely to replicate a person's day-to-day experience than are precoded quantitative surveys, which both impose the agenda and prescribe the range and form of response (e.g., Jensen 1987a; Lewis 1991). This may be true, but there is a real danger in endowing the everyday with a certain authenticity, with the implication that this is *the essence* of the real world in which people live, as opposed to the world imagined and imposed by opinion pollsters. As Ien Ang (1991) points out, all forms of research favor certain outcomes—there is no essential or privileged moment in which a public citizen expresses an opinion. People will express their opinions in different forms and in different contexts: we simply have to decide which of these moments we are interested in and choose our form of inquiry accordingly.

Any research into media influence on public opinion must therefore presuppose what public opinion is and how it can be measured. Although this is often seen as a methodological question, it is also a political one. So, for example, a field like cultural studies has emphasized the *political importance* of the everyday, such as the way in which children and adults experience and deal with the drudgery of school and work (Willis 1977) or the way in which soap operas (Hobson 1982) or romance novels (Radway 1984) are incorporated into everyday routines and practices. Janice Radway's well-known research on women romance readers is illustrative here. She argues that although romances as a genre tend to confirm a repressive, patriarchal view of the world, women are able to use them to create space away from—and thus temporarily free themselves from—the domesticity of their own lives. This, she argues, is politically significant. Not in the traditional sense of raising a politically active, feminist consciousness—the form of politics that is usually privileged in such analysis—but in the politics of everyday life. This political form may have absolutely no consequences in affecting legislative change, but it is no less real or important for that.

Deliberately or not, quantitative forms of mass communication research have often focused on a very different political arena—namely, statements made in response to prescribed notions of the public realm. This may implicate the politics of everyday life, but it may also bypass it completely. For example, someone may regularly engage in broadly political conversations or practices but be asked to address politics *as it is constructed in the news media* only on the one occasion she or he is asked by a survey interviewer to do so. A quantitative study, in turn, would privilege this one conversation and ignore the others. Someone may tell a pollster that the "most important issue" facing the nation is education; at the same time, the whole notion of "ranking issues" may have little influence on the way he or she talks about politics to anyone else.

But this does not mean that such a study is somehow missing the point. Even if this is a fairly limited way of understanding how people think about politics, it is important in the sense that opinion polls provide one of the few, potentially potent forms of public expression in contemporary culture. The focus of much quantitative research is therefore on the media's capacity to shift public opinion *as it is manifested in opinion polls.* Because opinion polls have the capacity to influence legislative struggles (albeit in the limited framework described in the previous chapter), this form of public opinion—regardless of its "authenticity" in day-to-day conversation—is of political consequence.

It is in this theoretical context—one in which we locate public opinion in different moments and constructions—that we can make sense of the debates about media influence. As a consequence, we cannot always assume that those making competing claims about the media's political power are talking about the same thing. My aim in this discussion is to avoid the common practice of privileging certain types of influence as *automatically* being of more political import.

Power or Empowerment?

In chapter one, I described how mass communication research began by exploring the relationship among masses, specifically the relation among mass communication, mass culture, and mass society (Beniger 1987). The focus on "mass" tended to create a bias toward quantitative or psychological forms of inquiry that assumed a certain homogeneity, that "mass society man" or "mass

society woman" would behave in ways that could be captured either by sociological aggregates—like polls—or by psychological studies. This notion was
modified but nonetheless retained by theories that differentiated between
"opinion leaders" (who, like Walter Lippmann's class of experts, offer guidance)
and the more capricious masses (Berelson, Lazarsfeld, and McPhee 1954;
Lazarsfeld and Katz 1955). This idea—which remains influential (e.g., Popkin
1991)—may enable one to make sense of quantitative data, but like any highly
reductive theory, it conveys a fairly crude understanding of media influence or
the way people interact and talk about politics.

Although the evidence they produced was somewhat contradictory (Hovland 1959), early studies of media influence were generally seen as allaying the
pessimism of "mass society" critics—from the Frankfurt School and elsewhere
(e.g., Adorno and Horkheimer 1979)—who feared that a propagandist mass
media might create a compliant mass society in its image. But the failure to
detect media influence beyond what have been called "minimal effects" was
partly a consequence of theoretical and methodological limitations rather than
the media's insignificance (Lewis 1991). More sophisticated models have, since
then, suggested ways in which the media *do* have a significant effect on the way
many people think in certain contexts. Indeed, commenting on this accumula-
tion of evidence, John Zaller has argued that the Berelson/Lazarsfeld era of
"minimal effects" is finally over, and that we now have a body of research that
obliges us to take the ideological role of the media extremely seriously (Zaller
1992).

Two of the most persuasive refinements of the quantitative tradition have
been cultivation analysis and agenda-setting research. Focusing on the broad
content of television—those ideas, people, or stereotypes that are repeated
across genres and over time—cultivation analysis has explored television's
long-term symbolic power to frame the way people define and interpret the
world. So, for example, while a number of individual television programs portray strong female characters, the more *systematic and sustained* representations
of men and women suggest profound inequalities (overall, men outnumber
women three to one on U.S. television—a ratio that tends to increase in more
traditionally authoritative genres like news and current affairs or advertising
voiceovers). The results of the cultivation studies indicate that—regardless of
other variables—the more television you watch, the more your views of the
world are likely to conform to television's dominant symbolic parameters.
These symbolic parameters, cultivation research suggests, tend to be conservative rather than progressive: heavy television viewers, for example, are more
likely to assume that men are naturally more authoritative than women and are

more likely to hold political views close to those of television's mainstream, which is generally to the right of center (Gerbner, Gross, Morgan, and Signorielli 1980, 1986; Signorielli and Morgan 1990). In the U.S. context at least, cultivation research has thereby identified a series of ways in which television plays a hegemonic role. Overall, we might say that cultivation analysis suggests that television prefers some meanings over others, and those meanings tend to favor the views of those with power (Ruddock 1998).

Agenda-setting research was conceived with the fairly modest goal of avoiding more overt forms of opinion formation, looking instead at the extent to which the media set the agenda in which opinions become important. This was initially, according to McCombs, Danielian, and Wanta, a way of circumventing "an argument ongoing at that time about the minimal effects of the mass media on opinions and attitudes by focusing their theory on the initial steps leading up to opinion change" (McCombs, Danielian, and Wanta 1995, 283). The results of agenda-setting research, however, significantly dented the notion of "minimal effects"—consistently indicating clear and sometimes dramatic patterns of media influence. In an early survey of undecided voters in the 1968 presidential election, McCombs and Shaw (1972) found an almost perfect correlation between their respondents' political issue agendas and the proportion of media content devoted to those issues. These findings have been supported in a number of subsequent studies (e.g., Funkhouser 1973; MacKuen 1981; Iyengar, Peters, and Kinder 1982; Iyengar and Kinder 1987) in which it becomes clear that responses to public opinion surveys *follow* rather than precede media agendas and often have very little to do with any evaluative analysis of the significance of an issue *outside* the arena of news reporting.

It might be said that early agenda-setting research was successful in locating media influence partly because of the modesty of the approach. It was, according to Silvio Lenart, "a humble endeavor, producing results that show the effects of the media to be narrow in scope and short-lived in duration" (Lenart 1994, 17). But as agenda-setting studies have become more sophisticated, the significance of media power actually appears to be *more* profound than initially imagined. As I pointed out in chapter one, agenda-setting has moved beyond Bernard Cohen's old adage—that the media tell us only what to think about, not what to think (Cohen 1963)—to acknowledge that the media are instrumental in providing information, and that "one's store of information shapes one's opinions" (McCombs, Danielian, and Wanta 1995, 295).

An important example of this approach is Shanto Iyengar's work, which suggests the media perform an agenda-setting function not only in the prioritization of issues but in the *episodic* framing of those issues (Iyengar 1991), whereby news consists of individual or particular events with little thematic context. This structure, Iyengar suggests, tends to exclude discussions of social causality. In the episodic framework, things—whether crimes or terrorist acts—just happen. Iyengar's research suggests that viewers supplied with thematic, contextual information are more able to turn their attention to social causes and possible forms of government intervention that might address those causes, while the episodic structure focuses viewers' attention on coping with only the manifestations of social problems.

Iyengar does not shy away from the political consequences of this finding, arguing—following William Gamson (1989)—that episodic framing serves the interests of political elites who are reluctant for government to address social problems. The center-right philosophy that dominates Washington benefits from a discourse in which poverty, crime, and environmental degradation have no clear causes or solutions. There is, as a consequence, little responsibility placed on political figures for addressing the structural causes of social problems.

While cultivation and agenda-setting focus on different forms of discourse, they both avoid simplistic notions of opinion formation in which opinions favored in the media are straightforwardly reproduced. Cultivation analysis is concerned with the media's influence on people's assumptions about the world, while agenda-setting has begun to explore the relation between different types of political discourse, of which "opinion," in its conventional sense, is only a part. The evidence they provide suggests that the media play a significant role in the construction of discursive or symbolic clusters that people use to define and understand the world. But their data are not absolute. Heavy viewers may be *more likely* to think in television's terms, but they will not necessarily do so. Television may encourage an episodic view of social problems, but it does not guarantee it. A statistically significant correlation indicates a tendency, not an inevitability. In short, while many people will replicate media frameworks in responding to survey questions, some will not.

If this point seems obvious, it is often forgotten, particularly by the critics of such research who see its findings—based, as many studies are, on quantitative aggregates—as insensitive to the multiplicity and complexity of ideological influences on a person. Certainly it is true to say that these studies tend to isolate media influence in order to assess its salience, but complexity is implied by the numbers themselves. Even when their findings suggest strong correlations between media content and survey responses, there will be 10, 20, or 40 percent of people who *do not* respond as the model implies they should. These models are therefore only *partial* descriptions of media influence—and they should not be interpreted (by practitioners or critics) as being more than that.

Qualitative audience research has tended to be more cautious in assessing media influence. Indeed, much of the work that has been conducted under the general rubric of cultural studies has been criticized in recent years for ignoring—or attempting to discredit—evidence accumulated by more traditional, quantitative approaches, and by focusing instead on the *instability* of meaning and on people's capacity to *resist* dominant messages. Whether in response to the postmodern turn, the development of "reader-response" theory, or work on "resistive readings," there have been a number of critiques of this development (e.g., Condit 1989; Carragee 1990; Corner 1991). Robert McChesney is particularly forthright in condemning the tendency of contemporary cultural studies to move away from an analysis of dominant hegemonic structures. This, in McChesney's view, has blunted the critical edge of contemporary cultural studies—particularly in the United States, where the comprehensive critical scope that characterized the emergence of cultural studies has been dismantled by the argument that "big issues" like the power of the media "do not exist or are impossible to understand" (McChesney 1996, 3).

There are three issues here. First of all, it is true to say that those who downplay media influence often fail to deal seriously—or, in some cases, at all—with the mounting evidence in its favor. The dismissal of evidence that comes, say, from cultivation analysis or agenda-setting research often rests upon a rather banal syllogism, namely: these studies are incapable of revealing the complex nature of the encounter between people and media texts; therefore, their findings can be ignored. This is much the same as the critique of public opinion polls that says that because the opinion poll is a contrived form of public expression, it tells us nothing about public opinion. All research into the way people think is a contrivance of some form; the issue is how we respect and interpret the limits of that contrivance.

Second, criticisms of this research often begin with the premise that, unless proved beyond every methodological and theoretical objection or quibble, media have no influence. The assumption, in other words, is that media are innocent of influence unless proved—beyond a reasonable doubt—otherwise. This, I would argue, is an odd—though in scientific discourse not uncommon—premise. Television, newspapers, magazines, radio, and other cultural forms are such a ubiquitous and important part of most people's semiotic worlds that the notion that media play little or no part in informing the way people understand and interpret the world is somewhat implausible. One might just as well begin by assuming widespread media influence unless demonstrated otherwise. For example, it is not enough to say that there are *other* ways of explaining the correlations in cultivation or agenda-setting research without demonstrating that those other explanations are, on the basis of available evidence, more plausible.

Third, qualitative audience research is often characterized as revealing the limits—rather than the extent—of media influence. And yet this is *not* what a thorough reading of qualitative studies would suggest. On the contrary, as Ann Gray has observed, any systematic review of the qualitative audience research literature offers at least as much evidence suggesting audience *consent* to dominant media frameworks as it does audience *resistance* to those frameworks (Gray 1987). Indeed, in the period since Ann Gray made this observation, there have been a number of qualitative studies published that implicate the media's role in the construction of social meaning (e.g., Philo 1990; Press 1991; Gamson 1992; Jhally and Lewis 1992; Heide 1995; McKinley 1997).

This body of research uses two of the key assumptions that often inform theories of audience resistance to media influence: first, audiences are seen as active rather than passive; second, media texts are seen as potentially ambiguous rather than monolithic (they can, in other words, be interpreted in different ways by different people). But the conclusions they draw do *not* suggest that audience activity or textual ambiguity diminish media influence. They simply make that influence more complex and diffuse.

For example, Greg Philo's research with news discussion groups in Britain asked various groups to write their own news story based on a fairly ambiguous set of pictures from the 1984/1985 British miners' strike. Participants could thereby replicate the dominant media frame, subvert it, or come up with a different frame altogether. The assumption behind such a method is that audiences are active in the construction of meaning. Philo's findings include moments in which audience members develop critiques of television coverage that draw from oppositional discourses outside television, as well as moments in which people replicate the assumptions and logic of dominant media frames (e.g., the assumption that it is striking miners rather than the police who are potentially violent). Thus, while different audiences negotiate with news in various ways, television supplies much of the symbolic or conceptual raw material for understanding the world, "limiting what audiences can see and in providing key elements of political consciousness and belief" (Philo 1990, 205).

E. Graham McKinley's (1997) study of teenage girls and their use and understanding of the show *Beverley Hills 90210* covers very different territory but comes to a similar set of conclusions. The girls in McKinley's audience were also active in their construction of the show's meanings, but those meanings tended to replicate rather than challenge the fairly stereotypical gender assumptions that permeate the show.

Equally, examples of audiences using different interpretative frameworks are not necessarily instances of audience power. Andrea Press's work suggests that while (predominantly white) working-class women interpret television very differently from middle-class women, both are implicated—in different ways—in dominant structures of meaning (Press 1991). While they are critical of television's realism in a general sense, middle-class women tend to assume a high level of identification with representations of women on television. Alternatively, working-class women are less inclined to identify with television's predominantly middle-class cast of characters, but they do not have the experiential resources with which to question the realism of those representations. In a similar vein, Jhally and Lewis (1992) found that while interpretations of *The Cosby Show* depended upon an audience member's race and class position, most members of the audience were inscribed within television's dominant discourse about race and class (Jhally and Lewis 1992).

Even some of the research most commonly associated with the notion of audience resistance to forms of media power reveals that audiences work within a hegemonic context. Janice Radway's classic study of romance readers—so often cited as a description of audience resistance (Radway 1984)—is also a study of hegemony and the *limits of* resistance. Henry Jenkins's work on the "textual poaching" of fans of *Star Trek* (Jenkins 1992)—work that is often regarded as an instance of the power of audiences to play with media texts and construct their own meanings—is also careful to acknowledge the limits placed on audiences. Jenkins thus argues that "fans' resistant reading occurs *within* rather than *outside* the ideological framework provided by the program" (Jenkins 1995, 263; my emphasis).

Overall, the notion of media power and hegemony *has not* collapsed under the weight of audience research within a broad cultural studies and/or qualitative tradition. On the contrary, it could be seen as demonstrating the complex and contested nature of media influence (see also Corner, Richardson, and Fenton 1990; Lewis 1991; Morley 1992; Heide 1995; Tulloch and Jenkins 1995; Press and Cole 1999). As Gramsci argued, hegemony involves struggle, not seamless domination (Gramsci 1971). Moreover, media influence is not something that is *experienced* as oppressive—on the contrary, it may be experienced as fun. Thus, as David Morley argues, "It remains necessary to analyze and understand the pleasures that popular culture offers its consumers if we are to understand how hegemony operates through the processes of commercial popular culture" (Morley 1992, 36).

If we can draw a broad conclusion from the very different approaches used to investigate media influence, it is to affirm the notion of media power but to recognize both its complexity and its limits. This may seem to be an unsurprising conclusion: indeed, it would be odd if the media, which constitute an important part—but only a part—of our discursive environment, had either a minimal or an absolute influence. It is, however, a conclusion that emphasizes the importance of various forms of research in identifying when, where, and how the media have power and under what discursive conditions. But if we might take for granted a degree of media influence, it is the nature of that influence that needs to be established.

MEDIA INFLUENCE ON PUBLIC OPINION

Let me briefly return to one of the notable findings of agenda-setting research—specifically, that while media coverage was found to influence public concern, public concern did not appear to influence media coverage (Behr and Iyengar 1985). The process being described here is therefore not a perfect circle of reproduction. There is agenda-setting, but there are also moments when media agendas and public opinion agendas drift apart.

Page and Shapiro's work on public opinion suggests that while it is possible to trace patterns of media influence, in many areas the aggregate response to public opinion polls is remarkably stable and consistent even when it is in marked opposition to the dominant perspectives in media coverage and elite opinion (Page and Shapiro 1992). In the previous chapter, I suggested that this mismatch is possible, in part, because the media tend to ignore or reinterpret poll responses in ways that create the impression that their coverage is generally *in line* with opinion surveys. This, in turn, is possible because the opinion data, as a whole, offer enough apparently contradictory evidence—like an astrological chart, it is a fairly open text—to allow interpretations that align poll results with elite opinion.

Perhaps the most persuasive way in which public opinion can be made to appear compatible with elite views of the world is in terms of broad ideological frameworks—defined (in the rather truncated lexicon of U.S. politics) as "liberal," "moderate," or "conservative." When people are asked to identify themselves with conventional political labels, polls tend to show the largest group nominating themselves as "moderate," followed by conservatives, followed by liberals (although in some polls in recent years, depending on how the question is asked, conservatives sometimes slightly outnumber moderates). The General Social Survey, for example, asks people to define themselves on a seven-point scale, from "extremely liberal" to "extremely conservative," with "moderate" in the middle. While the responses to this questionnaire have been remarkably consistent over the past few decades, the overall shift from the mid-1970s to the mid-1990s was in a slightly conservative direction, as illustrated in the following table.

General Social Survey Results

YEAR	LIBERAL	MODERATE	CONSERVATIVE
1974	29%	38%	28%
1984	23%	39%	35%
1994	27%	36%	38%

Opinion polls have thereby created a picture of the American population that might be interpreted as suggesting an increasingly robust conservatism, a solid—usually dominant—block of moderates, and a smaller group somewhere on the left. This image of the American public is well known. It is generally accepted by journalists and pundits regardless of their own political predilections and apparently vindicated in the electoral successes of "moderate" or conservative presidential candidates. Indeed, if we rely on people's political self-identification, the general shift to the right in Washington since 1980 appears to be in line with the ideological predilections of the U.S. public: thus, for example, in 1984 there appeared to be 12 percent more people on the conservative side than on the liberal side—figures easily lopsided enough to generate an electoral landslide. In this context, Reagan's reelection makes perfect sense.

If this neatly fits a democratic model of public opinion, it is also compatible with a hegemonic one—the key question being the media's role in these events. Did the media push public opinion to the right, or was it moving in that direction anyway?

And yet to take these choices at face value is to misconstrue the meaning of public opinion polls and, in particular, to substantially overestimate the use of the terms "liberal," "moderate," and "conservative" as taxonomic headings for the ideological preferences of U.S. citizens. If these responses fit fairly well with presidential election results in recent decades, they seem, at times, almost entirely *disconnected* from the general drift of other poll responses. As I have suggested, a number of studies have found that when Reagan was easily reelected in 1984, polling data on specific policy areas were generally moving in a liberal direction, with very little evidence of substantive support for—and a great deal of opposition to—Reagan's political agenda (Ferguson and Rogers 1986; Mayer 1992).

The ability of people to construct attitudes according to well-organized liberal-conservative belief systems has been the subject of much debate among
scholars of public opinion (see chapter eight). While the evidence suggests that
many citizens *may* think along ideological lines or, at least, be able to identify
where policies fit on a left–right spectrum, surveys have also tended to show that
only a minority can define the terms "liberal" and "conservative" in ways that
consistently match their usage in political science (Converse 1964; Delli Carpini
and Keeter 1996). This suggests that many people may well understand the basic
parameters of a classic liberal/conservative dichotomy but *not necessarily in
relation to those labels.* The terms "liberal" and "conservative," in other words,
may signify within a framework that is *connected to* but nonetheless *distinct
from* a left/right ideological framework. If this is so, it would explain why people appear more willing to embrace liberal policy positions than the term itself.

In order to understand these nuances, we need to think about the informational climate that might produce them. In the context of a broad cluster of poll
responses *moving to the left*, Ronald Reagan's victory in 1984 and the greater tendency of people to identify with the notion of conservatism rather than liberalism are both ideological victories with significant political consequences. Both
were carefully crafted and, I would argue, both relied upon *very specific* media
frameworks in which Reagan was signified positively and liberalism negatively
rather than upon a *more general* ideological shift.

Thus, for example, in their study of the 1988 election, Delli Carpini and
Keeter found that many voters not only failed to support details of a right-wing
agenda, but they were actually unaware of the conservative direction policy had
taken during the Reagan/Bush era, and thus: "only a quarter to a third of voters
knew that federal efforts on behalf of the environment, the poor, and the
schools declined during this period," while "a sizeable minority of this group
(from one-fifth to one-fourth) *thought spending had increased and thought that
this was a good thing.*" Among this group, "a large majority of these citizens
voted for Bush—in essence to continue policies that were the opposite of what
they wanted." This was even the case for those less well-off citizens normally in
the Democratic camp (Delli Carpini and Keeter 1996, 264). Thus Bush's election
appears to have been premised partly on the incorrect notion that he was following a liberal social-policy agenda. Whatever else this evidence suggests, it
clearly complicates simple notions of media influence on public opinion, or
lack thereof.

Moreover, such a contradiction indicates that the success of Republican
politicians pursuing an economic agenda may be based not on some form of
ideological persuasion but on the failure of a small but potentially significant

group of voters to make certain ideological connections. This is possible because the dominant media framework in which politics is covered very rarely makes such connections explicit. Janine Jackson's analysis of the media coverage of the 1992 Democratic primary, for example, found that only 2 percent of press articles covering the election contained any serious analysis of candidates' position on issues (Jackson and Naureckas 1996). In this framework, a politician is able to make symbolic gestures *as a deliberate strategy* to belie unpopular policy positions—Ronald Reagan's use of a "man of the people" persona and sympathetic imagery to counter policies whose immediate beneficiaries were corporate or wealthy interests is perhaps the prototype of such a strategy.

At the same time, many of those within the center-right mainstream that dominates Washington politics have, for some time, either conducted or tolerated a strategic assault on the term "liberal." This attack is important, because in the shorthand descriptions that dominate media discourse, the word "liberal" is taken to stand for the range of ideas on the political left. And yet the attempt to discredit the moniker "liberal" has *not been* a coherent systematic attack on concrete policies associated with liberalism. Indeed, the word itself has often been coupled with terms—notably the idea of a "liberal elite"—entirely disconnected from apparently popular liberal policies, such as government support for healthcare, the environment, public education, or the poor. Instead, the word "liberal" has been associated with, at best, naïve do-gooders and, at worst, a kind of indulgent, upper-middle-class tolerance of laxity or excess.

The success of these articulations has forced those who, in other circumstances, might be happy to accept the label to be somewhat defensive. In the Bush/Dukakis presidential race, for example, Bush repeatedly used the term to describe his opponent, while Dukakis not only avoided it, he chastised Bush for his use of the "liberal label." Indeed, the relative popularity of these labels neatly matches their usage in mainstream media discourse: the term "moderate" is usually given a positive association (moderates are good, extremists are bad[e.g., Morgan 1989]), the term "conservative" is generally more neutral and descriptive, while the term "liberal"—partly as a result of a sustained semantic campaign initiated by conservatives and accepted or tolerated by "moderate" Democrats—is often used pejoratively (to such an extent, at times, that it becomes almost ineffable, as in "the l-word," a politics that dare not speak its name).

The ability of those articulating the term "liberal" within a negative frame to inscribe this metaphorical structure into mainstream media discourse reflects, first of all, the dominance of those in the center or on the right in the political system. Those in Washington who might have desired to initiate a similar campaign against the term "conservative" have neither the political power nor the numbers to do so, being constrained by membership in a party many of whose leaders see themselves as moderate—or even conservative—rather than liberal. It also reflects a media framework willing and able to accept these terms of reference.

Indeed, a brief quantitative glimpse of media coverage of the term "liberal" indicates the degree to which the notion has been symbolically identified with privileged groups—of whom people on the left (especially working-class people) have generally been suspicious. A Lexis Nexis search found 127 articles in the U.S. press in the decade between June 1990 and June 2000 in which the phrases "working class" or "blue collar" were linked with (in this instance, within two words of) conventional ideological labels. Although polls suggest working-class people tend to be more left wing on most budgetary or economic questions (the main exception being civil liberties issues), in press coverage the phrases "working class" or "blue collar" were much more likely to be used in conjunction with the term "conservative" (71 percent of the time) than with the terms "liberal" or "progressive" (only 29 percent of the time). Conversely, in the same period, of the 248 stories in which the phrase "elite" was linked with (in this instance, within one word of) ideological labels, it was much more likely to be used in conjunction with the terms "liberal" or "progressive" (87 percent of the time) than with the term "conservative" (13 percent of the time). This symbolic environment is, to say the least, confusing for someone trying to grasp a lexicon in which the term "liberal" is supposed to be synonymous with left-wing positions and interests. This may begin to explain why working-class Americans are more likely to hold political positions on the left while being simultaneously suspicious of "liberals."

As I have stressed, a serious review of polling data would suggest that the relative popularity of the three labels, on one level, signifies little beyond rather shallow ideological semantics. As the popularity of a range of left-wing ideas (notably liberal government programs) indicates, it certainly does not enable us to graft a systematic—or even vague—ideological grid upon the American public. It has, nonetheless, a great deal of political significance in media discourse, where the term *is* often understood as a coherent ideological label. In this context, it has helped cement the notion among what Eric Alterman (1992) has called the "punditocracy" that liberalism *as an ideology*—rather than simply as a term—is generally marginal to mainstream American opinion.

Media influence on responses to public opinion polls is, in this instance, both shallow and profound: shallow inasmuch as it signifies little beyond itself;

profound inasmuch as it has an impact on the shape of political discourse. As I shall argue in the chapters that follow, this is symptomatic of the strategic way in which political elites influence public opinion. It also highlights what appears to be one of the central contradictions in the findings of public opinion polls, between abstract notions of political ideology or philosophy and more specific political concerns.

HEGEMONY IN ABSTRACTION

It is possible to identify in mainstream media and elite political discourse a number of indistinct, almost romantic notions that are rarely interrogated: an attachment to individual freedom, free enterprise, and moderation, and an antipathy to *self-defined* socialist notions of government. These abstractions tend to lend themselves to politicians on the right rather than those on the left, and polls dutifully show that majorities are prepared, when asked, to embrace all of them. For example, polling data over the past few decades suggest consistent and strong support for the idea of free enterprise as the basis for an economic system (Page and Shapiro 1992, 142–43—although it should be noted that there are signs that this support has, depending on how it is expressed, begun to wane in recent years). And yet it is a weak, gestural embrace that tells us very little about what most Americans think about political practicalities.

My attempts to understand what is going on in the apparently contradictory realm of poll responses were stimulated by Free and Cantril's instructive 1960s study, which found that while many Americans were inclined to support conservative principles in abstraction, they tended to lean leftward when those principles were given an immediate and specific context. After analyzing responses on general questions on federal interference in state and local affairs, regulation of business, local solutions to social problems, belief in economic opportunity, and belief in individual initiative, they categorized a national sample of 3,000 respondents thus:

Completely or predominantly liberal	16%
Middle of the road	34%
Completely or predominantly conservative	50%

On an abstract discursive level, conservative positions on the role of government, the individual, and free enterprise were likely to resonate with most Americans, while interventionist, collectivist philosophies were not.

The same sample also responded to questions about specific, mainly federal government programs: support for education, Medicare, the low-rent housing program, urban renewal, and efforts to reduce poverty and unemployment. When responses to these questions were sorted into political categories, Free and Cantril discovered a significant shift. The new political categories were tabulated as follows:

Completely or predominantly liberal	65%
Middle of the road	21%
Completely or predominantly conservative	14%

Nearly half of those who had endorsed abstract conservative philosophies were completely or predominantly liberal in their support of New Deal–style government activism, endorsing programs that, in theory, conservatives might have opposed. Or, as Kathleen Knight and Robert Erikson suggest, "U.S. public opinion may be philosophically conservative but it is operationally liberal" (Knight and Erikson 1997, 102).

Michael Moore's visit to Cobb County on his program *TV Nation* is, perhaps, one of the best-known demonstrations of the gap between the general and specific. This conservative stronghold also happened to be the recipient of significant sums of government money for various contracts and programs. The citizens of Cobb County, Moore discovered, were extremely receptive to antigovernment rhetoric in principle but understandably attached to the federal support their district received.

We find many of the same patterns in responses to opinion polls in more recent decades. When the concept of government is pitched against individual liberty, it resonates with an idea deeply embedded within a range of American practices and institutions. Its discursive power is undeniable. But it is also intermittent—severely compromised by its very generality. When it comes to practical instances—from environmental legislation to support for public broadcasting—suspicions of an active government often become, for many poll respondents, simply inappropriate. Unlike DNA, they are not the building blocks of larger, more complex structures. They do not translate into coherent political philosophies.

For example, a series of National Opinion Research Center (NORC) polls on the redistribution of wealth suggest that assumptions about the depth of American belief in the fairness of the free market are misplaced. When asked whether the government should do something to reduce income difference between the rich and the poor—an idea that is, after all, a basic tenet of democratic socialist philosophy—those supporting intervention have consistently outnumbered those who do not. While this reached a recent high in 1990 (51% to 25%), even the low point in 1994 (when Republicans captured both the House and Senate) indicated as many in support of egalitarian government intervention as opposed to it (39% to 38%).

It is interesting that if we focus on tolerance and civil liberties, there is evidence of the opposite trend: most people are inclined to support abstract notions of civil liberty and social tolerance, but they will often favor limitations on civil liberties or intolerant attitudes in specific instances. For example, most people will agree with the notion that people with minority views should be free to express their opinions, but they will be more inclined to limit freedom of speech for certain groups (Edy 1999, 365). In these cases, people tend to be progressive in abstraction and more reactionary in specific instances. This is notable, because it suggests that, in abstraction, people are inclined to be conservative on broadly economic questions (like those addressed in the Free and Cantril study) but more liberal on matters of tolerance and civil liberties. In other words, *on an abstract level of discourse, most people conform to the attitudinal pattern of the professional/managerial classes*, whether they be media professionals (Croteau 1998) or people who are major donors to the political system (Green, Herrnson, Powell, and Wilcox 1998).

Since media coverage of politics tends to revolve around generalities rather than the analysis of specific policy positions, this is highly suggestive. It indicates that the tendency in surveys to embrace liberal policies but eschew the term "liberal" may well be part of a more general pattern of media influence, whereby media play a significant role in winning support for an elite agenda in abstraction but are far less effective in creating enthusiasm for specific aspects of that agenda.

It is at this point that we can begin to see the complexity of the media's role in informing responses to public opinion polls. Above all, we cannot assume that the clusters of responses that make up the broad mass of opinion data easily cohere into discursive wholes. The notion of articulation—the idea that ideology works by connecting and disconnecting certain ideas or terms—is useful here (Hall 1996; Slack 1996). The appearance of ideas like free enterprise, deregulation, and individual initiative tend, in most mainstream media discourse, to be articulated with positive terms like "freedom," "efficiency," "dynamism," "America," and, more specifically, the "American Dream." For many respondents to an opinion survey, these articulations are likely to come to mind in response to a question that uses such abstractions. Since these abstractions are rarely articulated with specific policy proposals in media discourse, it is not surprising if they are also disconnected in opinion poll responses.

If we assume that these terms carry a fixed set of meanings that neatly correspond with the way in which pollsters and political commentators under-

stand them, then responses to public opinion polls are undoubtedly full of contradictions. But this assumption ignores the way in which people are addressed
in media discourse—a place where links between abstract concepts and specific
policies are rarely made in any systematic way. If polling responses are irrational
in terms of an "expert" evaluation of their meaning—if they are what Free and
Cantril call "schitzoid"—it may be that this evaluation misinterprets the popular meaning of poll responses. Indeed, if the media create an informational climate in which political abstractions are *not* articulated with specific policy ini-
tiatives, the failure of poll respondents to make such connections might be
regarded as an entirely rational response to the information available.

So, for example, we can say that the ability to tap into suspicions of government spending and regulation depends upon the way government is understood. When government is placed in opposition to the private individual—
whether in relation to, say, abortion or property rights—it is fairly easy to create robust majorities in support of forms of free enterprise and free agency. This
opposition is very much a part of elite/media framework in which abstract
ideas of government regulation are associated with meddling bureaucracy.
Accordingly, when a Harris poll in April 1995 asked the question, "Do you think
that the federal government should have the right to set certain regulations
affecting the use of private property, or do you think the use of private lands
should be left solely up to the property owner?" the response showed only a
minority (38%) supporting a government's power to regulate, with the majority (59%) opposed. This would appear to affirm a conservative ideology that
promotes the sanctity of private property.

Harris then asked the same question but in a different discursive form in
which the generality of the term is replaced by a specific instance:

*Do you think that the federal government should or should not have the right to pre-
vent owners of private land from developing the land if that development would involve
harming or polluting the environment?*

(*The National Journal*, May 20, 1995)

The notion of regulation is no longer abstract. It is therefore no longer so easy
to connect it to the dichotomous frame in media discourse. The negative associations with government regulation begin to fall away, to become less relevant.
Accordingly, the response to this question was quite different: 79 percent now
supported the government's power to regulate, and only 20 percent continued
to affirm the sanctity of private property. While this does, in some ways, invalidate the first response, it is perhaps more useful to see it as indicative of the
presence of another powerful (in this instance, more powerful) competing ide-

ology about environmental protection. In this case, the commitment to the sanctity of private property, in general, was compromised—and overridden—by the appeal of an environmentalist discourse.

This interpretation suggests that, for many people, the abstract notion of government regulation in the first of the two questions evokes unnecessary government interference rather than government as a representative of community interests. It therefore requires additional information—like that offered in the second question—to shift it away from this negative paradigm. If the first interpretation of the term "government regulation" is, in a technical sense, somewhat skewed, this may simply be a response—indeed, one might say a rational response—to the dominant use of the phrase in mainstream media discourse. Thus it is that "government spending" in its abstract form—a term frequently associated with waste and profligacy—is less popular as a term than a range of government programs that are generally signified within more benign discursive frameworks.

This becomes easier to comprehend if we see it as a product of very specific ideological campaigns espoused by elites in the news media. The notion of government spending or intervention (of "big government") *in abstraction* has a history of articulations within a well-constructed anticommunist or antisocialist discourse. Indeed, part of the success of that discourse was premised on the ability to *disconnect* it from popular or benign government programs—like Social Security, public education, and help for the poor—and signify it within a more sinister, authoritarian discourse. This disconnection, for many political leaders on the right, was entirely strategic and somewhat disingenuous. Thus, for example, Reagan was able to cut popular government programs in the name of a more abstract, populist, antigovernment discourse. Similarly, as I suggested earlier, the stigmatization of the term "welfare" has enabled elites to attack apparently popular antipoverty programs.

What this amounts to is a very specific form of hegemony—what we might call the hegemony of abstraction. It is the form of hegemony that allows many women to embrace basic feminist principles while rejecting the label for themselves (Douglas 1994). This is not to say that media influence can or will only take such a form, but it does tell us that the degree to which elites can create support—or antipathy—for certain abstractions is as conspicuous as their failure to generate support for the nuts and bolts of an elite policy agenda. In chapters six, seven, and eight, I develop this analysis in relation to some key ideological struggles in contemporary politics. However, before embarking on this somewhat hair-raising journey, I would like, in the next chapter, to take a step back and consider the discursive nature of responses to opinion surveys in greater detail.

CHAPTER 5

WHAT ARE OPINIONS AND
WHERE DO THEY COME FROM?

In democratic countries, the notion of turning words into numbers is well ensconced in traditions of voting. The technology of opinion survey research has been strongly influenced by electoral polls: what *counts* in these measures are clearly formed attitudes that allow people to make certain choices—the arena generally referred to as "opinion." This raises two questions: what, exactly is an opinion, and why do polls focus on opinions rather than on many other forms of public discourse?

If there are obvious answers to these questions, they are often tautological. It might be said, for example, that we focus on opinions because they are the central means of expression in democratic politics—but that is partly because of the way in which we have chosen to define democratic politics. If public opinion is often expressed by the results of public opinion polls, so democracy is often defined by the technology of voting. The idea of democracy is thereby reduced to the existence of voting mechanisms rather than other, more profound forms of civic participation in governance. In chapter eight, I argue that there are important consequences to this conflation—not least the lack of scrutiny given to the limits of electoral polls as a means of public expression, even when the electoral system is profoundly structured by certain economic and political interests. But in this chapter, I first want to consider the *limits* and *meaning* of opinions in the context of the vast residue of public discourses that are not generally classified under that rubric.

Knowledge and Opinion

Discussions of media influence *in* the media tend to be confined to marginal or excessive aspects of content—notably sex and violence—and outbreaks of deviant or antisocial behavior. Occasionally, these discussions also involve allegations of various forms of bias on political or social issues. Like many such discussions, these follow a familiar ritual, as a posse of commentators and academics complicate the picture, and media influence is rhetorically dissipated as a number of other culpable institutions (the family, the school, peer groups, etc.) are introduced. We are left with the impression that merely "blaming the media" is too easy an explanation in a complex world. And so it is. But in these discussions the significant relationship between the media and day-to-day cultural life—the ways in which people think about the world—is routinely ignored. The ease with which this takes place has been facilitated by the dominance of a research model in which, in a political context, the only kind of media influences under scrutiny are those that involve a straightforward, linear form of persuasion, whereby media-sponsored opinions are transferred directly onto the public.

In this context, we might say that much of the well-funded mainstream research on the influence of mass communications on political attitudes has been hampered by its narrow emphasis on opinion, and therefore on *specific moments* of political deliberation. In the case of research on voting and campaigns, this generally involves an emphasis on only those effects that register in the choices made in elections. In the early days of mass communication "effects" research, the focus on voting often meant a consequent focus only on overtly *opinionated* media (such as political advertising). The influence of what were seen as more purely informational or entertaining media texts was thereby downplayed, sidelining the importance of *ideas, assumptions, and beliefs* that could not be directly expressed as "opinions." In so doing, this kind of media effects research ignored most of television content and most aspects of the way people think.

In this model of media influence, where do opinions come from? At its simplest, this approach sees opinions either as products of direct attempts to persuade—by media or "opinion leaders"—or as independently formed, pregiven entities. I do not want to rehash a general critique of this approach (e.g., Hall 1980; Morley 1980; Lewis 1991; Gauntlett 1998); it is sufficient to say that in terms of an exploration of the media and public opinion, it involves two notable weaknesses—weaknesses that, in one form or another, we can still find lurking behind the assumptions of much of the research on media and public opinion.

First, formed as it was in the climate of fears about the effects of propaganda, early media effects research tended to assume a *pregiven, independent world* of public opinion, one that might or might not be contaminated or swayed by outside technologies like radio or television. Opinions that seemed to be formed "independently" were, implicitly at least, given a legitimacy that media influenced opinions were not, almost as if mass communications technologies were interfering in a natural, organic process. The idea that opinions are *always* formed through discursive processes involving an array of ideological agencies — of which the media are merely a part — was often submerged beneath the notion of media *intervening* in an otherwise independent realm. Or, to put it another way, the media were sometimes regarded as a rogue variable among a host of more legitimate "real-world" variables (such as race or education).

Second, while it could be argued that the content of mass media is propagandist, this analysis requires moving beyond a traditional notion of propaganda (as critical scholars like Edward Herman do). In short, the bulk of media content does not involve *direct* attempts to proffer or foist opinions on audiences. If we try to force media content into a simple persuasion model, most of it — even if we look only at news and current affairs — simply doesn't fit. As a consequence, if we are looking for media influence, it makes sense to begin by investigating those discursive categories that reflect media content — by looking *not* at people's opinions but at their images of and assumptions about the world. This may be a basic point, but it is one that still requires development.

The intervention of the agenda-setting approach in the 1960s and 1970s represents an important moment in this history. Bernard Cohen's famous assertion that the media "may not be successful in telling people what to think, but it is stunningly successful in telling [people] what to think about" (Cohen 1963, 13) is an interesting statement in this respect. The verb "to think" does not really refer to the practice of thinking at all, but the much more specific practice of constructing an opinion. His use of the word reflects the degree to which researchers — and academics and lay people alike — had restricted their practical understanding of thought in general to encompass only certain kinds of thoughts (i.e., opinions). But it also signaled a move away from these confines toward a different sphere of discourse — that is, frameworks ("what we think about") rather than opinions.

Since most media content consists of things other than overt attempts to persuade, this new approach provided a far more appropriate form for measuring media influence. Indeed, it was partly because it explored a realm of public response that more appropriately *matched* the nature of media content that agenda-setting studies yielded far more positive results than much of the media effects research that preceded it (e.g., McCombs and Shaw 1972; Funkhouser 1973; MacKuen 1981; Iyengar, Peters, and Kinder 1982).

Nevertheless, both media effects and some of the early agenda-setting research shared the same epistemological assumptions about what opinions are and where they come from. Although agenda-setting research was partly developed in the wake of the failure of these other approaches to find evidence of mass persuasion, its early formulations modified but still retained a certain innocence about a discrete world of opinions—one captured in Cohen's oft-repeated epigram. Behind the move away from opinion toward the broader arena of "what people think about" lies an independent, authentic, public opinion, tarnished but in tact. Indeed, some of the early agenda-setting research implicitly lapsed into an assumption that the world of opinions *was* an *independent realm* of discourse—existing in a universe parallel to the more *media contaminated realm* of frameworks and agendas. While some of those involved in agenda-setting saw it as a more subtle, circuitous route to media influence on opinions, there is a sense in which early agenda-setting took us to the verge of a theory in which the media (and other ideological agencies) are seen as active in the construction of public opinion, only to be held back at the last moment by the notion that the realm of discourse that *is* influenced by media—"what people think about"—is *entirely separable* from the world of opinions. Thus the media could be characterized as influencing one ("what we think about") without necessarily touching the other ("what we think").

In so doing, the early model of agenda-setting research—like much academic work in this area—maintained a rather coy relationship to a dominant media frame that tends to reject the idea that it has a direct influence on public opinion. As I have suggested, this position rests upon a distinction between certain discursive categories: what we think, it is argued, is epistemologically distinct from what we think about. The media, in other words, are able to influence the discursive structure of political thought while the independent category of opinion remains discrete and intact. This operates like Plato's distinction (rather than Aristotle's more discursive approach) between *doxa* (opinion) and *episteme* (knowledge)—two mutually exclusive realms whereby, Plato argued, members of the ruling class were informed by *episteme* in opposition to the wayward, fickle *doxa* of the masses.

Even in its own terms, this dichotomy is hard to sustain: once agenda-setting research began to explore the relation between information and attitude, it started to unravel. As agenda-setting research has developed, the idea that the world of opinions is elusive has, for many, been abandoned. Indeed, by distinguishing between two categories of discourse, agenda-setting research began to consider the *relationship* between the two (McCombs, Danielian, and Wanta 1995), at which point the fragile distinction between frameworks and opinions collapsed. So, for example, a study by Zhu showed a three-way relationship among media agendas, public agendas, and presidential approval ratings, thereby forging a direct relationship between the traditional categories of "what people think about" and "what people think." Specifically, George Bush's approval ratings went up when foreign policy concerns became the media's abiding issue (and subsequently the public's), and down when the rather amorphous question of "the economy" became predominant (Zhu 1991). The media "agenda" thus provided the *informational context* for an opinion about the president: when the agenda shifted, so did opinion.

As a consequence of such findings, agenda-setting research is now seen by many as neither innocent nor neutral, but something with direct political implications. Many researchers have thereby taken agenda-setting research to a new epistemological level by examining the political consequences of various forms of media discourse (such as those referred to as "priming" and "framing" [Iyengar 1991]). Even the results of opinion polls themselves become part of the discursive map that informs opinions (Patterson 1980; Noelle-Neumann 1993).

Agenda-setting research has therefore moved onto difficult terrain in which the whole world of public discourse becomes germane to the analysis of the more specific world of public opinion. Once this happens, it forces us to consider how politics is infused within all forms of public discourse rather than just "opinions." Opinion is, in short, no longer simply a matter of opinion. If the informational media can influence opinion simply by talking about X rather than Y—without, apparently, needing to express a single opinion—then information itself is deeply implicated in the construction of political ideology.

The notion that information is value-laden rather than value-free is scarcely new to social science, and yet it is still resolutely refused by the traditional boundaries of news reporting that fiercely defend the demarcation between fact and opinion (see chapter one). But it is also ignored by the dominance of an opinion-poll technology that measures "opinion" as if it were the only kind of value-laden speech—one that is somehow discrete from other forms of discourse. More recently, quantitative research by Bartels (1996) and Delli Carpini and Keeter (1996) has attempted to demonstrate how knowledge or knowledge frameworks have consequences on opinion formation (as measured by elections and polls), while Iyengar's work explores the way in which specific news frameworks encourage certain ways of understanding the world. Nevertheless, the relation between the information commonly made available within a culture through the media and the "will of the people" remains relatively unexplored.

THE POLITICS OF INFORMATION

Much of the research on political information and education looks specifically at public knowledge of social, political, and civic life. This work—worthy as much of it is—often takes place within an ideological vacuum. It is based on the premise that a healthy democracy requires an informed public and that civic knowledge will produce civic responsibility. Thus researchers have devoted themselves, for example, to a comparative analysis of different kinds of knowledge production—such as Zhao and Chaffee's (1995) or Brians and Wattenberg's (1996) comparison of the information communicated by TV news versus political advertisements—without seriously considering the ideological or discursive context that makes knowledge or assumptions intelligible.

While the premise of an informed citizenry is, in a narrow sense, both laudable and plausible, it is manifested in a form that clings to the idea that knowledge is an uncontaminated, apolitical category. Thus, for example, research by Brians and Wattenberg suggests that political advertising may be more informative than previously thought—a finding they see as a positive vindication of political advertising. In so doing, their study conforms to the notion that "more knowledge is good" without interrogating its ideological consequences. In these kinds of studies, information recall is, regardless of its ideological inferences, regarded as a social good, as evidence (or lack thereof) of a functional democracy—in so doing, it fails to consider in whose interests it is (or is not) functioning. To put it bluntly, information that is functional for political elites may be highly deleterious to the interests of people living on limited incomes.

It is possible, for example, that certain kinds of knowledge may actually be unhelpful to someone in identifying his own political interests. Thus a person who becomes well informed about the precise terms of elite debates may use this to construct an opinion that runs counter to her own immediate experience. Indeed, Edelman (1988) argues that ignorance of the kinds of facts elites regard as important may actually be seen as a positive act of resistance, since it means people are refusing to engage with elite discourse on its own terms. At the very least, as Carpini and Keeter suggest, conventional democratic theory often embraces the simple notion that "more knowledge is better," and therefore fails to explore more specific relations between knowledge and opinion (Delli Carpini and Keeter 1992). This is not to *discount* the utility of information in forming opinions that are compatible with a person's self-interest or sense of justice; it is merely to acknowledge that certain kinds of information may actually impede such opinion formation.

For example, knowing the First Amendment to the U.S. Constitution is seen as something of neutral value—it simply makes one a better citizen. And yet the First Amendment should also be seen as an ideological proposition—one that, on the one hand, promotes a liberal view of the world in which a diversity of opinion is regarded as healthy and, on the other, conflates freedom with freedom from government. These ideological contexts change what the First Amendment means. For example, attempts by government to regulate media in order to *increase* the diversity of available opinions would almost certainly be challenged by media corporations on First Amendment grounds. In this instance, the two meanings of the First Amendment are in direct conflict with one another, leading, as they do, in very different directions. Knowledge of the First Amendment in one context is therefore quite different from knowledge of it in another. The significant question in this instance is not *whether* people know the First Amendment but *how* they know it.

Since the traditional knowledge survey often rests on the assumption that "knowledge" and "opinion" are two discrete realms rather than interdependent forms of discourse, they tend to focus on facts that are considered value-free. As Neuman, Just, and Crigler point out: "When surveys do focus on knowledge rather than opinion, they tend to be based primarily on rather narrowly conceived questions that one might associate with high school civics" (Neuman, Just, and Crigler 1992, 13). This approach assumes a neutral store of information that, if dispersed equally among the citizenry, would guarantee a healthy democracy.

A common question asked by "civics"-style knowledge surveys, for example, involves the naming of a political representative. The implication of the question is that such information is both useful and important. Yet, while there are undoubtedly contexts in which it is helpful to know a politician's name, there are also contexts in which it is not. If, for example, one sees the political system in the United States as structured to produce representatives with leanings toward corporate and other moneyed interests, their names do not matter very much—the important issue is the political economy in which candidates emerge as "viable" rather than who they are. Thus the apparently value-free discourse of civic information is politically inflected. Knowing the name of your senator is, in one sense, part of a pluralistic discourse in which such things are paramount—where senators are seen to represent a range of opinions and where their individuality makes a significant difference. If the opinions of senators are bound by a system in which only certain views are likely to receive the financial support necessary to win elections, their names become a mere detail—a matter of nuance rather than substance.

Since these kinds of knowledge surveys often produce results that are—from their own perspective—extremely disappointing, the model of a functional democracy consisting of well-informed citizens remains a distant ideal. At its best, the "civics" approach blames a lack of what it sees as basic political knowledge—and, as a consequence, flaws in American democracy—on information systems, such as the media or schools. At its worst, it holds the citizens themselves culpable for their lack of effort in informing themselves. One should not underestimate the power of this second notion, which informs, from Walter Lippmann on (1922, 1925), important strains of democratic theory, as well as many discussions of mass or popular culture. As Laurie Ouellette argues in her analysis of the creation of PBS, the dominant critique of mass culture in the United States *holds the public rather than the system* responsible for its shortcomings—that is, the people get what the people want, the system merely delivers it (Ouellette 1998). The "vast wasteland" of American television is thus seen as a product of debased mass taste rather than the product of the special demands of an advertising-based, lightly regulated broadcasting system.

By the same token, the failure of citizens to make informed political decisions is often seen as a product of their own inertia. In this model, the many structural conditions that create differences in knowledge and political motivation—notably class and education—completely disappear. It is in such a context that Delli Carpini and Keeter's recent and comprehensive study of political knowledge in the United States—*What Americans Know About Politics and Why It Matters* (1996)—makes a significant contribution. The book is partly an attempt to show how the distribution of political knowledge is not merely a matter of personal effort or predilection but the consequence of structural conditions like social class, race, and gender.

In aggregate terms, Delli Carpini and Keeter's research is, in some ways, less pessimistic than most about the overall level of political knowledge among American citizens. Overall, their findings suggest the average U.S. citizen is not quite as bereft of political information as is often assumed. Their concern is with the distribution of that information. Like Pierre Bourdieu's analysis of "cultural capital" (Bourdieu 1984), their data suggest that the power and legitimacy that come with knowledge of contemporary politics are linked to social class (as well as to race and gender) in ways that benefit the advantaged.

Whether culpability is placed on institutions or on an insufficiently inquiring public, education is generally proposed as the solution to high levels of voter ignorance. Although they are working within a similar tradition, Nie, Junn, and Stehlik-Barry argue against this kind of model (which they term—albeit in a slightly different context—the "absolute education model"). They propose instead that participation in the political system is based on structural inequalities between those at the center and the periphery:

> Those seated close to the political stage can easily follow the actors and their actions and can readily gain the player's attention if they so desire. For those with seats at the periphery, the very opposite is true: following the action and identifying the actors requires much more careful attention, and making oneself heard by those onstage may be nearly impossible without creating a serious commotion. Whether expressed as "politics are too complicated for me," or "I wouldn't have any impact anyway," the implications of social distance are the same.   (Nie, Junn, and Stehlik-Barry 1996)

Again, like Bourdieu, they argue that education *is part of* this process simply because it is instrumental in sorting people out according to a class system with an unequal distribution of income and power.

So, while the question of what people know, believe, or assume is undoubtedly a vital one, there is a danger that, as Delli Carpini and Keeter argue, "attending only to 'informed opinions' might simply reinforce other inequalities in the political system" (Delli Carpini and Keeter 1992, 21). This forces us to examine how assumptions about the world work politically and to look at what kinds of information are available and how they are used.

Larry Bartels writes that the "political ignorance of the American voter is one of the best-documented features of contemporary politics, but the political significance of this political ignorance is far from clear" (Bartels 1996, 194). The only problem with this statement is that it implies a two-tiered system of political response—one based upon ignorance and one upon knowledge. Since few people will express opinions on a completely random basis—an opinion is usually based upon *some* kind of knowledge claim—the question is more a matter of what perceptions of the political world are available and how they operate in opinion formation.

I have suggested that assumptions, beliefs, and opinions are interdependent forms of discourse. One could go further to say that, as a consequence, any distinction between knowledge and opinion is essentially meaningless. So, for example, is a statement such as "People on welfare are lazy" a knowledge claim or an opinion? It is, on the one hand, something that could be verified—or not—by various forms of measurement, and yet it takes a form that implies an almost self-consciously subjective point of view (one that might easily be preceded by "I think that"). Indeed, it is the kind of statement that might find its way onto a pollster's repertoire (along the lines of "Some people think that people on welfare do not make enough effort to find work, while others feel that people on welfare are unable to find work—which comes closest to your view?").

Nevertheless, although they may be inseparable in discourse, it is useful to retain an analytical distinction between knowledge and opinion—as long as it is clear what we mean by these categories. Delli Carpini and Keeter define political knowledge as "the realm of verifiably correct information" (1996, 10–11). It is, I think, important to retain the notion of verification (a notion I shall return to in a moment). However, my own analysis of this realm is a little broader, incorporating knowledge *claims*—or what we could also call assumptions—statements that are, *on their own terms* (rather than in some essential or absolute sense), verifiably true or false. Thus the person who states that people on welfare are lazy might agree on how laziness is defined and on ways to measure it, and therefore understand the statement as one that might be independently tested. This is *not* to say that the statement can be verified for all time by some objective scientific procedure—the answer to the question will depend partly on how terms are defined (on what constitutes laziness) and the forms of measurement used for verification. It is simply to say that the statement implicitly *invokes* a system in which verification is possible.

Truth is, in this sense, a social construct rather than an absolute or essential phenomenon. This is not to belittle it. On the contrary, social construction encompasses a realm as vast as meaning itself—what Laclau and Mouffe call the realm of "being" (Laclau and Mouffe 1985). As Laclau and Mouffe point out, this kind of social constructionist perspective has often been misunderstood as a kind of skepticism about the existence of reality. But it is not an existentialist or a solipsistic position, simply an assertion that no scientific discourse can assert the truth or meaning of something *independent of socially constructed categories*. There is no ultimate truth to an oak tree or to an economy, for example, but there are many ways of understanding them in which we can distinguish between true and false statements. The fact that an oak tree is bigger than a daffodil rests upon a form of differentiation—the socially useful category of size—while the rate of unemployment rests upon socially constructed definitions and agreed (or contested) forms of measurement. The true or false statements that we can make about an oak tree or an economy depend upon how we want to understand them—not some essential, inner truth contained therein.

Assumptions or knowledge claims are, in this sense, dependent upon the categories used to establish their veracity. An opinion, on the other hand, might be seen as a statement that implies a degree of moral or political choice and which is *not* verifiable on its own terms. So, for example, the General Social Survey at the University of Chicago has perennially asked people to respond on a seven-point scale to the question: Should the government reduce income differences between the rich and the poor? While the response to such a question is clearly rooted in an array of assumptions, it is not, on its own terms, something that can be judged as either correct or misleading. This is not to say that opinions do not rest upon (as well as inform) assumptions that may be correct or misleading, only that those assumptions can be seen as analytically distinct from the utterance of an opinion.

To use a somewhat clumsy metaphor, an opinion is, in this sense, like the tip of an iceberg. The tip can be distinguished from the mass of ice below sea level, but it is nonetheless part of that mass. Opinions are moments of discourse that can be distinguished but not separated from knowledge claims or assumptions. If we are to make sense of these moments, we need to understand the assumptions that make opinions plausible or likely. In trying to understand the responses to public opinion polls—and the influence of the media on those responses—we therefore need to dip below the surface to examine the broader discursive mass below.

THE UNINFORMED CITIZEN AND OPINION CHOICE

From the early days of opinion research in the Unites States, surveys have shown large and significant gaps in public understanding of constitutional, social, economic, and current affairs. As Neuman, Just, and Crigler put it: despite "an intense and virtually uninterrupted barrage of video, audio, and print information on local, national, and world events, one finds a conspicuously large number of citizens with only marginal interest in and information about public affairs" (Neuman, Just, and Crigler 1992, xiv). This is, according to Delli Carpini and Keeter, particularly the case when it comes to information about contemporary political issues or government legislation or spending. For example, they report that even when U.S. involvement in Central America was a much reported political issue, most people were unable to distinguish the Sandinistas from the Contras or know which side the U.S. was supporting in Nicaragua, while only 8 percent knew the percentage of the federal budget spent on defense, 18 percent knew the percentage living below the poverty level and 9 percent knew the percentage of Americans with health insurance (Delli Carpini and Keeter 1996). The powerful enumerative discourse of public opinion polls may therefore, in its own terms, rest upon a feeble discursive foundation—as Lemert puts it, "popular knowledge can be so low about so many things that measuring preferences without first measuring knowledge can produce essentially meaningless percentages" (Lemert 1992, 41).

At first glance, the palpable existence of the apparently uninformed citizen might be what Paul Blumberg has described as "the dirty little secret of American democracy" (quoted in Delli Carpini and Keeter 1996, 23). Widespread public ignorance is consistently denied in the official forms of political and media discourse, where attempts to flatter audiences mean that the wisdom of citizens is, in public, generally exalted. Surveys by the Pew Research Center nonetheless suggest that political elites are privately somewhat contemptuous of levels of political knowledge: their survey reported that 77 percent of presidential appointees and 81 percent of senior civil servants felt that the public did not "know enough about issues to form wise opinions about what should be done." Indeed, such contempt can be expressed only under the cover of anonymity provided by survey technology—it is hard to imagine any of these officials going on record with such a dismissive characterization. We might say, in this respect, that elitist notions of democracy are practiced but not preached.

Certainly, alarmist stories about "how little Americans know" do appear in the press from time to time, but the dominant form of survey in media discourse tends to focus on public *opinion* in isolation. Questions about knowledge, once a staple of polling surveys, are increasingly rare. By the 1960s, Erskine noted that concern "about how much people know has decreased to almost vanishing point" (Erskine 1963, 133). More recently, Smith (1987) pointed out that knowledge questions in major surveys decreased from nearly one in ten questions in 1948/1949 to less than one in forty by 1984/1985.

There are practical reasons for this sensitivity. Testing respondents' knowledge on subjects they may know little about may make them feel uncomfortable and, as Neuman (1986) suggests, may jeopardize the rapport necessary for the completion of a successful interview. But on a more profound level, knowledge of the world in modern polling has almost become a philosophical taboo: if we begin to question the informational foundation of opinions, those opinions may seem compromised or even invalidated. Thus many opinion pollsters are inclined to ask people not what they know but what they *think* they know. So, for example, in a series of polls in 1990 and 1991, Gallup asked people, "Do you feel you have a clear idea of what the United States military involvement in the Iraqi situation is all about?" Polls done by the *Washington Post* and ABC/*Washington Post* similarly asked: "Do you feel you have a clear idea or not a clear idea why President Bush has sent U.S. forces to Saudi Arabia and the Persian Gulf?" (Mueller 1994, 215–16). These questions tell us nothing about what people do or do not know, merely that they may *claim* to know something. Delli Carpini and

Keeter's analysis of over 200,000 survey questions posed since the 1930s found that of the 5 percent to address issues of knowledge, three out of five are questions involving these kinds of self-assessments, while less than 2 percent directly measure specific knowledge or assumptions about the world (Delli Carpini and Keeter 1996, 66).

There are two basic problems with asking people to assess their own understanding or attention to an issue—not so much with the use of such questions but with the way they tend to be interpreted. First, since most people are prone to overconfidence or face-saving declarations, they are likely to collude in sustaining the notion that, while people may not know everything, they know enough to make relatively informed political decisions. So, for example, in response to twelve Gallup and *Washington Post* polls about military involvement in the Persian Gulf (taken from late August 1990 to July 1991), between 68 percent and 81 percent of respondents claimed to have a "clear idea" about events in the region (Mueller 1994, 215–16). And yet other research reveals significant areas of ignorance or misunderstanding (see chapter seven). Although it tells us nothing about what people actually know, such a confident response makes good copy because it allows the news media to claim it is informing the public well.

Second, while it may useful to ask people to make a rather vague knowledge claim, it tells us little about the informational context in which such a claim is being made. It may be that, even in their own terms, these knowledge claims are based on a series of mythic or incorrect assumptions.

THE RATIONAL PUBLIC THESIS

If many of those in the media and in politics are inclined, in their own interest, to publicly profess faith in an informed citizenry, scholars of public opinion have generally come to accept generally low levels of knowledge as a political fact of life. The response to this finding has not been as uniformly pessimistic as one might expect. Some influential scholars have questioned the conflation between the "uninformed voter" and the presumed inability to make rational political decisions. Sniderman, Brody, and Tetlock (1991), Popkin (1991), and Zaller (1992) have suggested that, even in a threadbare informational climate, citizens can behave both reasonably and rationally, using "information short-cuts" of "low-information rationality" to construct plausible and meaningful opinions. As Sniderman, Brody, and Tetlock put it: "People can be knowledgeable in their reasoning about political choices without necessarily possessing a large body of knowledge about politics" (Sniderman, Brody, and Tetlock 1991, 19).

In a similar vein, Page and Shapiro (1992) have argued that while there may be low levels of knowledge about constitutional politics or specific policy positions, surveys suggest that *individuals* may make poorly informed and ad hoc decisions, but the public *on aggregate* is able to articulate consistent and stable positions on basic long-term issues (such as government-spending priorities). These broad guidelines thus provide the ideological baselines for negotiating democratic decisions.

At times, versions of this argument employ a kind of cynical functionalism, using a cost-benefit analysis to suggest that for an individual citizen to spend time becoming politically informed is an irrational act, when that time might be better put to making decisions that will, on an individual level, be more meaningful than casting a single vote. As Popkin puts it:

> The resources expended to gather and process information before making personal consumption decisions have a direct effect on the quality of the outcome for the consumer, whereas time and money spent gathering information about candidates leads to a better vote, not necessarily a better outcome ... the expected gains from being an informed consumer remain higher than the gains from being an informed voter.   (Popkin 1991, 10)

There are a number of limits to such a position, the principal one being that it doesn't tell us very much. We can stretch this kind of rationality—as economists sometimes do—to explain most forms of human behavior. Thus someone who, in this model, takes the apparently "irrational" step of becoming well informed (despite the pointlessness of doing so) might also be recuperated as "rational" in the sense that he or she "gains" a sense of purpose and civic duty. The notion of "rationality," in this sense, does not reveal much more than the notion that most people, most of the time, do or think things for a reason. There is nothing good or bad about this kind of rationality—it might be selfish or selfless, depending on what forms of satisfaction a particular individual finds meaningful. If it partly explains the terms on which a particular version of democracy (one in which most people feel bored by and/or alienated from politics) reproduces itself, it tells us nothing about why that version is dominant or who it favors.

Nevertheless, as I suggested in the last chapter, there are aspects of the "rational public" argument that are both persuasive and important. At the very least, the argument forces us to explain the ambiguities in poll responses, rather than just dismissing them as contradictory. It does, however, either raise or bypass a number of significant problems.

First, as Page and Shapiro's work suggests, many surveys show that majorities consistently favor spending more on education, healthcare, and protecting the environment, and yet *these opinions often seem to bear little relation to voting behavior*—hence politicians committed to cutting spending in these areas often get elected. As Edelman puts it: "Regimes are able to obtain the support of electoral majorities while pursuing policies that those voters dislike" (Edelman 1995b, 113). This is possible, I have argued, because elections are political spectacles that have little to do with the rational working out of policy preferences. Public opinion, in short, fails to accord with the opinions and actions of the elite policy makers that purport to represent them (Page 1996). Or, as Kathleen Knight and Robert Erikson put it, "the meaning of elections are generally ambiguous" (Knight and Erikson 1997, 91). So, for example, Page and Shapiro's research leads them to reiterate Ferguson and Rogers's (1986) conclusion that "throughout the Reagan years and onto the Bush years, Americans favored *more*, not less spending on virtually all economic welfare programs" (Page and Shapiro 1992, 170; emphasis in original). Mayer's (1992) research on three decades of public opinion also suggests a generally weak—and sometimes contradictory—relationship between general movements right or left in public opinion and voting in presidential elections (see chapter three). In recent decades, overall swings to the right or to the left in response to specific policy or issue questions appear to take place quite independently of the ability of Democrats or Republicans to get elected to the presidency. Thus Republicans like Nixon and Reagan were elected when polls were registering a more general move to the left, and a Democrat, Jimmy Carter, appeared to be the beneficiary of a general swing to the right. In short, while most people may collectively know—or say they know—what they want, it is not at all clear that this corresponds easily with voting decisions.

Second, *the subtleties of the "rational public" analysis are generally ignored by policy makers*. In an earlier chapter, I referred to Page and Shapiro's point that "questions about programs for 'the poor' . . . often get a remarkable thirty or forty percentage points more support than questions about 'welfare' that are asked at the same time" (Page and Shapiro 1992, 126). Although this appears to be a contradiction (the principal programs for poor people in the United States *are* welfare programs), they argue that this reflects differences in the popular meaning of the terms, between the deserving poor, on the one hand, and the undeserving poor (i.e., welfare recipients), on the other. This nuanced reading is speculative but plausible: it is, however, entirely lost in a political process whereby political elites use the unpopularity of "welfare" (as a label) to cut programs for poor people. In other words, just because the attack on welfare has failed to significantly dent majorities favoring programs for the poor doesn't mean that the latter cannot be cut in the name of the former.

Third, although the ability to act in one's enlightened self-interest may not depend upon conventional forms of political knowledge, "*in most instances more information leads one to support policies that benefit one's own group*" (Delli Carpini and Keeter 1996, 250; my emphasis). Those forced to rely upon the briefest of "information short-cuts," in other words, may be laboring at a disadvantage. So, for example, among those people suffering economic hardship in Delli Carpini and Keeter's study, it was the better informed group in this section of the population who were more likely to be in favor of government spending on social welfare—a policy that might generally be construed as being in their interest. Similarly, women's support for women's rights increased among better informed women (regardless of other variables such as education or income), an articulation that explains the fact that the "gender gap"— women's greater propensity to support Democrats—applies mainly to well-informed women (Bartels 1996, 211).

This does not mean that poor people or women cannot construct well-informed rationales for more conservative positions, but it does imply that "the parameters of public discourse are affected by how informed or uninformed the public is" (Delli Carpini and Keeter 1996, 251), and that the discursive possibilities are not necessarily distributed equally. Again, this is not to replicate the notion that more knowledge is necessarily better, but it does emphasize the reliance of opinion on information.

This is, as Delli Carpini and Keeter argue at length, particularly troubling if we treat the public as consisting of different groups with different interests rather than as an aggregate. According to their study, the people with least access to conventional forms of political knowledge are precisely those who— whether because of race, class, gender, or age—are least powerful in making their voices heard. As a consequence, they argue that the

> political equality of all citizens depends fundamentally on the ability of citizens to discern their individual and collective interests and to act effectively upon them. Although inequality in other kinds of resources (such as money for contributing to interest groups or campaigns) renders some citizens more effective than others, the system still provides a substantial measure of power through such tools as the vote. But inequalities in political knowledge that correspond with those of more tangible resources can result in correspond-

ing inequalities in the effectiveness of even relatively simple or easy means of
participation.   (Delli Carpini and Keeter 1996, 137–38)

Those forced to rely on certain kinds of information short-cuts, in other words,
may have no other avenues available, while the better informed may have a
number of paths from which to choose.

Fourth and finally, it may well be that, regardless of demographic patterns of
information distribution, most people respond rationally to what is available.
But, as Delli Carpini and Keeter's work suggests, this should not lead us to suppose that the process is benign or that it favors the interests of those constructing rational responses. *Just because an opinion comes from the public does not
mean it is of the public.* To paraphrase an already oft-paraphrased comment by
Marx, people may make rational decisions, but not in conditions of their own
making. It may be that the available information leads to an opinion that, in
many ways, makes very little sense in terms of someone's perceptions of their
own interests. So, for example, Herman Gray argues that those white working-
class people who were persuaded that it was in their interest to vote for Ronald
Reagan (the "Reagan Democrats")—partly through a racially inflected discourse about welfare and fairness—were also, in a straightfoward and short-
term sense, voting against their own economic interests (i.e., most working-
class incomes stagnated under Reagan [Gray 1995]). Thus there may be
instances where a rational response appears to be premised on a series of misleading assumptions—it might be both rational *and* erroneous.

Moreover, as Bartels suggests in response to the aggregate rational-public
thesis, it is unlikely that these misleading assumptions will be random and
thereby politically neutral, merely canceling each other out in the aggregates of
public opinion surveys. Indeed, it is more likely that biases in the informational
climate would push opinions in particular directions (Bartels 1996). The generally sanguine drift of the "rational public" or "low information rationality"
argument is thus premised upon a benign view of the information that is available, one that assumes that if that information is partial, then it is so in arbitrary
ways that cancel out any prevailing ideological influences.

These points force us to consider exactly what rational thinking is, on what
grounds it is based, and where it leads. As I will argue in chapter seven, in many
ways the assumptions generated by media coverage of Iraq since the Gulf war
are such that they could be seen to lead inexorably toward support for various
forms of military aggression. The *informational structure* of media coverage, in
other words, made the case for bombing campaigns in 1991, 1998, and 1999 compelling. What rational thinking constitutes here is simply the ability to produce

readings in accordance with the meaning preferred by the structure of information. The nature of the informational climate is therefore critical to understanding and interpreting the responses to public opinion polls.

So, while the rational-public argument takes us beyond a dismissal of the
"uninformed citizen" as merely someone who is, for whatever reason, failing to
meet up to a civic ideal, it *should not* be seen as an implicitly optimistic argument about the independence of public attitudes from media influence. Rationality, as it is understood here, is an entirely dependent term, one that is not
necessarily commensurate with the pursuance of what are perceived as one's
own interests. To use a rather graphic and extreme example, people who have
been mistakenly informed that their loved ones have all perished in a plane
crash may reasonably decide that life is no longer worth living and make a rational decision to commit suicide. The fact that they were misinformed does not
make their actions any less rational, but it is clearly *not* the decision they would
have made had they been given different information.

Similarly, if people lack detailed or accurate knowledge of specific issues and
facts, this does not mean that they are unable to construct elaborate or meaningful ideological positions. But it might well mean that these positions rest
upon media frameworks that have little to do with people's broad understanding of their own interests. The question we should ask is not how do media
influence public opinion, *but how do media influence those assumptions about
the world that inform public discourse* (rational or otherwise). Or, as Delli
Carpini and Keeter put it, not "is the public well informed" but "who knows
what about what" (Delli Carpini and Keeter 1992, 19), and (I would add) to what
end?

The uninformed citizen is, from this perspective, a mythical figure. While
there may be instances in which polls encourage someone to make a choice on
a question on which he or she has no opinion—generally called the "problem
of nonattitudes"—these choices are rarely completely arbitrary. Herbert Asher
illustrates the problem of nonattitudes with the mischievous example of
respondents being asked about a nonexistent Public Affairs Act, a question to
which between a third and half of the respondents—depending on the survey
and the question wording—gave a response that registered support or opposition for the nonexistent piece of legislation (Asher 1998, 27–28). Although some
of these respondents may have done no more than mentally flip a coin in the
desire to appear informed, it is also probable that a number gave responses that
were *informed by something*—however vague or erroneous (such as a general
idea of what a Public Affairs Act *might* be). These responses may therefore mean
something more than a desire to appear informed.

To use a less amorphous example, on two occasions just before the beginning of the Gulf war in January 1991, an ABC/*Washington Post* poll asked
respondents whether they thought "the United States has done enough to seek
a diplomatic solution to the Persian Gulf situation, or not?" Those responding
positively (that the United States *had* done enough) outnumbered those
responding negatively by about two to one. And yet the media coverage of the
details of negotiations was decidedly skimpy (Mowlana, Gerbner, and Schiller
1992; Naureckas 1996b), and it is unlikely that many of the opinions recorded in
the poll were informed by any serious consideration of negotiating positions
(particularly as the Bush administration showed few signs of interest in a negotiated settlement of any kind and insisted not only on withdrawal but on withdrawal with various conditions attached). And yet the assumption of a reasonable United States and an intractable Iraq was not a matter of guesswork but the
product of an *informational climate that made such an assumption plausible or
likely.*

Although this may require us to question the solidity of the opinions proffered, it is wrong to imagine "uninformed citizens" behaving like so many mon-
keys at a typewriter and generating "nonattitudes" indiscriminately. It seems
likely, in this case, that many people were responding to a media framework that
presented the United States as earnest in attempts to reach a peaceful solution,
a sincerity thwarted by a belligerent Iraqi leadership. The poll reveals neither
authentic, independently formed attitudes nor incoherent nonattitudes. It indicates, instead, the presence of a *coherent ideological framework* that encourages
or prefers certain attitudes or knowledge claims. This raises the question to
which I shall now turn.

HOW INFORMED?

In their analysis of attitude and assumptions about welfare, Kuklinski and
Quirk (1997) argue that there is a significant difference between being uninformed and misinformed. Their study compared the attitudes of two groups:
the first group was asked a series of factual questions about welfare recipients
and the welfare system, while the second group was given this information. The
responses of the first group suggested a series of distorted perceptions: significant majorities overestimated the percentage of the federal budget spent on
welfare, overestimated the average annual payment each family received, and
overestimated the percentage of families on welfare. These misconceptions are
all consistent with one another, and they are all—particularly the first two—

easily linked to the view that welfare spending should be reduced. The power of this discursive link—or articulation—was suggested by the responses of members of the second group, who, when given the official statistics, were more sympathetic to welfare spending than members of the first group.

The wish to—in contemporary political parlance—"end welfare as we know it" is thus contingent upon the *way* we know it. Kuklinski and Quirk's research suggests that attitudes about welfare relate to a set of media stereotypes (who the welfare recipient is, how much they receive, their burden on the taxpayer, etc.). People's responses to factual questions are not wrong in an arbitrary sense but based upon assumptions that actively push them in a certain direction. Thus it is that when the survey respondents were given certain facts about welfare programs—when, in one sense, *welfare was redefined as a program for the poor* —they were more likely to express support for welfare spending. This vindicates Page and Shapiro's explanation of the apparent contradiction between the strong support in poll responses for antipoverty programs and the tepid support for welfare. The two are understood as meaning different things—"welfare," in particular, being a code word for rewarding the undeserving poor (Page and Shapiro 1992).

Discourses about "welfare" that proclaim welfare costs too much, creates dependency, promotes idleness, and should therefore be cut back are derived from clusters of facts and attitudes about welfare programs and recipients. They may also draw upon other discourses—about black Americans, the "American Dream," or an economic theory of incentives (Gray 1995)—and thereby invoke other clusters of facts and opinions. Every element is contingent. Opinion change, in this instance, is not a simple process but a consequence of a shift in these discursive clusters. Kuklinski and Quirk's work is an indication of the way in which questions about assumptions allow us a glimpse at the discursive framework in which opinions are constructed. The fact that many of the mistaken assumptions revealed in their study appear to reflect dominant media frameworks suggests that the relationship between media and public opinion consists less in telling people what to think than in sometimes providing them with a lopsided informational climate.

Testing knowledge claims, in this context, is not a simple question of seeing whether citizens are informed, uninformed, or misinformed; it is a way of probing into ideology, discourse, and media power. In the next three chapters, I attempt to do just that.

CHAPTER 6

THE IDEOLOGY OF ASSUMPTIONS

Although this is not their conventional use, surveys that explore public knowledge not only test what one might call "civic competence" but also tap into elements of popular discourse. My interest in developing this line of research stems from the desire to explore those discourses that sustain or resist systems of power. In the remaining chapters, I will use survey responses that allow us a glimpse at what people know, believe, or assume about politics—as it is expressed in the discourse of the opinion poll—in an attempt to explore ways in which these discursive clusters are linked to specific ideologies.

As suggested in chapter five, this is not simply a matter of opinion. To explore the operation of ideology, we need to trace the pattern of assumptions that makes opinions likely or possible. There is some scope for doing so in the existing poll data, but I shall also draw upon a series of surveys specifically designed to test the degree to which ideologies are manifested in misleading assumptions about the world. These studies are less surveys of opinion than a kind of "ideological indicators" project, a way of testing the power of dominant discourses—in the media and elsewhere—to create structural frameworks from which pollsters may pluck consenting opinions. In some of the questions described in the next three chapters, people were given the opportunity to opt for a "don't know" response; in others (notably the student surveys) people were asked to take "informed guesses" and could register a "don't know" response only by not answering the question, thereby strongly encouraging respondents to draw upon existing assumptions or else make a random guess. In the latter instance, although the percentages not answering were rarely more than 2 percent—totals sometimes add up to less than 100 percent.

Three of the surveys described in the chapters that follow are general population surveys: the first was a survey of 250 people conducted in the metropolitan Denver area in February 1991, designed to explore the context of people's attitudes toward the Iraqi invasion of Kuwait and the Persian Gulf war; the second was based on a national sample of 600 likely voters in October 1992, during Clinton's first successful presidential campaign (this, since it excluded self-declared nonvoters, is slightly skewed in class terms), as well as a series of focus groups with people from a range of class backgrounds; the third was based on a national sample of 600 in February 1998. The 1991 and 1998 surveys were carried out by a research team of myself, Michael Morgan, and Sut Jhally. The 1992 survey was conducted by myself, Michael Morgan, and Andrew Ruddock. All these surveys were based on samples gathered by random digit dialing and telephone interviews (see Appendix). While the sampling techniques used in these surveys were fairly standard, the aim was not to forecast something as precise as the result of an election but to provide a general discursive picture of ways of thinking—especially in relation to the news media's dominant ideological constructions.

These studies are complemented by a series of written surveys completed by students at the University of Massachusetts between 1992 and 1998, with sample sizes varying from 125 to 550 (see appendix). The student surveys are much less formal and are bound by the limits of using an undergraduate population, who are obviously a rather specific population grouping—particularly in terms of age, class, and education (while students at the University of Massachusetts are by no means an elite group in class and education terms, they tend to be a more middle-class and formally educated grouping than the population as a whole). Moreover, since most of these student surveys were gathered during large introductory lectures in communication, they are not necessarily representative of students in general. What makes these surveys useful, I would argue, is that as a population the students are likely to be a little to the left of and, in some areas, better informed than the general population (a point confirmed when the same questions were put to general population surveys and the student surveys). We would therefore expect this group to be more likely to possess information that might problematize mythic, right-wing discourses. So, while the student surveys should be regarded as limited endeavors, they are nonetheless suggestive—particularly if we are interested in exploring the role of media in constructing discourses that favor right-leaning political attitudes. In short, if most members of this group are unable to construct oppositional discourses, it is unlikely that access to such discourses would be widespread among the general population. In some cases, the results of these student surveys formed the basis for a subsequent discussion in which it was possible to probe the thinking behind responses.

Let me begin this last part of the book with a both a claim and a caveat. Having conducted several of these surveys over the past ten years, it has become clear to me that the power of dominant ideological frames to create misleading or incorrect assumptions about the world is highly predictable. Even among a student population, some of whom may be trying to second guess the motives of the survey, it has become depressingly easy to devise questions that will elicit responses in tune with dominant ideologies but that are verifiably wrong. I would, nonetheless, want to stress the suggestive nature of these studies. They offer some preliminary ideological sketches and, I hope, a direction for further work.

The Political Inflections of Misinformed Guesses

The power of an ideological framework can be revealed in the presence and absence of particular assumptions about the world. A statement that contains a knowledge claim—say, the naming of a politician or the association of that politician with a specific policy—tells us very little on its own. The ambiguity of these statements is lessened by the presence or absence of other statements around it, and this pattern may well be organized in discursive clusters that indicate a specific ideological premise. So, for example, someone who can name a series of politicians but who is unable to identify where those politicians stand on basic matters of policy, might be operating in an ideological framework in which politics is signified as a question of persona rather than a struggle of ideas and or competing interests.

The clarity of these ideological parameters is often brought into even sharper focus by the presence of knowledge claims that are, on their own epistemological terms, verifiably false. For example, King and Schudson have demonstrated how the popularity of Ronald Reagan was greatly exaggerated in media discourse, particularly during his first two years. While the media's construction of a mythic discourse about Reagan's popularity can be established through forms of textual and content analysis, its subsequent presence in public discourse is more vividly established if it can be linked to the widespread occurrence of incorrect knowledge claims. Thus, if people are asked the question:

According to polls, which of the following presidents was the least popular during his first two years of office: Jimmy Carter, Richard Nixon, Gerald Ford, or Ronald Reagan? the *power* of the media's mythic discourse about Reagan's popularity would be most clearly indicated by a reluctance to choose him as "least popular." This question thereby sets up a conflict between the correct response (Ronald Reagan) and the media preferred response (anyone but Reagan). Thus, regardless of its veracity, it is the "anyone but Reagan" option that we might expect to be more significant in informing public response: accordingly, when this question was posed to surveys of students in 1998, fewer choose Reagan (only 19%) than any other option. Similarly, when a 1999 student survey was asked to name the most popular of the four, the most common response (41%) was also Reagan.

Although this example seems rather specific and somewhat trivial, Noelle-Neumann's research (1993) on the "spiral of silence" suggests that the increase in Reagan's popularity after 1982—and his reelection in 1984—may have been facilitated, for some, by the *perception* of popularity—an example, perhaps, of a self-fulfilling prophecy based on specific misinformation.

A more enduring example involves perceptions of the media itself. The weight of research on political bias in the news media (this book included) suggests that while the structures informing media coverage involve a complex array of determinations—from the political economy of the news media to the professional codes of news making—the overall drift (with the exception of civil liberties issues) is toward a center-right mainstream generally defined by political elites (see chapter three). However, the most *prominent* discourse about the news media in the news media itself is the right-wing assertion of a "liberal" or "left-leaning" media.

A sample of 1,963 newspaper stories derived from a Lexis Nexis search (over a ten-year period, from June 1990 to June 2000) in which the phrase "media" was linked with (in this instance, within two words of) ideological labels demonstrates the degree to which the media tend to replicate the liberal media claim. The terms "liberal" or "progressive" were linked to the term "media" 84 percent of the time, while the more plausible link in terms of scholarly research—with the term "conservative"—was made only 16 percent of the time. Indeed, a further analysis of a random sample (of fifty articles) within these two groups found that of the 16 percent which linked the terms "media" and "conservative," the proportion that suggested the media *was* conservative was about the same as the proportion that rejected the notion (as in "a conservative media watchdog claimed that"). This suggests that the "liberal media" claim is widely reported, while more well-researched claims of a conservative tilt receive far less attention.

The evidence for the liberal media claim is generally fairly flimsy—it rarely involves any systematic analysis of content, of the political economy, of media, or of the structural factors that inform mainstream journalism—relying instead upon the conventional wisdom that journalists themselves tend to be liberal. As it happens, even on this count, the evidence suggests that journalists, like other members of an educated, professional class, are inclined to be more liberal than the general population on only civil rights and tolerance issues (see chapter eight), while they tend to be more conservative on most other issues (Croteau 1998). Indeed, the prominence of the "liberal media" critique is—perhaps ironically—partly a function of the power of conservative political elites (rather than "liberal journalists") to inform media frames. Hence the "liberal media" claim tends to be reported while counterclaims are not.

As various scholars have pointed out (e.g., Zaller 1992, 1994), the ability of elite claims to influence public opinion is often increased when those claims are uncontested within elite discourse. If the "liberal media" claim has been fairly comprehensively discredited by media scholars (e.g., Gans 1985), it is rarely refuted by prominent Democrats, and even more rarely countered by elite claims of a conservative tilt (rather tellingly in this regard, President Clinton is among those who have used the term to complain about the "liberal" news media). Accordingly, while surveys indicate that most people tend to have a reasonable degree of faith in the "objectivity" of the news media, those who identify a bias tend to replicate the dominant media frame. In the 1992 general population survey, for example, a majority (52%) said that they felt the media to be "pretty balanced," while the rest were over four times more likely to see the media as liberal (39%) rather than conservative (9%). The same pattern emerged when people were questioned about an indicator of media bias that is straightforwardly verifiable:

There has been some debate about the role of the media in politics. Overall, in presidential elections over the past thirty years, would you say more newspapers have endorsed: the more liberal candidates; the more conservative candidates; or is there no systematic pattern of support?

A clear majority—57 percent—assumed a liberal bias (as opposed to 27 percent who assumed a conservative bias). Even responses to this question in the 1998 and 1999 student surveys (among a fairly liberal population, some of whom have been exposed to evidence on this issue) fell in the same direction, 41 percent to 45 percent assuming a liberal bias and only 21 percent to 25 percent assuming a conservative one. As most of the scholarship on this issue would predict, newspaper endorsements have, with rare exceptions, actually fallen heavily on the side of Republicans rather than Democrats. For example, even when Jimmy Carter beat Gerald Ford in 1976, 411 dailies backed Ford and only 80 backed Carter (Lewis and Morgan 1996, 100).

The editorial pronouncements of newspapers are, of course, a fairly flimsy indicator of the ideological leanings of its news pages. The conservative tilt of editors may not be in sync with the more liberal inclinations of its journalists. It is even more notable, in this respect, that even when questioned about this verifiably conservative group, assumptions still drift toward the "liberal media" frame. We should not underestimate the importance of this perception—if nothing else, it reinforces the media frame and marginalizes arguments (this book included) that counter it. However, my aim here is not to suggest overarching forms of media power (a point I take up in chapter eight)—even in terms of the media's power to invoke a discourse about itself. As I have indicated in the first part of this book, the gap between elite opinion and opinions signified by public polls means that the media do not necessarily produce or reproduce consent in any comprehensive or straightforward sense. It is notable, in this respect, that despite the obscurity of claims of a conservative or elite bias in media content, over a quarter of respondents did, in fact, assume such a bias—albeit in relation to editors rather than journalists—thereby suggesting an ability of a significant minority to respond *outside* the dominant media frame. It is, on the other hand, absurd to assume that the media play no part in informing the frameworks, assumptions, or beliefs people draw upon when responding to polls, whose questions are often designed to be compatible with media frameworks. My interest, in what follows, is to explore those moments when the media's informational or discursive content *does* appear to influence public opinion—albeit in the limited form in which it is generally measured.

ASSUMPTIONS WITH CONSEQUENCES: STRATEGIC ATTACKS ON THE WELFARE STATE

One of the most successful ideological projects in the past two decades has been the move away from "Great Society" notions of an active public sector toward a diminished set of expectations of what the public sector can or should do, and a gradual relinquishing of the public domain back to private corporations. Perhaps the best example of the success of this transition is the ease with which politicians and pundits in Europe and the United States declare that the public sector *can no longer afford* the ambitions or largesse that characterized the 1960s and 1970s, even while economies and rates of productivity have continued to grow.

This hegemonic project is most clearly identified with the Thatcher and Reagan years, which constituted a turning point among political elites, pushing those parties more traditionally associated with the advocacy of the public sector toward an embrace of privatization and a curtailing of ambitious public sector regulation or spending. Even while it reversed the overall flow of the twentieth century, this general drift has assumed an air of inevitability, so much so that the capitalist backlash against the growth of welfare states is often taken for granted as if it were preordained. Those who might wish to celebrate the gains made by activist governments up until the 1970s are generally derided as being backward or old-fashioned.

And yet, as I suggested in the first half of this book, what is remarkable about this shift is that it has happened without any clear mandate from public opinion polls. Certainly, there are areas in which the public sector has failed in terms of public support (Hall 1988), but the electoral successes of Thatcher and Reagan were not based on a desire for a less activist government—particularly in areas of social justice—or support for privatization or deregulation (Ferguson and Rogers 1986; Taylor-Gooby 1995). This is not to say that there are *no* manifestations of this ideology in public opinion polls. For example, the National Election Studies in the United States indicate that "trust in government" has generally declined in recent decades (although since much of this decline took place in the 1960s and early 1970s, it is not at all clear that this has much to do with lack of support for government regulation or spending, or that it is reflected in attitudes toward state or local governments where attitudes have generally moved in a *more* supportive direction). Similarly, since the mid-1960s, surveys show clear majorities respond to questions about government profligacy by agreeing with the proposition that "people in the government waste a lot of money we pay in taxes."

There is, nonetheless, a distinction drawn in polling surveys between the idea that government is not what it could be and the desire for an efficient *and* activist government. Thus support for most government programs—and moreover, the desire for government to do *more* in many areas of social and economic life—remains strong. So, even if rhetoric against "big government" has made an impact on poll responses, support for most areas of progressive social spending remains high, while some aspects of faith in the corporate or business sector (to which responsibility has generally been passed) has been declining— a remarkable trend, since it generally goes *against* the dominant discourse of faith in market solutions.

There is, in other words, no clear evidence of popular consent for the rightward drift of mainstream political parties—or, by the same token, for the abnegation of the public realm to private, corporate sectors and institutions. Media influence, in this context, takes two forms.

First, resistance to the rightward drift has been diminished or softened by an informational climate that portrays government spending on social programs as generous and downplays the success of the corporate sector in reducing its relative tax burden. For example, the 1998 and 1999 student surveys asked the following question, designed to measure the extent to which people are aware that the tax burden has shifted away from the corporate sector and toward individuals and households.

The Federal Government raises money from various sources, such as income tax on families and individuals and corporate income tax. Over the past forty years, the proportion of revenue raised from corporate income tax has a) Increased; b) Remained the same; c) Decreased.

Even though this is a student population that might generally be expected to be more critical of the corporate sector, in both surveys (of the three options) most—39 percent in 1998 and 44 percent in 1999—said the corporate share had increased, and only 35 percent in 1998 and 32 percent in 1999 knew or guessed that the corporate share had gone down (part of a trend since the late 1970s in which the tax burden has shifted significantly away from the wealthy; see Harrigan 185-87). The success of the corporate sector in reducing its share of the overall tax burden is an unlikely topic for a corporate media system to dwell upon, and even elite claims about "corporate welfare" have played a fairly minor role in media agendas. In this instance, in spite of popular cynicism about the ability of the wealthy to find tax loopholes, we might say that the failure of the news media to report this trend has *limited the possibility* of citizen discontent in the face of this shift.

The 1998 and 1999 surveys also repeated a question put to a group two years earlier which asked students to assess the generosity of the U.S. welfare state in an international context. How aware were they, in other words, that the United States government—and the amount it spends on antipoverty programs in particular—is proportionately smaller than that of most other Western nations? The responses were as follows:

How does the U.S. Government compare with most other developed countries in terms of the amount it spends, proportionately, on Welfare and tax relief for the poor?

	SEPT. '96	SEPT. '98	SEPT. '99
	N = 121	N = 280	N = 201
a. It spends less	38	32	32
b. About average	10	19	12
c. It spends more	50	46	54

Only around one-third were able to guess the correct answer, while around half assumed *the opposite* to be the case (i.e., the United States was seen to be *more* generous toward the poor than other developed nations). The 1998 and 1999 surveys also asked them to assess the comparative size of government spending, with the following responses:

A modern economy can be divided into two main areas: those that involve government (education, defense, social security, health care, criminal justice, the environment, welfare, foreign aid, etc.) and those parts of the economy in private hands (big business, small business, etc.). In which of the following countries is the government proportion of GDP the largest?

	SEPT. '98	SEPT. '99
	N = 280	N = 201
Canada	11	10
France	13	6
Germany	15	17
Great Britain	13	7
The United States	46	49

While these guesses appear to be fairly scattered, nearly half assume, once again, that the United States is at the top of the list (rather than, as economic data indicates, firmly at the bottom). What these responses suggest is a discursive climate in which attacks on "big government" spill over into assumptions—about the size and generosity of the U.S. government. These assumptions will tend, for many, to either validate these attacks or diminish the strength with which they might be repudiated.

A second area in which elite campaigns work their way into popular assumptions is in terms of *strategic areas of symbolic significance*. In the first part of this book, I discussed the way in which the generally popular idea of "programs for the poor," or "antipoverty programs," was superseded in elite discourse by a focused campaign against specific antipoverty programs, notably welfare. Thus polls suggest a degree of popular support for limiting welfare payments, a view that would seem to be at least partly based on various media stereotypes of feckless recipients who gain more than their fare share of government handouts (Kuklinski and Quirk 1997). The presence of these myths was also manifested in the 1992 general population survey, in which people were asked to estimate the average number of children that women on welfare are likely to have. The actual figure (fewer than 2) is in marked contrast to a media stereotype of irresponsible women who blithely produce children at the public's expense. The average figure given by respondents however (3.3) would appear to be informed by this stereotypical image. This response is also reflected in a series of student surveys, where responses tend to be clustered around or even a little above the 3–3.5 range.

How many children, on the average, would you say women on welfare have?

	SEPT. '95	FEB. '96	SEPT. '96	SEPT. '98
	N = 125	N = 120	N = 121	N = 280
Between 1 and 1.5	7	5	6	3
Between 2 and 2.5	28	27	25	20
Between 3 and 3.5	28	37	38	35
Between 3.5 and 4	25	22	22	27
Between 4 and 4.5	12	8	10	13

These responses provide a glimpse of the power of media stereotypes to create what we might call "assumptions with consequences"—in this case, a set of assumptions that make an antiwelfare discourse more plausible than a pro-welfare discourse.

In much the same way, the regressive structure of state and local taxation in the United States tends to exacerbate rather than diminish poverty, but once again, the degree to which this is the case is not generally understood. On the contrary, despite the existence of various forms of middle- and upper-class tax relief, it is the middle class, rather than the poor, who are thought to be especially beleaguered by taxes. If this assumption was marked in the general population survey, it also clearly present in a series of student surveys. The following question (used in both the 1992 general population survey and the student surveys) was designed to assess the extent to which the disproportionate share of state and local taxes paid by poor people—often as a result of regressive taxes, notably taxes on the sale of goods—was generally appreciated.

Which income group pays the highest percentage of their income in state and local taxes?

	GENERAL POPULATION	APRIL '92	SEPT. '95	FEB. '96	SEPT. '96	SEPT. '98
	N = 600	N = 550	N = 125	N = 120	N = 121	N = 280
The richest 20%	3	11	16	19	17	20
The middle 20%	86	71	72	71	70	64
The poorest 20%	11	14	12	10	12	15

This response—particularly in the general population survey—is a fairly dramatic indication that the poor are not regarded as disadvantaged. Although 85 percent to 90 percent of responses in these surveys are erroneous, the shape of those responses correspond to a media discourse in which the *middle* classes are seen to bear the brunt of the tax burden—a discourse that is perfectly in line with the rhetoric of political elites from both parties, both claiming to alleviate the problems of the middle classes (which is, in terms of self-identification, where most of the votes are). This is, in one sense, a populist discourse, inasmuch as it implicates the rich as getting off lightly, but it also works as part of a discourse in which recipients of antipoverty programs might *also* be seen to be getting "a good deal" on the backs of the middle classes.

In chapter four, I argued that media discourse appeared to resonate in responses to surveys more in terms of abstractions than specificities. So, for example, the attack on the idea of government in general (as wasteful, inefficient, and cumbersome in its size) has not prevented the persistence of majority support in surveys for increased public spending on a range of programs. But in certain strategic instances, this abstract discourse *can* be used to mobilize public opinion (as it is currently measured) against forms of public intervention. This is notable in the case of health care. Over the past forty years, polls have shown consistent and sizable majorities in favor of more government spending on health care and in support of a national, universal system. When questions *specifically* refer to federal government control, however, support still generally outweighs opposition, but it drops considerably (Page and Shapiro 1992, 129–31). As befits their thesis, Page and Shapiro rationalize this response by suggesting it mandates support for a mixed public/private universal system. This may be so, but since public- or government-run healthcare systems are considerably more efficient than a private system (a point clearly acknowledged by both the U.S. General Accounting Office and the Congressional Budget Office but almost entirely ignored by the news media during the health care reform debate in 1991 [Canham-Clyne 1996]), it is also based on flawed assumptions. Put simply, it seems plausible that the suspicion of government in these poll responses is based on the erroneous assumption that government healthcare systems are *more* bureaucratic and wasteful rather than less. An abstract, negative discourse about government, in this instance, can be articulated to refer to a specific policy program.

This is hardly a trivial point. Research suggests that the wastefulness of a private, corporate health-care system is profound: a study by Woolhandler, Himmelstein, and Lewontin published in the *New England Journal of Medicine* (1993) found that the overhead costs in a private insurance system were 13 percent, compared with 3.5 percent with Medicare and Medicaid and less than 1 percent in the Canadian single-payer system. In other words, under a single-payer system, the cost of *universal* health care would, in the long term, be cheaper than the existing private system in which substantial sections of the population are under- or uninsured (Canham-Clyne 1996). The costs of a private universal system, on the other hand, are enormous. If the comparative costs of the two systems were allowed to slip past the corporate gatekeepers (in this case, the health insurance companies) of the "conventional wisdom," and thereby entered into popular political discourse, it seems very likely that support for a universal government-run system of some kind would solidify in poll responses.

The maintenance of the existing system — the last (and most expensive) of its kind in the developed world — is thus based *not* on a popular mandate, or on the ability of elites to persuade people of the superiority of the U.S. system, but on the ability of elites to use *a well-developed abstract discourse* (against wasteful government bureaucrats) to help undermine popular pressure for reform. This occurred at two strategic moments in elite discussions of health care reform — during the Truman and Clinton administrations — when insurance industry and Republican campaigns mobilized the "wasteful government" discourse, and polls registered a drop in support for government involvement in reform efforts (Page and Shapiro 1992, 130; Naureckas and Jackson 1996, 157–70). In this way, the long-term support for a national, universal health care system is either ignored or, in rare instances (where the hegemony of the system is threatened), diminished by campaigns to articulate wasteful government with a government-run health-care system.

To extend the argument made in chapter four, this suggests that while media influence on public opinion is far more clearly manifested in abstract political ideas (like "government is wasteful") than in specific areas of policy, the ideological baggage attached to these abstractions *can* be connected to specific policy areas by highly visible public relations campaigns, of which the attack on welfare is a notable example. These raids on public assumptions may make only small dents in general patterns of public opinion, but they are done at moments and in contexts that maximize their political significance. As we shall see, this tells us a great deal about the strategic nature of media influence.

Sustaining the Myth of a Benign Foreign Policy

In many ways, the ability of elites to create consent in public opinion polls is most marked in areas of foreign policy, where elite control of information is likely to be most stringent and where, in the face of elite consensus, the news media tend to be most compliant (Herman and Chomsky 1988; Page and

Shapiro 1992; Zaller 1994). Since most people tend to rely on mainstream media and are unlikely to consult alternative information sources, there is little information available with which to dislodge the assumptions that inform elite frameworks. However, what is notable about public support for U.S. foreign policy—insofar as it exists—is that it is *not* based on straightforward support for U.S. hegemony. Instead, public support depends heavily on a powerful mythic frame that dominates media coverage: a framework that sees U.S. foreign policy as informed by the desire to promote the principles of peace, democracy, and human rights.

In some ways, the ubiquity of this myth in media and public discourse is remarkable. It is not merely that there is so much evidence to contradict it, but that any sober analysis of U.S. foreign policy in the twentieth century would indicate that support for peace, democracy, and human rights is almost *entirely irrelevant* to U.S. foreign policy (Herman and Chomsky 1988; Hellinger and Judd 1991; Herman 1999). In general, U.S. foreign policy has always been motivated by a fairly simple set of imperatives that involve the protection—and extension—of U.S. corporate interests and a system of corporate capitalism in general. This is neither surprising nor, in elite policy circles, a closely guarded secret, and yet the solidity of the notion that U.S. foreign policy is informed by a higher set of principles remains firmly enshrined in media discourse. When Hellinger and Judd state bluntly that "the overriding concern of U.S. elites has been the construction and maintenance of a system of governments that will protect inequality and class privilege at least as effectively as in the United States" (Hellinger and Judd 1991, 221), they are speaking entirely outside the realm of mainstream media discourse, and yet there are very few instance of U.S. intervention—whether directly or through the "structural adjustment" policies of the IMF—that have not had precisely the outcome they describe.

This is not to say that there are not moments of candor—usually encapsulated in the less altruistic but often vague notion of "national interests." On an occasion when *Nightline*'s Ted Koppel was forced by one of his guests to discuss the U.S. government's complicity in supporting the Khmer Rouge in Cambodia, he acknowledged that "sometimes foreign policy logic doesn't bear a whole lot of resemblance to what we like to think of as interpersonal ethics" (*Nightline*, January 9, 1990). But such examples tend to be regarded as lapses or even mistakes in the context of the broad thrust of support for peace, democracy, and human rights.

To be frank, there are so many examples of the U.S. government establishing or supporting undemocratic regimes with brutal human rights records, including countries (such as Chile, the Dominican Republic, Iran, and Guatemala) where the U.S. government has been involved in overthrowing democratic, fairly benign governments to install such regimes, that sustaining this mythic framework might seem rather difficult. It is achieved by a form of acute selectivity, focusing on those instances when the economic and political interests of U.S. elites *happen to coincide* with notions of democracy and human rights. These selective coincidences are then elevated to the status of principles.

Thus a concern for "human rights" elicits broad degrees of elite concern only in countries whose governments are considered undesirable (usually for their failure—whether because they are too left-wing or too independent—to be compliant with U.S. strategic or economic goals). During the cold war, this meant pointing an accusatory finger at leftist governments—whether in Vietnam, Angola, Cuba, or Nicaragua—while simultaneously supporting client states regardless of their human rights record.

For example, the United States has a history of support for brutal regimes in Latin America when those regimes support certain economic—generally corporate—or strategic interests, a history that, despite extensive documentation by various human rights agencies and international commissions, U.S. elites are not inclined to draw attention to. As a consequence, the abuses of these regimes tend to receive little media attention (Hellinger and Judd 1991), while the sins of leftist governments—such as Castro's Cuba or the Sandinista governments in Nicaragua in the 1980s—are amplified (Herman and Chomsky 1988; Herman 1999). My interest, here and in chapter seven, is to see how powerful this framework is in eliciting support for U.S. foreign policy.

So, for example, from an elite perspective, the longest standing enemy in the region is Cuba, whose system of government has traditionally been seen as antithetical to the interests of U.S. corporations, or corporate capitalism in general. Human rights abuses in Cuba are fairly mild when compared with those of regimes in countries like Guatemala and, at various times, El Salvador, Nicaragua, Honduras, or Haiti. Cuba's record on human rights is, however, rarely examined in such a context, and it has, at various times, received a great deal of elite condemnation, its flaws being subject to a degree of media scrutiny from which others in the region have been spared. In terms of popular assumptions, the effect of this selective coverage can be revealed fairly clearly. In surveys in 1996 and 1999, students were asked to compare levels of human rights abuse in three countries, with the following responses:

Where, over the last decade, were citizens most likely to be tortured or assassinated because of their political beliefs, and which has the worst record on providing health care, education, and employment to its citizens?

	SEPT. '96	SEPT. '98	SEPT. '99
	N = 121	N = 280	N = 201
El Salvador	29	34	27
Cuba	54	51	51
Guatemala	16	13	21

In terms of the criteria outlined in the question, Cuba has the best rather than the worst record, while Guatemala's record for torture and assassination was particularly egregious in the early 1990s. Nonetheless, Cuba is undoubtedly the most popular choice in all three surveys. In this context, many of the responses in this survey would seem to be informed by a media framework in which Cuba is the only country in the region identified with human rights violations.

This suggests a picture of the world in which those governments picked out for elite and (therefore) media criticism are *assumed* to be especially and distinctively worthy of condemnation. Since most people do not have the discursive resources to be able to make serious comparisons, they are forced to rely on a fairly simple *associative framework* (Lewis 1991) in which certain leaders or countries are signified within a largely symbolic realm constituted by an array of negative terms. In the context of a small amount of available information, this can create a variety of assumptions in which the "bad guys" in foreign policy terms—in this case, the Castro government in Cuba—can be easily linked to any number of "bad acts." This associative process is implied by the following question:

Which prominent public figure is banned by the government of Costa Rica, because of his or her involvement in international drug dealing?

	APRIL '92	SEPT. '95	FEB. '96	SEPT. '96
	N = 550	N = 125	N = 120	N = 121
a. Oliver North	14	12	12	9
b. Fidel Castro	56	62	54	53
c. Donald Trump	5	2	1	1
d. Imelda Marcos	18	22	31	37

As Martin Lee and Norman Solomon have documented, most major media have been reluctant to cover Oliver North's relationship with international drug traders (Lee and Solomon 1990), so it is not surprising that so few knew or guessed the answer to this question. Instead, responses are drawn from a media landscape in which Fidel Castro—and to a lesser extent, Imelda Marcos—is the most plausible candidate to be slotted into a negative associative frame.

This associative perception is also present in responses to media coverage of the Middle East. Critics such as Edward Said (1978) and Edward Herman and Noam Chomsky (1988) have, in different contexts, argued that U.S. media portrayal of Palestinians is framed within a negative discourse—part of a broader set of stereotypes that Said refers to as "orientalism." Representation of the conflict between Israel and the Palestinians, they argue, has been informed by a bias in U.S. foreign policy in favor of Israel. While knowledge surveys of Middle Eastern politics generally indicate low levels of interest in such issues (Morgan, Lewis, and Jhally 1992), the power of an anti-Palestinian ideological frame might be explored by probing expectations of culpability. The following question attempts to trace the degree to which assumptions about blame in the conflict might form part of a mythic, anti-Palestinian or orientalist discourse:

Before the recent peace process, who was repeatedly condemned in the United Nations for the occupation of other people's land in the Middle East?

Respondents were given five possible answers: Iran, Syria, Jordan, the Palestinians, or Israel. The most accurate answer, in terms of the number and weight of UN resolutions on the issue, is Israel. The question was phrased thus because, regardless of whether one agrees with most UN member states, the answer is verifiable. The question was posed in five different student surveys, and the general pattern of response was fairly consistent:

	SEPT. '95	FEB. '96	SEPT. '96	SEPT. '98	SEPT. '99
	N = 125	N = 120	N = 121	N = 280	N = 201
Iran	25	18	24	22	21
Syria	7	7	2	13	3
Jordan	4	3	1	7	8
The Palestinians	47	47	43	31	45
Israel	16	22	28	24	20

What is noticeable, first of all, is that the answers are not distributed at random but consistently move in the same directions: the Palestinians are the most popular choice in every case, while Israel and Iran are always second or third. Iran, which has a long history of receiving bad press in the U.S. media—as a "rogue" or "terrorist" state—was placed on the list because the country might be seen as a plausible answer by those who know little about the region but who might nonetheless be inclined to associate Iran with international condemnation. The pattern of responses indicates that for approximately 20 to 25 percent of students, this logic may have been operating. Nevertheless, a majority (between 54 percent and 69 percent) correctly see this question as relating to the Israeli–Palestinian conflict. What *is* remarkable, in this respect, is that respondents are consistently more likely to assume that the occupying force being condemned in the UN *are the Palestinians rather than the Israelis.*

On one level, such a response suggests an understanding that turns the conflict on its head. While there is an argument in support of Israel's occupation (although, as subsequent discussions made clear, one that very few of the students in these surveys were informed enough to make), it is difficult to see how one could accuse a stateless people of being an occupying force. Equally, although the U.S. government and news media might be pro-Israel, this bias amounts to a justification for the Israeli occupation rather than a denial of its existence. In light of what we know about public knowledge, this response suggests two things: first, general understanding of the Palestinian–Israeli conflict is hazy and somewhat confused; second, amid this confusion, there is a *general impression* that it is the Palestinians who are the aggressors in the conflict.

This would appear to support the argument that the news media have created an informational climate in which people are, regardless of evidence, likely to see the Palestinians — rather than Israel — in a negative light. It also suggests that media influence has more to do with general ideological frames than more specific forms of information recall. The use of such ideological frames as "information shortcuts" is not, therefore, innocent or benign. In this case, it allows the promulgation of a mythic discourse that helps sustain the partisan views of political elites.

The same principle is at work in response to a more general question. Thus, even among a fairly liberal group of college students, the World Court's decision in favor of Nicaragua against the Reagan administration does not fit within an associative framework in which the United States is seen as an enforcer rather than an abuser of international law.

Which of the following countries was taken to the World Court in the 1980s for subversive activity in another country, found guilty, fined, and refused to pay the fine?

	SEPT. '95	FEB. '96	SEPT. '96	SEPT. '98	SEPT. '99
	N = 125	N = 120	N = 121	N = 280	N = 201
a. Soviet Union	12	12	14	17	17
b. Libya	34	33	42	30	26
c. Iraq	18	21	12	23	21
d. Cuba	12	11	14	7	17
e. The United States	20	22	17	17	15

Since media coverage of this event was minimal, it is hardly surprising that few students knew the answer to this question: neither is it surprising the most consistently "likely" suspect appears to be Libya, a country whose regime was, in the 1980s, generally portrayed as being in violation of various moral or legal codes of behavior, and whose "rogue" presence in news discourse has been sustained by coverage of the bombing of the Pan Am flight over Lockerbie and its aftermath.

Instead, the United States is more likely to be seen as playing a benign role in a demanding world in which it often asked to "help out" rather than as an imperialist nation acting in the interests of its elites. The United States and other Western nations are thus regarded as having a charitable rather than an exploitative relationship to the third world, an attitude that many policy makers might regard as gratifying but naïve. The following question (asked in the 1998 and 1999 student surveys) was, in this vein, designed to test awareness of the extent to which money flows from poor to rich countries.

The United States and other industrialized countries give aid to countries throughout Africa, and they receive money back through the repayments on debt and interest payments. What would you estimate the ratio of money given to money received to be?

	SEPT. '98	SEPT. '99
	N = 280	N = 201
a. Africa pays out more than it receives back in aid.	18	14
b. Industrial nations give in aid about the same as they receive.	17	15
c. Industrial nations pay out more in aid than they receive back.	63	70

The responses to this question not only suggest very little awareness of the size and effect of third-world debt, they indicate the presence of an ideological frame in which the West—and the United States in particular—is seen as benevolent rather than exploitative.

Foreign policy is thus translated from a story of money and power to a simple moral tale—a narrative that is, I have suggested, well ensconced in both media and scholastic discourses. It has spawned a succession of subsidiary images that assume its truth. For example, discussions of U.S. foreign policy in the post–cold war world often revolve around the question of the degree to which the United States should help resolve other peoples' problems. In this formulation, support for interventionism rather than isolationism can even appear to be altruistic. Thus when various pollsters (such as the General Social Survey and Gallup) put the following question:

Do you think it will be best for the future of this country if we take an active part in world affairs, or if we stay out of world affairs?   (*quoted in Mueller 1994, 323–24*)

the meaning of this question, for most people, works within a moral narrative. So it is that, according to the National Election Studies at the University of Michigan, self-declared liberals have, since 1990, been slightly more inclined than conservatives to support the United States playing an international role. This implies that, for many, the question is read more as "Should we help out on behalf of moral principles?" than "Do you support U.S. hegemony?"—even while such responses (which tend to favor "playing an active part" rather than "staying out") are more likely to be used to justify an imperialist rather than an altruistic foreign policy. This view is generally reflected in the discourse of opinion poll questions themselves, as this Gallup question indicates:

How much confidence do you have in the ability of the Unites States to deal wisely with the present world problems?   (*quoted in Mueller 1994, 323–24*)

Here, the sagacious intent of the United States is assumed, the only question being the *ability to enact* that intent.

The operation of this moral discourse often manifests itself during isolationist moments in public opinion. So, for example, during the 1992 presidential election, a common theme—encapsulated in various polls—was that George Bush spent too much time on problems elsewhere and not enough on those at home. This idea was repeated many times during a series of focus groups conducted during the October 1992 study. As people in the focus groups put it: "He's over worrying about what's happening in these other countries. Take care of home," "Why are we giving billions of dollars in aid to countries when people are starving here?" (Lewis, Morgan, and Ruddock 1992, 9). What is notable about this discourse is that it rests *entirely within a moral framework*—one in which the idea that U.S. foreign policy is guided by imperialist or self-interested goals plays no part.

This is an important point, because public support for U.S. imperialism—or related discourses that put patriotism above principles—no longer receives majority support. For example, while two-thirds of respondents to a Gallup poll in 1955 agreed that "The United States is the greatest country in the world, better than all other countries in every possible way," after the much celebrated Gulf war in July 1991, the proportion of people agreeing to such an absolutist expression of patriotic faith was down to 37 percent, compared to a majority who agreed to the more moderate assertion that: "The United States is a great country, but so are certain other countries" (Mueller 1994, 300). It is therefore *necessary* to portray U.S. foreign policy within a moral rather than an imperialist or purely patriotic ("my country right or wrong") framework in order to gain majority support in opinion surveys.

Thus we see that support for U.S. foreign policy is based, to a large degree, on a mythic version of that policy, one sustained by the selectivity of media coverage and the lack of access most people have to contextual information. Within this framework, understanding the world often depends upon an associative logic, whereby a people, leader, or regime is generally associated either with democracy and human rights or the abuse thereof. In the next chapter I shall consider how this framework has been developed within the specific confines of the post–cold war world.

CHAPTER 7

FLICKERING THE EMBERS OF CONSENT: PUBLIC OPINION AND THE MILITARY INDUSTRIAL COMPLEX

In the previous chapter, I argued that consent for U.S. foreign policy is predicated on a moral narrative that has little to do with the facts or objectives of that policy. In this chapter, I develop this point by asking how it is that the United States is able to maintain a cold-war military budget—at the expense of various other programs—when public opinion polls generally suggest support for quite different priorities. Part of the answer, I will argue, is that in the post–cold war era, a global military gains much of its credence from creating the conditions in which it is deemed necessary to use its power. In other words, without a global "threat" to replace the Soviet Union, it will be necessary to fight wars to justify spending priorities in which the military budget continues to dominate discretionary spending in the United States

Unbalanced Budgets

The United States is the most powerful nation on earth. If such a statement sounds glib, it is not as a result of hyperbole. The Unites States is not simply at the top of the list of wealthy nations; its political leaders have established a degree of global hegemony that goes well beyond the comparative size of its GDP. Thus the United States is able to dominate powerful international institutions—such as the International Monetary Fund (IMF), the World Trade Organization (WTO), or NATO—in such a way as to create global economic structures favored by U.S. elites. The establishment of this hegemonic position involves various forms of strategic influence, but perhaps its crudest guarantor is the U.S. military.

In the United States, the armed forces are not designed for defending it from invasion or attack by outside forces. Even if such a scenario were plausible, current levels of spending for such a purpose would be absurd. The U.S. military budget is over five times the size of the next biggest spender in an overall climate in which most of the other military powers (eight of the top ten) are not potential enemies but U.S. allies. Even in those areas generally regarded as potentially volatile, U.S. allies generally outspend others in the region on their own—for example, South Korea spends significantly more than North Korea, and Saudi Arabia easily outspends Iran and Iraq combined (as does Israel). In other words, from the U.S. perspective, the balance of military power is well in its favor without spending a dime. And yet the Pentagon outspends the combined military budgets of the seven countries it most often identifies as likely adversaries (Cuba, Iran, Iraq, Libya, North Korea, Syria, and Sudan) by a factor of eighteen to one. If the budgets of close U.S. allies are included, these seven potential enemies are outspent by more than thirty-three to one (Hellman 1997). Thus the military budget could be reduced to *one-fifth* of its present level and the United States would still be the world's foremost military power in a relatively secure world (i.e., one in which its allies are significantly stronger than its potential enemies).

Although the overall size of the military budget has dropped during the post–cold war period (part of a global trend), this marks a decrease from the record spending levels of the Reagan era (responsible for much of the budget deficit that became a political issue in the 1990s). The current budget is, in real terms, roughly at the level it was in the late 1970s following the Soviet occupation of Afghanistan. It is, in essence, a cold-war budget without the cold war. This use of resources clearly limits the money available for other purposes: nonetheless, by 1999, the only matter of debate among political elites in Washington was *not* how to redirect military spending to other uses, or even whether to increase the Pentagon's budget, but the *size of the increase* (as a *Washington Post* headline on May 29, 1999, put it: "Consensus Builds for Increased Defense Spending"). This amounts to either a substantial commitment by political elites to a military capable of enforcing U.S. hegemony on a global scale, or a rather corrupt and inefficient form of Keynesian economic policy (in which military spending becomes an extravagant job creation scheme). In practice, it is a bit of both.

The extent to which the collapse of the Soviet Union and the "communist threat" created a crisis for the Pentagon or NATO is debatable. It could be argued that even if some of the particularities have shifted, the overall focus of U.S. foreign policy remains broadly the same—namely, the extension of a favorable climate for U.S. or Western business interests, with various political or military structures established to support those ends. As Peter Rodman of the Nixon Center put it: "The Cold War may be over, but the laws of strategic geo-politics have not been repealed" (*New York Times*, March 15, 1998). Indeed, it is only in these terms that it makes sense to maintain a budget designed to fight a global adversary even when that adversary disappears. While the cold war had its own logic, competing with the Soviet Union allowed the United States to establish its own empire (of client states and cooperative global institutions like the IMF). The collapse of the Soviet Union simply makes the maintenance and expansion of U.S. influence a little easier.

I do not, however, want to give an impression of a unified U.S. elite sharing a clear and agreed commitment to the military enforcement of Peter Rodman's "strategic geo-politics." The basis of the commitment to a global military is rather more complex than unanimity among U.S. elites in support of a clear set of goals. From an elite perspective, for example, one could argue that economic and political forms of power are more elegant and effective ways of encouraging cooperation among recalcitrant nation-states. But the creation of any large infrastructure creates its own imperatives—a series of interlocking economic interests that encompass, in President Eisenhower's famous phrase, "the military industrial complex." Thus there are large and powerful institutions—such as the Pentagon, NATO, and the various corporations that supply them—with the means and the motives to maintain their positions of dominance, while the tentacular reach of the military infrastructure into most congressional districts and into the media system (through ownership of media empires) facilitates attempts to mobilize bipartisan support for military spending and makes most politicians resistant to significant cuts. In 1984, nearly all of the 3,041 counties in the United States received money from the Department of Defense, and while this was a period of unusually high military expenditure, it remains true that, as Hellinger and Judd put it: "Few congressional representatives can afford to attack waste and fraud vigorously or to challenge the Pentagon's priorities without fear of retribution" (Hellinger and Judd 1991, 209).

In other words, the creation of large government and corporate bureaucracies will involve such myriad beneficiaries that support for its survival will, regardless of "strategic geo-politics," be both powerful and difficult to unravel.

But whatever its raison d'être, what is striking about the elite consensus for maintaining a vast, imperialist military is that it operates *autonomously from public deliberation or sentiment*. If we look at public opinion polls as a guide to public spending priorities, in the past few decades we see consistent majority support for increasing a whole range of social welfare programs, whereas support for increasing military spending remains a *minority* response. Thus the military budget continues to dominate the discretionary budget even though it is not, according to polls, a popular priority.

There is a range of areas in which a majority of poll respondents consistently say they want to see increased spending—notably education, healthcare, urban problems, and the environment (Page and Shapiro 1992)—but the military is not one of them. Apart from the brief period in the late 1970s and early 1980s (following the Soviet invasion of Afghanistan and the election of Ronald Reagan in 1980 on a wave of cold-war rhetoric), the percentage stating that "too little" is spent on the military has rarely risen above 25 percent, and has often dipped well below that (Page and Shapiro 1992, 262–66). Gallup, for example, has recorded only one occasion when the proportion articulating support for more spending rose above 50 percent (51 percent during the height of support for defense spending in 1981), a peak of support that dropped off sharply by the subsequent year to just 16 percent, with 41 percent in 1982 saying that *too much* was spent (Gillespie 1999).

While we cannot treat these or any other responses as authentic or independent expressions of "true" public opinion, they raise a significant question: How, in an era when polls suggest people want more resources going to education, healthcare, and the environment, is increasing the already huge military budget *ideologically* possible? Or, conversely, to what extent do elites simply ignore public opinion polls in continuing to expend huge public resources on the armed forces? If the answer to the first of these questions was once straightforward, it is no longer so. From the 1940s to the end of the 1980s, high levels of military spending and widespread U.S. intervention around the world was justified as a global effort against a global threat. By its own logic, the collapse of the Soviet empire in 1989 made it possible to contemplate a large-scale conversion of military to domestic spending, to dream of ambitious but popular schemes—from subsidized childcare to rebuilding a modern mass transit system—that such a conversion might allow. Before exploring how this shift in resources was avoided, it may be helpful to briefly reprise the role anticommunism played in public opinion surveys and its relation to support (or lack thereof) for military spending.

ANTICOMMUNISM AND THE MILITARY BUDGET

The selling of the cold war rested upon decades of ideological work that portrayed communism of any kind as a creed so repressive and so threatening that almost every act of U.S. aggression was justified in its name. It is hard to understate the influence of anticommunism in the United States: it was, quite simply, one of the most successful propaganda campaigns of the twentieth century. State-sponsored anticommunist propaganda was at its most virulent during the 1950s, and the degree to which this ideological campaign is manifested in public opinion polls is, from a propagandist perspective, impressive. For example, Stouffer's well-known survey in 1954 indicated that most people were prepared to abandon a range of civil rights in order to alleviate the "communist threat": 89 percent agreed that "a man who admits he is a communist" should be fired from teaching in a college, while 91 percent favored firing a communist high-school teacher, and 66 percent stated that a book written by such a person should be removed from a public library. In perhaps the most remarkable indications of the fearful intolerance of popular anticommunist ideology, over two-thirds (68%) stated that an admitted communist should even be fired from working as a clerk in a store (hardly the most politically sensitive occupation), while the same percentage felt that an "admitted communist" should not be allowed to speak in the local community. Although support for these expressions of antipathy declined in the following decades, anticommunism remained a powerful presence in poll responses. By 1988—one year before the collapse of the Soviet Union—as many as 47 percent agreed with firing an "admitted communist" college teacher, 38 percent said that such a person's books should be removed from the public library, and 37 percent agreed that he or she should not be allowed to speak in the local community (Niemi, Mueller, and Smith 1989, 115–17).

   Poll support for various expressions of anticommunist ideology would appear to reflect the nature of elite discourse, in which the only question at stake is the degree of virulence with which communism is condemned or attacked (Herman and Chomsky 1988). Polls also reflect the nature of anticommunist propaganda, in which communism was signified with a series of vague and sinister metaphors rather than seriously debated. For example, when the 1954 Stouffer survey exchanged the words "admitted communist" to a person "favoring government ownership of all the railroads and big industries," levels of intolerance dropped considerably (thus 31 percent agreed that such a person should not be allowed to speak in the community, and 35 percent stated that such a person's books be removed from the public library). Since widespread public ownership of the means of production is a core principle of communist ideology, this suggests that anticommunism was not necessarily popularly understood as a political critique. This is certainly commensurate with a propaganda campaign that tended to avoid addressing communism in terms of principles or ideas.

And yet, for all its discursive power, anticommunism was limited in terms of generating support for military buildup and intervention—if anticommunist ideology manifested itself in *elite* support for high military spending and widespread global intervention, public support for such measures was often decidedly shaky. As Terence Qualter observes, even in the Stouffer study in the 1950s, when asked what most concerned them, less than 1 percent mentioned the internal communist threat (Qualter 1989). Moreover, support for vast military spending justified largely in its name waned considerably during the 1960s and has—apart from the brief period in 1980/1981—remained lukewarm. Similarly, the use of anticommunist ideology to justify specific military interventions has, in terms of public opinion, a patchy history. While support for U.S. intervention in Korea appeared strong at the beginning and end of the Korean War (in 1950 and 1953), a series of polls between December 1950 and October 1952 suggested that public opinion was fairly divided, with small majorities stating that the war was "a mistake" (Niemi, Mueller, and Smith 1989, 69). Support for the Vietman War, while initially strong, steadily weakened from 1967 onward, and between 1968 and 1973 polls showed that those calling the intervention "a mistake" consistently outnumbered those who did not (ibid., 70). Poll responses to the Reagan administration's "anticommunist crusade" in Central America also indicated only weak support at best (Page and Shapiro 1992). Indeed, it was the realization among elites that public support for military intervention could not be guaranteed—even in the name of anticommunism—that made covert interventions (in places like Guatemala, Iran, or Chile) a more desirable option.

But if anticommunism was not always successful as an ideological project for securing support for high levels of military spending and activity, *it was successful enough*, and apart from vague references to "international terrorism," elites invariably invoked the threat of communism as the reason for devoting considerable public resources to a global military. The "need" for massive military spending, moreover, did not rely on the "need" to use military force—the existence of a well-armed Soviet empire, in rhetorical terms, was a sufficient explanation. Still, if anticommunism often failed to translate into support for military intervention, it amplifies the ideological difficulties of winning such support without it. To recapitulate: without "the evil empire" to contend with, on what ideological basis can a cold-war military budget be maintained?

The answer, I shall suggest, is illustrative of the complex nature of hegemony, the media, and public opinion. Support for maintaining the United States's military power is composed of a patchwork of absences and ambiguities rather than any clear or overriding establishment of consent—a pattern of survey responses that we might say *permits* but does not sanction or mandate such a policy. Since 1989 the two main pillars of ideological support involve the absence of contextual information about the size of the military budget and the ability of elites to win support for specific military interventions abroad.

THE QUIET COLOSSUS

As I have suggested, support for high military spending—apart from a brief period between 1979 and 1981—is based more on the *absence* of a significant and sustained polling majority in favor of cutting the defense budget than on any popular enthusiasm for increasing it. Given that polls show significant and sustained majorities in favor of increasing many areas of government spending, this is a very weak form of vindication. Indeed, support for *cuts* in military spending has sometimes reached the 50 percent mark (in the late 1960s/early 1970s and, as I will argue shortly, during a particularly critical period in the late 1980s and early 1990s), a level of opposition far higher than is *ever* registered for programs like education, heathcare, or tackling urban problems (Page and Shapiro 1992). In general, in polls since the 1960s, those favoring cuts in military spending have tended to be more numerous than those favoring increases. It is only the number of people favoring the status quo—often a kind of "default response" in polling terms—that generally prevents their being in a majority.

Even this weak level of support may be dependent upon a context in which few people possess a comparative knowledge of the size of the military budget, in relation either to other countries or to other areas of public spending. In Delli Carpini and Keeter's study, questions about the defense budget—or any other area of government spending—tend to yield very low percentages of correct responses (Delli Carpini and Keeter 1996, 94). Instead, such questions are more likely to elicit some notable misconceptions. When a Gallup poll taken in May 1999 asked people whether "the United States is number one in the world militarily" or "only one of several leading military powers," responses were fairly evenly divided (51 percent said "number one," and 46 percent said "only one of many"). Given the enormous disparity between the United States and everyone else, this suggests widespread ignorance of the extent of U.S. military dominance (i.e., nearly half of those polled assumed that the military budget is *several times smaller* in comparative terms than is the case). Lack of knowledge here is hardly surprising: the media rarely provide this kind of information, and when budget areas are discussed, it is usually in isolation and rarely in an international context.

I would argue that it is precisely the absence of such a context that is significant in *limiting* the number of people who might favor cutting the military budget. Unless one is in favor of cutting military spending on principle, it is difficult to proffer such an opinion without some notion of how large the budget actually is, of how it compares with other areas of government expenditure, and how it compares with the budgets of other countries. The lack of such knowledge may well incline many people toward the status quo option on survey questions such as these. This applies, of course, to all areas of government spending, but what makes it notable in this instance is that while the lack of support for areas like welfare and foreign aid tend to be linked to a significant *overestimation* of their comparative costs (Kuklinski and Quirk 1997), the weak public support for (or indifference to) military spending is linked to an *underestimation* of its cost.

In the 1992 presidential election survey, for example, people were asked which of three areas received the greatest proportion of federal spending: foreign aid, the military, or welfare? These three categories were chosen because the differences among them were fairly marked— expenditure on foreign aid and welfare being fairly small in comparison with the military budget. Nonetheless, only 22 percent of respondents correctly identified the military budget as the largest of the three, while 72 percent named either foreign aid or welfare. These figures suggest more than an uninformed response selected at random. Even if we assume that *everyone* was guessing, the pattern of responses suggests an informational climate in which high spending is more commonly associated with welfare or foreign aid than with the Pentagon (Lewis and Morgan 1996). The same survey also suggested that people overestimated the extent to which politicians—notably Bill Clinton—intended to reduce military spending. When given a list of options, nearly three-quarters of those asked stated that Clinton intended to reduce the military budget by over 50 percent—considerably more than he intended at that (or any other) time. It seems plausible, then, that the degree of public resistance to devoting such heavy resources to the military is attenuated by the lack of contextual information which might counter the image of a modest and rapidly shrinking military.

The extent to which the comparative size of the U.S. military is understood was explored in the 1999 student survey. Previous surveys suggest that this population is much more aware than those in general population surveys of the size of military spending. Nevertheless, the following responses suggest the limits of that understanding:

If the U.S. military budget is compared with the other countries, we find that:

a. The United States is now the third biggest spender in the world.   15%
b. The United States is first, equal with two other countries.   17%
c. The United States is the biggest spender in the world,
   spending twice as much as the next biggest spending country.   48%
d. The United States is the biggest spender in the world,
   spending five times as much as the next biggest country.   19%

In this instance, most students demonstrate an understanding that the United States is the world's biggest spender, although the degree of imbalance is less generally appreciated (by less than one in five).

The responses to the following question demonstrate a similar underestimation of the size of the U.S. military budget in relation to those of other nations:

The U.S. State Department has identified seven countries it regards as potentially dangerous adversaries: Cuba, Iran, Iraq, Libya, North Korea, Syria, and Sudan. The total military spending of these seven countries adds up to roughly:

a. More than five times what the United States spends
   on the military.   11%
b. Twice what the United States spends on the military.   16%
c. About the same as the U.S. military budget.   23%
d. Half what the United States spends on the military.   34%
e. Less than one-tenth of what the United States spends
   on the military.   14%

Responses tend to weigh on the side of U.S. dominance, although in this instance, the degree of the imbalance is even less clearly understood (only 14 percent getting the answer right, while half either underestimate U.S. spending or overestimate the power of the stated adversaries by sizeable margins).

For some years I have conducted a class exercise in which students work in groups to allocate the federal budget as they see fit. Each group is given information about the needs and scope of each budget area but is *not* told how current budgets are allocated. Invariably, every group—even those whose members are committed to a strong military—*substantially* cuts the proportion of the budget going to the military. Most are, as a consequence, taken aback by the size of the actual military budget in relation to their own priorities. This response is indicative of a discursive climate where the lack of comparative information—such as the extent of the imbalance between the United States and other nations or the degree to which the military dominates the discretionary budget—works in favor of the status quo.

This is not to discount the degree to which many people appear, in poll responses, to find the idea of a strong military appealing. Polls record a majority in favor of the proposition that the U.S. military should be "number one in the world." Although the proportion who agree with this statement is sizeable, it is worth noting that, given the unanimity among U.S. elites on this issue, the number who disagree with this proposition is also fairly high—39 percent in a May 1999 Gallup Poll (Gillespie 1999). Even for those who declare support for the idea of military supremacy, it is also not entirely clear what such a response means. Since such a desire could be achieved with spending at *one-fifth* the current level, this response could therefore be seen as much as a mandate for reducing the budget as increasing it. Moreover, the moral narrative described in chapter six means that support for U.S. military strength is *not* equivalent to support for U.S. imperialism.

A global military is also ideologically at odds with various other strains in public opinion polls: surveys consistently show people prioritizing "national problems" over "international issues," as well as favoring a multilateral approach to the resolution of international disputes (Niemi, Mueller, and Smith 1989, 54–55). As Douglas Kellner points out, research on this issue suggests most people are, in general, suspicious of unilateral U.S. military interventions (Kellner 1995). For example, criticism of the United Nations voiced by more conservative elites (and manifested in U.S. policy, such as the failure to pay its UN dues) has little relation to survey responses, which show clear and consistent support for the United Nations. Indeed, it seems plausible that the unpopularity of foreign aid, combined with the tendency to significantly overestimate the size of the foreign aid budget, may be a negative reaction to certain *military* functions, since these are often presented to the public as attempts to help, assist, or rescue other nations from various perils.

Overall, poll responses highlight the ideological vulnerability of the military budget. It is also easy to see how a different informational climate—one that stressed the comparative size of the budget—might increase popular resistance to current spending levels. Consent, inasmuch as it exists, is thereby achieved as much by the *absence* of information as by its presence. The media's role in this process thus has less to do with what is said than what is ignored. The elite consensus for increasing the budget at the turn of the century is reflected in media coverage in the sense that such a policy is the subject of little controversy or scrutiny, while stories of Pentagon waste or excess are rarely covered outside the alternative media. For the rest of this chapter, I argue that it is also through such absences that public support is garnered for various forms of military action.

A New Rationale for Military Intervention

Since 1989 U.S. military intervention in other countries has tended to be portrayed as specific responses to certain conditions. Indeed, it might seem that the decline of Soviet communism has meant that each new conflict has to be justified with a new rationale—a cumbersome ideological project that potentially limits the scope for military intervention. And yet in the decade since the fall of the Berlin Wall, the U.S. military has fought three wars on three continents—in Panama, the Persian Gulf, and Yugoslavia—not a record that suggests restraint. On the contrary, the ability of elites to demonstrate public support for such interventions has become an integral part of a political strategy to maintain military spending at cold-war levels. The "need" to fight wars at reasonably regular intervals is a way to signify that, even without the cold war, *the world is a dangerous place*—what we might call a shift from an anticommunism discourse to a "dangerous world" discourse. But while it was possible to represent the threat of Soviet communism as a constant presence, the discourse that "the world is a dangerous place" is partly constructed *by* events like the Gulf war and the war against the Serbs in Yugoslavia.

In other words, whether by accident or design, fighting wars has now become *a necessary part* of an ideological strategy to diminish public opposition to the size of the military budget. Regardless of intention, elites are able to use support for *specific* military endeavors to maintain *generally* high levels of spending. The Gulf war was especially critical in this respect, occurring in a year in which the notion of a "peace dividend" was becoming prominent in media discourse, and when polls were showing increasing support for conversion to various forms of social spending. Even after the Gulf war, the *Washington Post* (December 4, 1991) published a Times Mirror poll indicating that 61 percent of respondents favored shifting resources to programs like healthcare, education, and the environment—far more than the 27 percent who favored shifting resources to deficit reduction or the 10 percent who wanted the money back in tax cuts (although, in yet another example of the disparity between popular and elite priorities, it was the latter options that were, albeit on a modest scale, favored and pursued by elites). A Lexis Nexis search of major media for the phrase "peace dividend" suggests that the term emerged at the end of 1989 (with 58 references that year, 46 of which were in December) and entered into common usage in 1990, with 589 references to the term. And yet during the 1990s the phrase began to disappear from media discourse, with 237 references in 1992, declining to 47 references by 1997 (all of which, by that time, referred to other contexts).

While the Gulf war did not create majority support for *increasing* defense spending, it seems to have halted the trend toward majority support for decreasing it. As Tom Smith has pointed out, polls suggest that "the Persian Gulf War notably increased confidence in the military . . . expectations of future wars (and) support for defense spending" (Smith 1993). The key element in the discursive cluster Smith describes involves the increase in expectation of future wars, or the "dangerous world" discourse. From the Pentagon's perspective, the survival of the Hussein regime has been useful in this regard, since it maintains the existence of his "threatening" presence. Indeed, polls show a *gradual rather than a sudden* shift of public opinion in the 1990s away from favoring cuts in defense spending. By 1999, support for the military budget, albeit for maintaining rather than increasing it—or, more specifically, whatever people *imagine the military budget to be*—was as high as it has been since 1981 (Gillespie 1999). The Gulf war was, in this context, not so much a transmogrifying event as the beginning of a shift in consciousness.

What is also notable about the Gulf war is the importance of the act of war itself in generating public support. As John Zaller (1994) points out, depending on how the question was asked (since responses varied widely depending on the discursive context), polls suggested that support for the war increased and solidified once battle commenced. While this was partly a product of a bipartisan effort to "support our troops," support for various prowar discourses was clearly intensified by a narrative context that pitched two sides against each other (in what the networks called the "Showdown in the Gulf"; Kellner 1992) rather than one that hypothesized various options for dealing with a "problem." Thus the media's rhetorical context shifted from the question "what to do?" to "which side are you on?"

If the ideological conditions for maintaining cold-war military budgets rely upon—and are constructed by—the act of war itself, this raises more specific questions about the way in which those wars are constructed as both worthy and necessary. As I have suggested, public opinion polls suggest that survey respondents do not automatically support elites in the use of military force for global intervention. Public support for such intervention has historically been contingent upon the success of specific elite campaigns. While these campaigns often *are* successful, they are campaigns nonetheless. Consent for military interventions, in other words, needs to be won. As John Zaller points out, the chances of achieving compliant responses in opinion polls is considerably increased if they are seen to be bipartisan, since without serious disagreements between political elites, the news media tend to fall into line behind an elite consensus (Zaller 1994). While this bipartisanship is often forthcoming in foreign policy, some of the conditions that favor widespread political support for high military spending in general—that is, significant sums of public money going into most congressional districts—do not necessarily translate into support for specific military interventions. The processes I am tracing here are not therefore the work of a well-orchestrated elite but one in which various elite interests coalesce to achieve certain hegemonic goals.

The first direct post–cold war U.S. military intervention came very quickly after the collapse of the Soviet Union when President Bush ordered the invasion of Panama in December 1989. As an exercise in winning consent, the invasion was extraordinarily successful—it suggested not only that public support for military intervention in the post–cold war world was feasible, but that such interventions, even if in blatant violation of international law, could bolster the popularity of the governing administration (polls suggested sizeable public majorities in favor of the invasion, while Bush's approval ratings immediately after the invasion showed a significant upward bump).

The Panama invasion was a comparatively small-scale operation (although fairly devastating to parts of Panama) and had many specific features. Most important, perhaps, it formed part of a "war on drugs" narrative that was prominent in elite and media discourse (and hence a matter of public concern) at the time. The Panama invasion and the capture of Manuel Noriega (although it had no verifiable effect on levels of drug availability or use in the United States) provided the simulation of "closure" in that narrative. But from a hegemonic perspective, the success of the Panama invasion contained some key elements for the development of a public relations strategy for selling intervention in the post–cold war world.

Most notably, it demonstrated how the *vilification of a country's leader*—in this case Manuel Noriega—could be used to enlist public support for military intervention, *regardless of history or context*. Thus, despite the history of U.S. support for Noriega (in which George Bush himself played a role as head of the CIA), and despite the fact that Noriega's alleged offenses against the general principles of legality, democracy, and human rights were less egregious than those carried out by many regimes in the region supported by the United

States, the Bush administration was able to carry out a campaign unencumbered by such information. As Cook and Cohen point out, the administration's use of the "evil, dangerous dictator" framework was an easy one for the media to work with—hence, for example, CBS anchor Dan Rather was able to put Noriega "*at the top of the list* of the world's drug thieves and scums" (emphasis mine) without any qualifying statement about the basis for such a comparative evaluation (*CBS Evening News*, December 20, 1989; quoted in Cook and Cohen 1996, 14).

The establishment of this framework is made possible by the media's *general tendency* to ignore the history or context of a news event (Iyengar 1991), an exclusion that provided the ideological conditions to set the vilification campaign in place. This is not to say that the history and context of U.S. relations with Noriega were entirely absent, but that reports invoking it were marginal enough to avoid destabilizing the dominant narrative (Cook and Cohen 1996). Uncomplicated by more awkward or contradictory stories, the "evil, dangerous dictator" framework was powerful in moving public opinion (Manheim 1994), depending as it does upon widely agreed moral principles and a good guy/bad guy structure that is, for most people, an extremely familiar narrative context. Like anticommunism, the advantage of this framework—from a hegemonic perspective—is that, without the constraints of history or context, it can be repeated and used in a wide variety of instances.

The Panama invasion also indicated the advantage of using overwhelming force to ensure a reasonably quick resolution and/or one with minimal U.S. casualties, as well as the need to pay careful attention to maximizing media complicity (through a mixture of press restrictions, well-produced propaganda, and the media's reliance on "official" U.S. sources). The problem with Panama, as a discursive model for reproducing global intervention, was its size—it did not require substantial military force—and its location, as the quaint imperialist expression puts it, in "the United States's backyard." If the Panama invasion suggested possibilities, these factors limited the extent to which Panama-style interventions could be used to offset discussions of a "peace dividend." Indeed, polls on military spending after the invasion continued to show increasingly high levels of support for cutting the Pentagon budget.

The fact that the Bush administration was, within a year of the fall of the Berlin Wall, prepared to engage in a *second* highly publicized military engagement is indicative of the urgency with which many of those within the military and political elite regarded the need to avoid pressure for a significant transfer of resources to a peacetime economy. To be blunt, without a war, there was no obvious counterargument to calls for widespread conversion of military resources to peacetime use. This made polling trends especially ominous, since they showed support—to a symbolically significant 50 percent mark in 1990—for cutting the military budget (Gillespie 1999).

While there may have been some possibilities for substituting the communist threat with notions of "international terrorism" or "Islamic fundamentalism," these threats were neither new nor, in a purely abstract or theoretical form, immediately compelling as a basis for massive military expenditure. A war against a major country in the Middle East, on the other hand, provided a more practical opportunity for winning support for a large-scale military intervention in the short-term and a model for maintaining high levels of defense spending in the longer term.

The significance of the Gulf war surpasses the event itself: it provided the ideological groundwork for generating public support for military action and military institutions in the postcommunist era. The Iraqi invasion of Kuwait in 1990 and the subsequent Persian Gulf war in 1991 was, in this sense, a seminal moment in recent history: one in which the United States and its Western allies were able to adapt to the new postcommunist world and redefine a public rationale for the use of military force in the imposition of U.S. or Western hegemony. Thus current military strategy is now premised on the need to fight two "Gulf wars" simultaneously, an imperialist premise that might not have been politically viable had the Gulf war never occurred.

Although the Gulf war itself was fairly short-lived (after a month of bombing, the ground war lasted less than a week), the buildup to the fighting allowed it to form part of an eight-month news narrative. It was, in this sense, the biggest international news story of the decade. It not only dominated media coverage in 1990 and 1991 but appeared to create an increased interest in news in general. During this period, twenty of the twenty-five largest newspapers enjoyed circulation gains, while CNN, at key stages, increased its audience ratings dramatically—to such an extent that at times it was receiving ratings over ten times higher than normal, higher even, than the three main networks (Hallin and Gitlin 1994). This apparent enthusiasm for news was, perhaps, not surprising: events in 1990 and 1991 involved the buildup and execution of the first *major* war in which the United States was overtly engaged since Vietnam—an event accorded enormous significance by political elites.

If the significance accorded to these events by both the press and the public seems self-evident, it rests upon a questionable premise. As William Dorman and Steven Livingston put it:

How was it that an Iraq constantly at war with its own people, or for eight years with Iran, did not pose a clear and present danger to world peace, while an Iraq at war with Kuwait suddenly did? Similarly, why was Saddam Hussein not only tolerated by the Bush and Reagan administrations but even given vital economic and military support by them for a decade if he was a character as evil as Hitler?   (Dorman and Livingston 1994, 65–66)

In other words, since Iraq's invasion of Kuwait was *entirely consistent* with its recent history, why did it go from being a recipient of military support to the worst of enemies? There has been a great deal of critical analysis of this question (Kellner 1992; Mowlana, Gerbner, and Schiller 1992), from which it is clear that the answers have little to do with the narrative that dominates media discourse of foreign policy.

As I have suggested in the previous chapter, U.S. foreign policy has little to do with moral or ethical imperatives, despite widespread assumptions to the contrary. Illegal and brutal occupations—such as the Chinese occupation of Tibet and the Indonesian occupation of East Timor—may be either tolerated or ignored if they do not interfere with (or if they promote) U.S. economic or strategic goals. Similarly, any notion that U.S. hostility or support is contingent upon a concern for human rights is untenable: the list of brutal regimes supported by the United States since the 1950s—whether in Africa (e.g., Mobutu's Zaire), Asia (e.g., Suharto's Indonesia), Central America (e.g., a series of genocidal regimes in Guatemala), South America (e.g., Pinochet's Chile), or the Middle East (e.g., the Saudi Arabian theocracy)—is both long and well documented.

It would therefore be a mistake to see U.S. policy toward Iraq in 1990 as a shift in any grand or morally binding sense. If the switch from a supportive to a hostile stance on Iraq seems incoherent from a human-rights perspective, it is because *neither position* was informed by such laudable goals. The Iran–Iraq war may have been an enormous waste of human life and economic resources, but for U.S. policy makers it usefully constrained two of the major powers in the region from leading any regional moves that might threaten U.S. strategic or economic interests. Hence the decision by the U.S. government to supply arms to Iraq (and, indeed, to both sides at various times) was one that helped to maintain U.S. and Western hegemony. The border between Kuwait and Iraq was drawn by the British in precisely this spirit of colonialist containment, in order to restrict a potentially powerful state like Iraq access to the Persian Gulf. Iraq's invasion of Kuwait was therefore not only a more lopsided encounter than the Iran–Iraq war, but one that potentially upset the "stability" of Western hegemony in an economically significant oil-producing region.

Even so, it is plausible to see how U.S. or Western interests might have been maintained by pursuing a policy of "constructive engagement" to encourage an Iraqi withdrawal in exchange for a resolution with Kuwait on the question of oil prices (the issue that sparked the Iraqi invasion). A transcript of a meeting between Saddam Hussein and U.S. representative Joseph Wilson on August 7, 1990, suggests that the Iraqi leader was open to U.S. overtures for a negotiated solution. Media interest in the dispute would certainly have waned in response to a policy of quiet diplomacy (rather than noisy hostility), while the U.S. administration might have strengthened its alliance with Iraq, something that, until the invasion, it appeared to be keen to do. And yet, as Douglas Kellner documents, the Bush administration decided to characterize the Wilson–Hussein meeting as a hostile encounter signifying not only Iraqi intransigence but its ambitions to attack other neighbors—notably Saudi Arabia (Kellner 1992). This thereby set in motion the deployment of half a million troops to "defend" Saudi Arabia (a strange but rarely challenged premise, since Saudi Arabia was already the biggest military power in the region), in the name of "Operation Desert Shield."

The sudden adoption of a more aggressive posture—one whose hostility increased with intensity in the ensuing weeks—was therefore notable in that it did not obviously serve the interests of U.S. elites in any broad geopolitical sense. What made this dramatic about-face both plausible and ultimately attractive was a series of other elite concerns and interests, all of which might be advanced by a war with Iraq. First of all, the Pentagon and the arms industry were facing the possibility of significant cutbacks and needed to justify its global scale of operations; but this was not the only form of pressure on the Bush administration. The Kuwaiti regime not only had close ties to the administration and to U.S. business interests, it was adroit in its use of the public relations firm Hill and Knowlton to drum up support for U.S. intervention on its behalf (Manheim 1994). Moreover, the Bush administration had already experienced an increase in support following the Panama invasion, while polling data indicated the agenda-setting benefits to Bush of displacing economic concerns with a "foreign policy" narrative (Zhu 1991). In the longer term, the Gulf war provided an opportunity for the United States to assert its political dominance as a world power during a period of economic and geopolitical uncertainty, as well as erasing the constraining image of the Vietnam War. In short, apart from the involvement of the Kuwaiti elite, what made a war with Iraq appealing had little to do with Saddam Hussein.

Truth or Dare: The Gulf War

In terms of media coverage, Iraq's emergence into the world of headline news began with the invasion of Kuwait. Although Iraq had fought an eight-year war with Iran, and although the brutality of Saddam Hussein's regime—particularly toward the Kurdish minority—was well documented, the volume of media coverage of Saddam Hussein and Iraq prior to the invasion of Kuwait was sporadic and, by the standards of events following August 1990, minimal (Dorman and Livingston 1994). As a consequence, surveys indicate that most people had little knowledge of Saddam Hussein and U.S.–Iraqi relations before August 1990 (Wilcox, Ferrara, and Allsop 1991). From a public relations perspective, this meant that the Bush administration was not, in terms of public understanding, burdened by the history of U.S. support for Iraq.

Media interest in the Iraqi invasion of Kuwait was clearly predicated on the prominence of the issue in elite discourse. As a variety of scholars in mass communication and political science have pointed out, the media take their cues from political elites in deciding which issues or stories to cover (Herman and Chomsky 1988; Kellner 1990; Page and Shapiro 1992; Zaller 1992). This is particularly notable on foreign policy, where there is a heavy reliance on domestic government sources. For example, the Indonesian occupation of East Timor might have been seen as an important precedent in evaluating U.S. policy during the media coverage of the Iraqi occupation of Kuwait, but since it was not in the interests of political elites to make such comparisons, this particular occupation by a major regional power went largely unnoticed in the U.S. media.

In the case of Iraq, the problem for U.S. elites was not necessarily one of drawing media attention to the issue but doing so in a way that *obscured the motives* of political elites and of U.S. foreign policy in general. Most people were unlikely to appreciate the more self-serving goals of the Pentagon or the Bush administration: to put it bluntly, fighting a war to boost presidential approval ratings or to provide a rationale for high levels of military spending was—and is—hardly likely to engender popular support. The extent of the ideological and political task was suggested by a poll taken two years earlier, in which people were asked to respond to a scenario in which Iran invaded Saudi Arabia. Despite the history of negative coverage of Iran (from the hostage crisis on), only 18 percent of respondents supported the option of sending U.S. troops to assist Saudi Arabia in this hypothetical instance (Wittkopf 1990).

Even if people were persuaded of more general hegemonic or economic imperatives (i.e., the need to assert U.S. power in the uncertainties of the post–cold war period), these were unlikely to prove compelling in polling discourse. To illustrate, polls suggested weak support for a war fought to ensure the flow of oil supplies to the West, a reluctance that was apparent from an early stage. A *Los Angeles Times* poll on August 29, 1990, explicitly explored the conditions necessary for creating popular support for military action. Thus, when people were asked

Do you think it's worth risking the lives of American soldiers (in the Middle East) to protect our oil supplies, or not?

only 29 percent responded positively, while 61 percent said no. A general unease with the notion of economic self-interest was further revealed when the poll asked a similar question, but in a way that more clearly underlined a notion of economic self-interest:

Do you think it's worth risking the lives of American soldiers (in the Middle East) in order to keep down gasoline prices, or not?

Put this way, only 5 percent supported going to war, with 91 percent opposed. By contrast, when a moral principle was invoked, the degree of support rose dramatically:

Do you think it's worth risking the lives of American soldiers (in the Middle East) in order to demonstrate that countries should not get away with aggression, or not?

In this instance a clear majority—53 percent, with 37 percent opposed—supported going to war, even at this early stage. A similar response was recorded by a Harris poll (conducted August 17–21, 1990), in which a majority opposed risking money and "American lives" to protect U.S. oil supplies but supported (by 62% to 35%) doing so "to serve notice on Iraq and other aggressor nations that they cannot militarily invade and take over other nations and get away with it" (Mueller 1994, 250–51). Similar questions were asked in polls throughout the build up to the Gulf war, and while the figures vary depending on the question wording and context, the pattern is the same, with certain moral imperatives consistently registering far higher levels of support than appeals to economic self-interest or other less altruistic objectives (Mueller 1994, 250–60).

This point was also clarified in a more abstract context. The Gulf war study conducted in February 1991 (see chapter six) gave respondents a series of three hypothetical situations (in unspecified countries) in order to gauge the *principles* that lay behind support for U.S. military intervention. The study indicated clear majorities favoring U.S. military intervention to protect human rights against a brutal regime (58%) or to restore the sovereignty of an occupied country (53%), while less than one in five (18%) favored military intervention against an oil-producing nation pursuing policies antagonistic to U.S. interests (Morgan, Lewis, and Jhally 1992).

It is, of course, possible that, even to an unknown interviewer in a survey, people are simply more reluctant to admit to being informed by more self-serving economic motives or the desire to assert global dominance than they are to endorse more high-minded concerns for world peace and human rights. Nevertheless, even if this is so, the fact that people feel the need to articulate *public expressions* of more principled motives to justify war is itself significant. This is partly because what appears in opinion polls is generally taken at face value in mainstream political discourse, but also because it implies that people will feel more comfortable if their political leaders use similar justifications. Overall, the polls taken during the late summer and autumn of 1990 suggest three areas of particular potency in engendering support for military action: first, to punish aggression (in the form of an oppressive occupation); second, to punish a dictator responsible for egregious abuses of human rights; and third, to prevent a brutal dictator like Saddam Hussein from developing nuclear or chemical weapons.

The question wording in most of these polls implicitly denied the presence of inconsistencies in U.S. foreign policy. Both the Harris and the *Los Angeles Times* polls, for example, proposed the idea that military action will demonstrate that aggressors "cannot militarily invade and take over other nations and get away with it." Since the United States and other Western nations routinely tolerate other such invasions and occupations (in places such as East Timor, Tibet, and the West Bank), it is difficult to see how a general principle can be invoked in this particular instance. The question itself makes sense *only* in the narrow discourse promoted by the Bush administration and military elites, a discourse that relies on the absence of contextual information.

The lesson for political elites in these polls is fairly straightforward. In order to create public support for a war—in this case against Iraq—the need for military action must be cast *within a moral framework*, notably one in which the aggressor is seen as posing a unique and rampant threat to notions of national sovereignty, human rights, and world peace. As I suggested in the previous chapter, this kind of moral narrative is familiar territory for most people, who are used to understanding foreign policy in terms of the pursuit of lofty principles. After some initial floundering—during which the Bush administration was criticized principally for its failure to make a clear and compelling case for intervention (Entman and Page 1994)—this discursive strategy was consistently employed. To be plausible—and thus to avoid awkward questions such as those posed by Dorman and Livingston—this strategy required the use of *hyperbole* and *suppression*: Saddam Hussein's brutality must be exaggerated, while corresponding cases of toleration for other violations of national sovereignty, human rights, or the development of nuclear or chemical weapons (including, notably, Iraq before July 1990) must be ignored.

The image that best encapsulated these elements was the notion that Saddam Hussein was an incarnation of Adolf Hitler. The Hitler analogy not only stressed the threat to human rights and world peace, it implied a view of history in which the awkward list of brutal dictators supported or tolerated by the United States—such as Mobutu, Pol Pot, Pinochet, the Samozas, Suharto, and Saddam Hussein pre-1990—drift into insignificance. The comparison also suggests a truncated and strangely elliptical history of dictatorship in the twentieth century: first, there was Adolf Hitler; then, there was Saddam Hussein. President Bush and other prowar officials were therefore liberal in their use of the analogy. Bush, in particular, used it on an almost daily basis, to such an extent that his *failure* to use it during a brief period in early November became the subject of news stories in the *New York Times* and the *Washington Post* (Dorman and Livingston 1994, 71). The Hitler comparison—to be revivified later by Clinton in the war against Serbia—thereby became the main operational metaphor in media coverage. Hence, in their analysis of preinvasion and postinvasion coverage, Dorman and Livingston report: "After the August 2 invasion, the Hitler analogy exploded. Between August 2 and January 15, the *Washington Post* and the *New York Times* published 228 stories, editorials , or columns . . . which invoked the Saddam Hussein-Adolf Hitler analogy" (Dorman and Livingston 1994, 71).

In a more critical media environment, one of the dangers of the Hitler analogy was that it might have implicated Bush—and Reagan before him—in the role of appeaser. Indeed, it became apparent during September 1990 that April Glaspie, the U.S. ambassador to Iraq, had, in a meeting with Saddam Hussein just prior to the invasion of Kuwait (on July 25), reacted to the possibility of an attack on Kuwait by declaring a position of neutrality—a position *entirely consistent* with the administration's position up until that point but dramatically out of kilter with subsequent condemnations of the invasion. Fortunately for the administration, the news media paid little attention to this remarkable inconsistency, or to the many years of support for Saddam Hussein before the summer of 1990 (Dorman and Livingston 1994; Naureckas 1996b). For example, in their study of 4,214 articles in the *Washington Post* and the *New York Times* (between August 2 and November 8, 1990), Dorman and Livingston found only 20—*less than 1 in 200*—that dealt with the ten-year history of U.S. support for Saddam Hussein.

The issue here is one of volume. When an article in the *Washington Post* on November 1 revealed that between 1985 and 1990, the United States approved $1.5 billion worth of equipment for sale to Iraq—all of which could have been used for the development of nuclear weapons—its significance was negated by a well-established and oft-repeated framework that ignored this history and emphasized the need to do something to contain Saddam Hussein. This framework was so well established in the period immediately preceding the outbreak of war (in December 1990 and January 1991) that the Associated Press, CBS/*New York Times*, Gallup, the *Los Angeles Times*, NBC/*Wall Street Journal*, and *Time*/CNN all ran polls asking people whether war was justified to remove Iraq's capacity to produce nuclear or chemical weapons (a majority responding positively in every case). Again, such a question makes sense only in the context of a narrative in which the United States's role prior to July 1990 is suppressed. Needless to say, this question—or any version of it—was not asked during the decade in which the United States assisted in Iraq's military development.

Overall, the emphasis by political elites of threats to world peace and Iraq's "naked aggression" were repeated fairly uncritically in the news media. A content analysis of the early period of the Iraq/Kuwait story by Timothy Cook suggests that official government sources—the White House, the Pentagon, and the State Department—dominated the news frame (these three news beats comprised 79 percent of the domestically derived lead stories on ABC, CBS, and NBC), while oppositional voices—protestors, peace activists, conscientious objectors, and Arab Americans—"had virtually no access to the news" (Cook 1994, 119; Naureckas 1996b).

The way in which this framework informed the responses to public opinion polls was suggested by the 1991 survey of people's assumptions. The survey's aim was to probe the extent to which the apparently strong support for the war was based on a mythic narrative in which moral inconsistencies and contradictions were suppressed. There are two discursive domains whose absence is particularly significant, not only in this instance but in the coverage of foreign policy in general: these involve an understanding of *history* and *context.*

In terms of history, perhaps most critical to the mythic narrative of moral consistency was an assumption that Saddam Hussein's history of brutality was accompanied by a history of U.S. disapproval, that the only movement in U.S. policy had been from irritation to outrage. In this version of events, the recent history of U.S. support for Iraq would be replaced by a more morally consistent history of U.S. opposition. Thus, when respondents were asked a question about April Glaspie's meeting with Saddam Hussein, they were given the opportunity to support two kinds of answers, one that would reflect U.S. tolerance for Iraqi acts aggression prior to July 1990, and other answers that assume a mythic, morally consistent history. The question and answers were as follows:

In July 1990, just before he invaded, Saddam Hussein indicated he may use force against Kuwait. How did the United States respond?

    a. The United States said it would impose sanctions against him.   74%
    b. The United States said it would regard it as a threat
       to the United States.   47%
    c. The United States said it would take no action.   13%
    d. The United States said it would support Kuwait
       with the use of force.   65%

Since the U.S. position before the invasion received such scant media attention, it is not surprising that so few—just 13 percent—were able to identify it. But to see this is as merely a manifestation of an uninformed public would be to miss the point. Most responses move very clearly toward answers that are *compatible with the mythic narrative*—indeed, nearly two-thirds assume that the U.S. government went as far as threatening military action.

This is a powerful example of the way in which media coverage can influence public assumptions—not by deliberate misinformation or mendacity but simply by highlighting certain facts (those compatible with the mythic narrative) and neglecting others (those that contradict that narrative).

The same can be said of the absence of *context* in media coverage. Since the power of this mythic discourse is dependent upon the absence of comparative cases, the survey asked about other occupations in the Middle East. It is, of course, possible to regard the Israeli occupation of the West Bank and the Iraqi occupation of Kuwait in different moral contexts—the first being portrayed as an act of defense in a hostile Arab world, the second being regarded simply as a brutal act of aggression. But what was notable was that most people—70 percent—appeared to be *unaware* of the Israeli occupation (even fewer people—15 percent—had heard of the Palestinian Intifada).

Perhaps the most egregious contemporary example of a foreign invasion and brutal occupation that might have provided an instructive comparison is the Indonesian occupation of East Timor (one in which one-third of the Timorese population were killed.[Herman 1999]). Knowledge of this occupation was tested in two of the student surveys, which asked about the occupation and given a series of possible answers:

Which country invaded East Timor, slaughtered many of its citizens, and continues to suppress the native population?

	APRIL '92 N = 276	SEPT. '96 N = 121
China	31	26
North Korea	26	45
Vietnam	16	10
The Soviet Union	13	6
Indonesia	13	12

As the responses suggest, the numbers correctly designating Indonesia are so low that all of them could be accounted for by random guesses (or an informed guess based on a basic knowledge of geography), while "informed guesswork" appears to lead them toward China or North Korea. If these responses make little geopolitical sense, they match a news framework in the 1990s in which the occupation of East Timor was ignored while the governments of both China and North Korea were generally signified as oppressive and possibly dangerous regimes.

The history of U.S. support for Indonesia in this context may seem somewhat removed from the Persian Gulf, but since the two cases are, *in the moral terms* used to justify the war against Iraq, so directly comparable, its absence from media accounts is a necessary part of the mythic history that gave the Gulf war its moral force. Had journalists repeatedly asked why the administration was expressing such moral outrage in response to the invasion of Kuwait while tolerating the occupation of East Timor, the appeal to principle in much of the prowar rhetoric would have been very difficult to sustain.

Overall, responses to questions in the Gulf war survey suggest the forceful presence of this morally consistent narrative. For example, when people were asked

How would you compare the number of civilian casualties in the U.S. action in Panama and the Iraqi invasion of Kuwait

we can be reasonably sure that they were unlikely to have been in a position to give an authoritative response. Figures of casualties in these two engagements were generally conflicting and hard to come by—estimates of Kuwaiti casualties are around 500 to 700 (Mueller 1994), while estimates of Panamanian casualties varied between an early "official" U.S. estimate of 254 to subsequent estimates of several thousand. Although allegations of thousands of Panamanian casualties were made on the popular news program *60 Minutes*, it is more likely that most people would need to rely on more general guidelines to make a comparison (Lewis 1991). Since the overall thrust of media coverage tended to emphasize Kuwaiti victims and play down Panamanian victims, we would expect responses to reflect a framework that implies the *moral superiority* of the United States—symbolized, in this instance, in purely quantitative terms. Thus a majority—57 percent—said that Kuwait casualties were higher, compared to 20 percent who assumed more Panamanian deaths (despite the technical nature of this question, only 16 percent said that they did not know).

Another indicator of the discursive structure of the mythic moral narrative was the translation, by some, of U.S. allies into democracies. This did not form an explicit part of the media coverage, apart from general, rather vague statements about "fighting for democracy," and yet faith in the mythic moral discourse about U.S. foreign policy would be likely to push some responses in this direction. Thus, when asked to identify whether Iraq, Kuwait, or Saudi Arabia were democracies, less than 5 percent said Iraq, while 23 percent said (preinvasion) Kuwait, and 22 percent said Saudi Arabia. This suggests that, for some, the impression had been created that the United States was defending democratic regimes against a dictatorship rather than intervening in a dispute between dictatorships.

Conversely, information about Saddam Hussein that might complicate his image as a megalomaniac bent on regional domination was *not* part of a popular knowledge framework. Only 2 percent of respondents in the survey were aware of the fact that the invasion was predicated by Kuwait's noncooperation over regional oil prices. This motive for the invasion may be morally indefensible, but it is at least suggestive of a precise economic rationale of limited ambition rather than a more general "Hitlerian" desire for power. And yet the majority of respondents (53%) *were* aware—or guessed—that he had already used chemical weapons, information that *is consistent* with the "Hitler revisited" narrative.

While the numbers in the Gulf war survey are small (250), the relationships in the data are suggestive. For example, various studies indicate that more educated respondents are able to demonstrate more political knowledge on surveys than those with less formal education (Delli Carpini and Keeter 1992, 1996). In the Gulf war survey, the strongest predictor of knowledge of certain responses—such as the U.S. position articulated by Ambassador Glaspie—was not education or news viewing *but opposition to the war itself* (only 10 percent of those who strongly supported the war knew or guessed the correct response, while 27 percent of those who opposed the war did so). Similarly, 71 percent of strong supporters of the war—compared with 46 percent of opponents—

erroneously assumed a morally consistent answer to this question (i.e., that the United States had vowed to support Kuwait with the use of force). This suggests a *discursive relationship* whereby contextual knowledge is articulated with an ideological position—in this case, opposition to the war—while the absence of such knowledge is related to support for the war.

As we might expect, this relationship was particularly apparent when that knowledge tended to undermine the administration's morally unambiguous case. Strong supporters of the war, for example, were more than twice as likely than nonsupporters to wrongly assert that Kuwait was a democracy (28% to 12%). In relation to the Palestinian uprising on the West Bank, opponents of the war were more than twice as likely to be able to identify the Intifada than strong supporters (24% to 12%).

This is not to say that war supporters were simply more ignorant than opponents. War supporters were, for example, slightly more likely than opponents to be able to identify the "Patriot missile" (as the weapon used to intercept incoming Scud missiles). Clearly, the ability to name a missile celebrated at the time (although subsequently discredited) for its clinical efficiency does little to undermine the case for military intervention—on the contrary, such knowledge might seem to support a faith in the ability of "smart weapons" to minimize the loss of human life (it is notable, in this context, that when it came to estimating Iraqi casualties, opponents gave a mean response that was over four times higher than war supporters—over twelve thousand as opposed to fewer than four thousand).

In this sense, the popularity of the Persian Gulf war was not a simple matter of people being told what to think. It was predicated, instead, on a set of discursive conditions—the presence of certain kinds of information and (more conspicuously) the absence of others—in which support for the Gulf war seemed to be in confluence with a set of moral or high-minded principles about democracy, human rights, international law, and world peace. In this sense, many of those who supported the war responded both *morally* and *rationally* to the information made available to them.

The most subversive forms of discourse, in this sense, is one that disrupts the politics of principle espoused by elites. Since critics of the Gulf war were given so little access to media discourse, this may be a mute point. Nevertheless, this analysis suggests that some of the slogans of the peace movement in 1990 and 1991 were unlikely to be persuasive. Specifically, the cry of "No blood for oil" or allusions to Vietnam did little to disrupt the discourse of moral principle promoted by elites and absorbed into the narrative of popular understanding. Indeed, they could be dismissed as irrelevant (as the driver of a Texaco truck put it to the local news media during an antiwar demonstration in Boston: "It ain't [about] Texaco. What about freedom? What about the Kuwaiti people?").

Onward and Upward

By the summer of 1991, the mythical history of a United States committed to the containment of Saddam Hussein was so firmly established that polls in July 1991 (by ABC, Gallup, NBC, and *Time*/CNN) indicated strong support—around three-quarters in favor—for the continued bombing of Iraq in order to destroy any chemical or nuclear weapons capability (Meuller 1994, 274–75). This position actually hardened in the aftermath of the much celebrated victory: those supporting "resumed military action" against Iraq to "force Saddam Hussein from power" increased from a range of 51–58 percent in April 1991 to 65–70 percent in August 1992 (ibid., 271). Willingness to support intervention proved remarkably robust, and the subsequent bombing campaigns against Iraq in 1998 and 1999 to "force compliance" over this issue were, according to polls, widely supported. The role of the United States in creating Iraq's military infrastructure—or in supplying the region with weaponry—has thereby receded further into a forgotten history. While U.S. elites fail on counts of moral consistency, public response is, by contrast, steadfast in adhering to the narrative constructed by those elites.

Public support for George Bush in the wake of the Gulf war was, by comparison, decidedly short-lived. Bush's approval ratings dropped fifty points in little more than a year (from 89 percent in early March 1991 to 39 percent in April 1992 [Mueller 1994, 179–81]). The consequences of the Gulf war for the hegemony of U.S. military power, on the other hand, have been more profound.

In sum, opinion poll data during the past four decades would suggest that it is difficult for elites to build majority consent for increased military spending (even if support for cutting the military budget has declined, support for increasing it has rarely risen above 30 percent). Thus, while such a policy has often been both advocated and enacted by the U.S. government, it is generally without a clear mandate from the polls. What we have seen, instead, is a more indirect example of hegemony, one that creates the discursive conditions in which such increases are *ideologically viable*. Since 1990, these conditions have been informed by three repeatedly told stories that we can see reflected in popular assumptions: first, the military budget is not especially large and is in decline; second, the need for a strong military is indicated by the need to contain brutal dictators like Hussein and Milosovic in a dangerous world—a need most vividly signified by the act of war; third, this containment fits within a moral narrative in which U.S. foreign policy is guided not by imperialist aims but by the adherence to moral principles and the need to counter egregious violations of those principles. The presence of those stories, in turn, depends upon the absence of information in the media that would make these mythic narratives utterly incoherent. This is not to imply that events since 1989 are part of a well-crafted, meticulously planned campaign by military elites and their political allies; it merely illustrates *how* the ideological consequences of patterns of information, knowledge, or assumptions have worked in their favor.

These discourses all have their own distinct structures of absences and appearances, perhaps the most alarming of which is the way in which *war itself* gives credence to the notion that the world is a dangerous place. Thus, in 1999, the Clinton administration was able to replicate many aspects of the "Hitler revisited" framework in a vilification of Slobodan Milosevic and the Serbian treatment of Albanians in Kosovo. Once again, comparable instances—such as the Turkish treatment of its Kurdish population—were generally ignored in media coverage, while U.S. policy in the region was generally characterized as consistent. And, once again, it is easy to see how the "crisis in Kosovo" might have been resolved diplomatically—or even simply ignored. Whatever the motives for declaring war on Yugoslavia might have been, the bombing campaign helped to suppress questions about the continued existence of the NATO alliance constructed to fight a Soviet empire that no longer exists. More insidiously, if the Gulf war killed the "peace dividend," the military campaign against Yugoslavia helped to cement the notion of a "dangerous world" full of eratic and brutal dictators. It thereby created the political conditions for *increasing* the military budget.

In chapter three, I stressed the comparatively "open" nature of the opinion polls in contrast to the much narrower representation of public opinion in media discourse. It is this disparity that allows us to see how moments of popular consent have been adapted and used by political elites. Reading opinion polls about Iraq and Yugoslavia in the 1990s, one gets the slightly eerie sense that opinion pollsters are unwittingly exploring these disparities in ways that amount to a kind of "research and development" role for the construction of elite media campaigns. Thus, in 1990 and 1991, we had a slew of polls probing a series of discursive conditions upon which people would support a war with Iraq, where it became clear that the way to align the war with popular responses to polls was to portray it in moral terms.

But the polls conducted by various agencies during events like the Gulf war also demonstrate the limits of polling data. The tendency of poll questions to reflect elite discourse meant that moral contradictions in U.S. foreign policy tended to be suppressed in poll questions themselves. Thus the many questions asked about Saddam Hussein or motives for military action tended to assume the "Hitler revisited" framework, offering responses that made sense only in terms of that discourse (rather than in terms of an evaluation of comparable cases or the history of U.S. foreign policy). One notable exception was a question asked in a *Los Angeles Times* poll of registered voters taken in October 1992, which asked the following:

Have reports that the Bush administration supplied aid to Saddam Hussein's government in Iraq in the months and years prior to the Gulf war made you more likely to vote for Bush in November, less likely to vote for Bush, or haven't they affected the way you might vote one way or the other?

Indeed, the question itself demonstrates how long it took for information easily available to journalists from the day Iraq invaded Kuwait to enter into media discourse (the phrasing conveys the erroneous impression that this information had only recently been unearthed). Once asked, nearly half the sample (47%) suggested this information made it less likely that they would vote for Bush (Mueller 1994, 334).

Since these "reports" may not have been as widely known as the question implies, it is difficult to know whether this is in response to the "reports," or to the report of "the reports" in the poll question. Either way, the fact that 47 percent stated that this information was critical at a time when the political agenda had changed to domestic economic concerns is, perhaps, suggestive. A Gallup poll two months earlier indicated that even if Bush were to preside over a successful military operation that resulted in Saddam Hussein being removed from power (something that polls showed most people supported), four-fifths of respondents stated that it *would not* effect their vote (Ibid., 334). The more sizeable response to the *Los Angeles Times* poll is perhaps the only direct indication in mainstream polling discourse of the power of contextual information to disrupt the dominant interventionist narrative. Had these "reports" been widely circulated in 1990, the coherence of the case for the Gulf war would, in terms of popular discourse, have been directly undermined.

Finally, I do not want to overestimate the degree to which it was necessary to create the right ideological conditions for maintaining or increasing a cold-war military budget. As I have argued in chapter three, public opinion polls can be contained in media discourse by ignoring those who are outside the confines of elite discourse. In the final chapter, I shall explore the extent and limits of consent in the United States today.

CHAPTER 8

SELLING UNREPRESENTATIVE DEMOCRACY

In what follows, I shall explore a pivotal political question: *How is a procorporate, center-right hegemony sustained in the U.S. political system?* If this question evokes the beginning of Louis Althusser's famous essay on ideology—namely, how are capitalist relations of production reproduced ideologically (Althusser 1971)—my aim is not to provide a grand, functionalist model. The purpose of this endeavor is to look for connections rather than assume them, and thereby examine *specific* ideological mechanisms in media representations that support or are connected to forms of political power in contemporary society (e.g., Hall 1996; Laclau and Mouffe 1985).

RESISTANCE AND CONSENT IN PUBLIC OPINION

In the United States, one of the most overriding instances of hegemony in action involves the maintenance of a political system dominated by corporate interests with no significant left-leaning, social-democratic presence. Most social-democratic parties in Europe—even Tony Blair's "New Labour" Party— are well to the left of the U.S. Democrats. The U.S. government is notable among industrialized countries in this respect: civic programs that are taken for granted in most other industrialized countries—such as a government-run, national healthcare system or a form of public service broadcasting—are rarely promoted within the U.S. political mainstream. The "welfare state," inasmuch as it exists, is meager in comparison with that of most other wealthy nations, and even in the post–cold war era, the chief area of government spending (excluding social security) is on the military. As Thomas Streeter argues in relation to broadcasting policy, anything that questions the basic premises of a corporate model (and that favors notions of public service) is, within the corridors of power, simply beyond the boundaries of discussion (Streeter 1996).

It is often assumed that there is a significant level of citizen consent for this model: that the government broadly reflects the generally conservative wishes of the people. Thus it is that, in the United States and elsewhere, reactionary politics are associated not just with the U.S. government but with a more general idea of the United States—a right-wing, probusiness strain than runs through the country's citizenry and its institutions like a kind of genetic imprint. This might seem self-evident: since governments are elected by citizens, the two might be expected to hold similar views. And yet, as I have argued in the first half of this book, the evidence for a simple confluence between citizens and those who govern them is, at best, highly contradictory. Opinion polls are often constructed around elite concerns with a narrow framework of response (Herbst 1993b; Lipari 1996), and yet it is difficult to squeeze the mass of public-opinion poll research into a form that demonstrates straightforward consent for policies favored by political elites.

Although popular opinion is remarkably stable—in the aggregate terms measured by polls (Page and Shapiro 1992)—it often fails to accord with the opinions and actions of the elite policy makers that purport to represent the public. Among all its many ambiguities and apparent contradictions, opinion research indicates the presence of a series of popularly held political positions that are to the left of those of the Washington mainstream. Thus, while most people will respond positively to abstract notions of free enterprise and small government, polls also show majority support for forms of economic and social equity or justice, even when political leaders are advocating parsimony and reductions in public intervention or government largesse.

As discussed in chapter five, Page and Shapiro's research confirms Ferguson and Rogers's (1986) contention that "throughout the Reagan years and onto the Bush years, Americans favored *more*, not less spending on virtually all economic welfare programs" (Page and Shapiro 1992, 170). In other words, the period in which a rightist, procorporate hegemony was—depending on your perspective—established or solidified exemplified a time in which government policies had little to do with popular consent (Paletz and Entman 1981; Mayer 1992).

This suggests a substantial degree of popular resistance to elite agendas. Page and Shapiro write:

> Public opinion is quite resistant . . . particularly when a few elite voices dissent, or when policy preferences are based on personal experience, or when events are inherently easy to understand. [Thus] the failure of barrages of publicity in the late 1970s and early 1980s to dislodge Americans from their advocacy of social welfare programs and arms control, or to persuade them to aid the Nicaraguan Contras.   (Page and Shapiro 1992, 395–396)

It is nonetheless worth noting that this resistance *may* have modified but did not prevent a massive arms buildup, the dismantling of social welfare programs, or the destabilization of the Nicaraguan revolution.

In other words, popular resistance within the discourse of public opinion polls has failed to manifest itself in the form of a more progressive body politic. Elites have repeatedly failed to see their endorsement of a probusiness model of governance transformed into popular common sense. This suggests that a pro-corporate, right-leaning system of government is *not sustained in any simple sense by ideological consent.* The system is more securely delivered by its political economy, which consists of a loosely regulated system of campaign finance, a weak party system (whereby those individuals with the most successful campaigns will become their party's standard bearers), and few spending restrictions on political advertising. This gives a significant advantage to those candidates who can win the financial backing of wealthy, corporate donors, and who can therefore afford the sizeable marketing budget required for a successful campaign. Corporate backing is further stimulated by the freedom given to legislators to directly pursue the interests of their corporate supporters—whether Philip Morris, Gallo, or the health insurance industry.

This favors not only right-wing, probusiness parties (Republicans have outspent Democrats in all but three presidential campaigns in the twentieth century) but also right-leaning contenders for the Democratic party nomination. Unless they are already independently wealthy, political candidates must therefore pass through an economic filter to become viable, a right of passage granted, in effect, by an elite group with the financial wherewithal to do so. If the formal right to choose their representatives is bestowed upon the populace, it is from a shortlist skewed toward certain economic interests and in an informational climate structured by privately paid advertising. In the early stages of any election campaign, the significant data are not provided by opinion research but by those who track campaign contributions.

It is this process—perhaps more than any other—that pushes American politics to the right and guarantees a procorporate hegemony in the body politic. Hellinger and Judd argue that this is particularly notable in the Democratic Party, the only agency available for the promotion of left-leaning ideas in the political mainstream: in recent decades, rising campaign costs have meant that congressional Democrats who are not primarily supported by business have become a dying breed (Hellinger and Judd 1991, 149).

This two-tier system, in which those with money whittle down the field for a more general population to vote for or against, was highlighted by a survey conducted by the Center for Responsive Politics. The study compared the views of political donors with those of the general population. Not surprisingly, given the data on wealth and political attitudes, the results put the general public considerably to the left of the people who shape their political choices, pointing out that "donors tend to be mainly wealthy, upper-status men, who tend to have conservative views, especially on economic issues" (Green, Herrnson, Powell, and Wilcox 1988). Since it is donors who largely determine the field of viable candidates, a procorporate hegemony is thereby achieved before a single ballot is cast.

If further guarantees of corporate hegemony are needed, they are supplied at the legislative level by the lobby system, in which groups are granted access to political representatives involved in writing and voting on legislation. As Hellinger and Judd put it, "corruption is endemic to this system" (Hellinger and Judd 1991, 189). The superior resources of the corporate sector in assembling professional lobbyists means that they will also be the dominant voice in crafting the details of legislation or the allocation of budgets (Hellinger and Judd 1991). For example, it was the National Association of Broadcasters—rather than citizens or viewers groups—that played a dominant role in writing the 1996 Telecommunications Act (McChesney 1997).

At this point, it might be inferred that I am arguing both for and against the presence of popular resistance to elite agendas: resistance is manifestly present in public opinion polls, but it is *essentially useless*—at least in terms of its impact on political decisions. And yet the political system still relies upon the presence of forms of ideological consent, not only in terms of approval through the electoral system but by voting for candidates (such as Ronald Reagan) who do not necessarily reflect the public's political concerns. My argument, thus far, is simply that this consent is neither straightforward nor simple.

It is partly achieved (as discussed in chapter three) by the *appearance* of support in the media representation of public-opinion poll data—such that polls tend to be reported when they reflect the agenda of political elites and disregarded when they do not. But it also depends upon an ideology in which the system's inequities are suppressed by a powerful and elaborate mythic discourse establishing the fairness of democracy in the United States. As Lance Bennett puts it, while it may not be defensible empirically for media and institutional gatekeepers "to assume that elites in the system somehow represent public interest and popular reason," it is defensible culturally, since this notion is so imbued in dominant ways of thinking about democracy (Bennett 1989, 324). In this discursive context, the system's bias, when it is seen at all, is regarded as either inevitable or as a mere glitch rather than a more fundamental flaw.

DEFLECTING CYNICISM FROM POWER

This is not to say that there is not widespread suspicion of government and a degree of alienation from it. If rates of participation in U.S. elections are not low enough to precipitate a crisis, they are scarcely an endorsement of popular faith in the process. Although some—such as conservative columnist George Will— have advanced the notion that nonvoting merely signifies a lazy contentment (DeLuca 1995), research on the sociodemographic status and inclinations of nonvoters belies this sanguine (and in some cases, opportunistic) conclusion (Nie, Junn, and Stehlik-Barry 1996). As John Harrigan (1993) and Hellinger and Judd put it, the "skewed pattern of turnout heavily favors the Republicans" (Hellinger and Judd 1991, 99). Low turnout, in other words, is an ideological phenomenon with measurable political effects.

In broader terms, the National Election Studies at the University of Michigan show that trust in government declined precipitously in the period between the mid-1960s and the early 1970s, and that it has remained at a fairly low level (with minor fluctuations) ever since. Since the early 1970s, the question "Would you say that the government is pretty much run by a few big interests looking out for themselves or that it is run for the benefit of all people?" has consistently generated majorities opting for "a few big interests," with these majorities growing to over 70 percent in the 1990s. Similarly, the proportions agreeing with the proposition "People like me don't have any say in what the government does" has, with some minor fluctuations, generally increased to over 50 percent in the 1990s.

As one might expect, those who regard themselves as powerless in these polls tend to *be* more powerless—notably in class terms, with 44 percent of professionals agreeing that they "don't have any say" compared with 80 percent of unskilled workers. In focus groups carried out for the 1992 election study

(Lewis, Morgan, and Rudduck 1992) this difference manifested itself clearly. Faith in the system was most consistently articulated by those with more power—as one member of a group of upper-middle-class male professionals put it: "I happen to believe that the political system . . . is responsive to the people. There's always that carrot out there, so that if you don't like it, there's something you can do to change it. So it's more participatory, more open. It allows you that ability." By contrast a working-class, African-American woman expressed very little confidence in a system dominated by people quite unlike herself: "This is the first year I'm saying, should I vote? Whoever they want gets in there. I've always believed that if they don't want you in there, then you don't get in. If they want a person in there, if I vote or nobody votes, they'll get in there." Regardless of whether her decision to abstain from the process is in her best interests, she is quite right to see the system as stacked against her.

One might anticipate that this pattern would also be reflected by those who say that they see the government as run by "big interests"—and yet, according the NES surveys this group of respondents have no clear demographic profile. The relationship between voting and antigovernment cynicism is therefore a complex one. Overall, cynicism about the role of "big interests" is as likely to come from a liberal or a conservative, a black person or a white person, a man or a woman, a professional or a blue-collar worker. In other words, this response seems to bear little relation to one's distance from or proximity to positions of power. Since members of more powerful social groups tend to be more ideologically in tune with and more responsive to elite political discourse (Zaller 1992; Nie, Junn, and Stehlik-Barry 1996), this uniformity of response requires an explanation.

On one level, the widespread suspicion that government is dominated by a few "big interests" would seem to be somewhat subversive. And yet its subversive connotations are ameliorated by a form of displacement, whereby the notion of "big interests" is disconnected from those *with* power and rearticulated with groups *struggling* for power. In this rather unlikely connotative field, the likes of General Electric or Time Warner mingle with labor unions, environmentalists, and advocates for gay rights. As Stuart Hall argued in the context of Thatcherism, this discourse allows those inside the "power bloc" to conveniently disappear from view (Hall 1988).

This is partly a product of ideological work carried out on the very notion of "big interests" or "special interests," whereby the term is portrayed as including not only those with economic power (who constitute the great majority of powerful lobbyists in Washington) but pressure groups representing certain citizen interests, such as NOW or the NAACP. The term is thereby "loaded" in a way that appears to dilute corporate power, and thus corporations become just one of many "special" or "big" interests attempting to influence government. Indeed, the use of the term in media discourse tends to refer to *noncorporate* citizen groups. Thus, for example, the Democratic Party is often discussed in terms of the influence of "special interests"—like black groups, women's groups, or labor—but rarely in terms of the business interests that are actually the Democratic Party's main donors. Similarly, the debate about NAFTA pitched corporate interests against labor and environmentalists, but it was the latter who tended to be described as "special interests" (Lee and Solomon 1990; Jackson and Naureckas 1996).

The tendency to link the Democratic Party with these kinds of "special interests groups" is reflected by a response to a question in the 1992 election study. While most people in the survey correctly identified the Republican Party with money from business sources (87%), in response to the question "Who do you think gives more money to Bill Clinton and the Democratic campaign," over two-thirds (69%) chose labor and only 16 percent chose business (3 percent said both and 13 percent said they did not know). I would argue that this erroneous response is partly shaped by the structure of the questions, in which it is assumed that if the Republicans get their money from one set of interests, the Democrats must get theirs from somewhere else (a point I shall take up again shortly).

Public understanding of the term "special interests" reflects this loaded ambiguity, in which "special interests" cover the ideological spectrum rather than coming disproportionately from the business sector. In the 1992 election survey, people were asked in an open-ended question to identify who they first thought of when they heard the term "special interests." The question generated a wide range of responses—38 percent mentioned various citizens groups (women/feminists, minorities, labor, environmentalists, gay rights activists, or groups campaigning for or against abortion), while 28 percent made general or specific references to powerful business sectors (Lewis, Morgan, and Ruddock 1992). This ambiguity of the term was also indicated by the student surveys, with the following responses:

Much has been said about the influence of "special interests" on the U.S. government. When you hear about "special interests," who do you tend to think of?

	SEPT. '95	FEB. '96	SEPT. '96	SEPT. '99
	N = 125	N = 120	N = 121	N = 201
a. Citizens groups representing minorities, the disabled, gay rights, etc	37	42	46	63
b. Big business and corporations	34	23	23	34
c. Both	28	35	39	n/a

These answers indicate how the notion of big or special interests may be inflected in various ways—as an all-inclusive term, as one that implicates those with economic power, or within a more reactionary discourse that sees well-organized minority groups as exerting too great an influence on politics. This suggests that the ambiguous and/or inclusive use of the term in media discourse works to *deflect* the power of corporate interests. In other words, advocates for poor people, women, or minorities may not actually be powerful Washington insiders, but they can get to play one on TV.

These various survey responses illuminate the NES data in which a poor black woman is as likely to see government as the property of a "few big interests" as a rich white man. Thus for many people—particularly those on middle or higher incomes—cynicism toward government may be, but is *not necessarily*, part of a political critique in which the system is structured in favor of those with economic power.

If cynicism about politicians and government is, for many, thereby disconnected from a critique of corporate power, this displacement is combined with a degree of faith in the fairness of American democracy. According to the National Election Studies, most people (particularly those sections of the population inclined to vote) "care a good deal" who wins presidential elections (75 percent in 1992 and 78 percent in 1996,), while a plurality think that elections make the government pay "a good deal" of attention to what people think, with the proportion saying that government pays "not much attention" being generally well below 20 percent. Similarly, Pew Research Center surveys report around two-thirds agreeing that "voting gives people like me some say in how the government runs things."

This indicates that alongside various forms of antigovernment cynicism lurks a time-honored discourse emphasizing the fairness and transparency of American democracy. This discourse, I would argue, is *crucial to creating consent*—or, at least, *enough* consent—for a system whose structure guarantees the dominance of corporate interests. This is a very particular form of hegemony, one that has less to do with ideological struggle in its traditional sense and more to do with winning consent for a *certain form* of governance, one in which various powerful interests are simultaneously enshrined and effaced. This is an idea that has been developed in different ways by Tony Bennett in his account of the role of museums (1995) in circumscribing particular notions of citizenship, culture, and polity, and variously by Toby Miller (1993) and Laurie Ouellette (1999) in their accounts of the ways in which public television in the United States works to promote a notion of "good citizenship"—one that works within the boundaries of elite political discourse rather than questioning its terms or its codes of conduct. For example, Ouellette describes how PBS has traditionally seen its function as one in which it conveys the issues that concern political elites to a professional/managerial-class audience of "opinion leaders" rather than broadening the scope of democratic debate. This notion of civil or enlightened political discourse was encapsulated by a PBS spokesperson in the 1970s describing its approach to the coverage of the Republican convention: "If Gerry Ford is giving a very dull speech and a riot is going on outside," he stated, "we will stay with Gerry Ford" (Ouellette 1999, 77). Civility, in this context, becomes a form of ideological constraint—the possibility that those protesting outside the convention hall might be closer to popular opinion than Gerry Ford is simply inadmissible within the discourse of civility.

While this particular example is specific to public television in the United States, the belief in the efficacy and fairness of the electoral system is a more general and widespread ideological project that helps to maintain a system of power. While such a discourse is undoubtedly nurtured in the schools where accounts of American democracy tend to be celebratory rather than critical (Hellinger and Judd 1991), it is also sustained by a series of media frameworks. For the rest of this chapter, I shall explore the nature of these frameworks and their influence on public assumptions.

FRAMEWORKS OF ASSUMPTION:
THE ESTABLISHMENT OF CONSENT

The idea that the U.S. political system is representative rather than dominated by powerful corporate interests consists of a number of discursive elements, three of which are particularly instrumental in sustaining the necessary degree of support for a system with ideologically limited electoral options.

THE LEFT VERSUS RIGHT FRAMEWORK OF POLITICAL REPORTING

Given the political economy of the electoral system, we would expect the U.S. political system to tilt to the right. If this seems blatantly obvious to some, it is nonetheless difficult to make such a straightforward observation within the structures of political reporting. Political battles in Washington are routinely framed as right/conservative versus left/liberal. Although this discourse can become cluttered by other terms (such as "moderate" or "new Democrat"), the mainstream leaders of the Democratic and Republican parties, as well as the field of "experts" who inform media discourse, are generally transposed onto this framework without caveat or scrutiny (Herman 1994; Naureckas 1996a; Dolny 1996). Michael Dolny points out, for example, that while the Brookings Institution is commonly used by journalists to "balance" conservative experts (from groups like the American Enterprise Institute, Cato, or Heritage), Brookings itself has center-right leanings, and its senior staff includes a number of former members of Republican administrations. Like many leading Democrats, its corporate, centrist credentials are redefined by a structural framework that places it on the left. The framework is solidified by an emphasis on conflict: political differences are stressed, while areas of agreement are assumed to take place somewhere in the political center.

For example, although Bill Clinton emerged from the right wing of the Democratic Party (via the Democratic Leadership Council) and has governed as a centrist (at the center, in other words, of a probusiness political mainstream) with economic priorities that differ little from those of his Republican predecessor, he is routinely situated as the principal representative on the "left" side of the political debate. This is not to say that journalists have ignored the conservative drift of Clinton's politics, simply that these details are conceptually submerged within the more general framework. Statements by individual journalists that refer to Clinton's adoption of a series of conservative positions are liable to get lost or become unintelligible within a larger associative structure that places Democrats on the left and Republicans on the right. In describing political battles between President Clinton and a Republican Congress, it is assumed that the public more or less inhabits *the same political space* as their representatives. The substantial areas, as signified by public opinion polls, to the left of both mainstream Democrats and Republicans implicitly disappear.

While reporters will occasionally report on public disaffection with the two main parties, they rarely do so in overtly political terms. Indeed, as I have suggested in chapter three, it is generally assumed that any viable alternative (such as Ross Perot, Colin Powell, or even Jesse Ventura) will occupy the space *between* the two parties.

The ideological effect of this framework is to sustain the notion of a pluralistic democracy in which the political breadth of public opinion is represented by the two main parties. The structural factors pushing the system to the right are thereby suppressed.

We can catch a glimpse of this conceptual framework in survey responses by comparing questions in the 1992 and 1998 general population surveys. I have already described how a two-part question about the two political parties and campaign money generally leads to a response in which Republicans are seen as backed by business and Democrats by labor. The same pattern of responses was also consistently reflected in the student surveys. While labor certainly gives far more money to Democrats than Republicans, this response tends to conceal the degree to which both are predominantly funded by business. A similar question was asked in the 1998 survey, this time *without* the Republican/Democrat dichotomy:

Republicans and Democrats raise money for their campaigns from big business and from organized labor. During the last presidential campaign, who gave more to the Democratic party, was it labor or big business? Or was it about the same?

On this occasion, the responses were much more evenly distributed: 27 percent said labor, 29 percent said big business, 24 percent said about the same, and 21 percent said they did not know. While this may have indicated a change of perception between 1992 and 1998, a more plausible explanation is that in the 1992 survey, people were responding to the assumption that if the Republicans got their money from one source, the Democrats must receive it from another. They were, in other words, responding to a framework in which political differences between the two parties are stressed, thereby putting the Democrats on the left. By asking only about the Democrats, the 1998 survey did not encourage respondents to adopt this conceptual framework—hence responses were more scattered (albeit mostly incorrect).

THE DOWNPLAYING OF ECONOMIC ISSUES IN DEFINING POLITICAL DIFFERENCE

The left-versus-right framework is also made possible by the selection of indicators used by mainstream—and often alternative—media to define political difference. The economic bias within the political system tends to allow for greater plurality of opinion in government around issues—such as abortion or tolerance for minority groups—that are often tangential to economic and corporate interests. The emphasis on issues that involve degrees of respect or tolerance for civil liberties tends to limit any serious interrogation of the restricted nature of political differences on broadly economic questions. (By "economic" I mean the broad range of issues that implicate government spending or private sector regulation, from healthcare to the environment.)

A survey of major political donors conducted by the Center for Responsive Politics found that while major campaign donors were much more likely than a sample of the general public to favor conservative economic policies, they tended to be moderate to liberal on questions of tolerance or respect for civil liberties, or what are frequently (and somewhat misleadingly) termed "social issues." For example, they report that "more than one-half support tax cuts even if it means reducing public services, but only one-quarter would prohibit abortions unless the life of the women is at stake"(Green, Herrnson, Powell, and Wilcox 1998). If most donors are against increasing antipoverty programs, most are also in favor of some form of civil liberty protection for gay people.

Thus, if we were to ignore broadly economic issues entirely, it could be argued that the elite group that funds political campaigns is not especially unrepresentative. Indeed, on some civil liberties issues—such as abortion—they are more likely than the general public to give more liberal responses to poll questions. Given the very specific economic interests that define this elite group, this is not surprising. It is not to say that the class position of this elite group has no other manifestations in terms of race, gender, or age (the study found that donors are overwhelmingly white, male, and over forty-five), but they appear to be less likely to feel threatened by certain progressive social trends. Since this group is also likely to have had more formal political education, this may also reflect a relationship between *knowledge* of civil liberties and various expressions of tolerance (Delli Carpini and Keeter 1996, 220–23).

The dominant media representations of political difference confuse or disguise the hegemonic structure of the political system less by downplaying economic questions than by downplaying the degree to which economic or budgetary issues are *indicators of political ideology*. In media discourse, issues of tolerance or civil liberties (usually, and often erroneously, implying that an issue has few budgetary or economic implications) thus become emblematic of political philosophies. As a consequence, it is often assumed that the "socially liberal/economically conservative" couplet is generally in tune with public opinion in general—a notion espoused by such diverse figures as former Governor William Weld of Massachusetts and Governor Jesse Ventura of Minnesota. And yet it is, according to opinion research data, typical of only elite or upper-middle-class opinion (Harrigan 1993). Diversity of opinion in this formation tends to be expressed by this ideological couplet.

The use of the liberal positions held by some elites on "social issues" to create the impression of a broad, representative political spectrum is, as Ouellette points out, well enshrined within media discourse. Her account of the early PBS current-affairs program *The Advocates*—in which topics of the day were debated and subsequently voted upon by PBS's upscale audience—describes this conflation whereby the views of the professional/managerial classes are seen to represent a more general range of opinion:

While political participation did not extend beyond the ritual of voting, the 22,000 plus votes received each month were taken as public opinion that mattered. Neither the sociodemographic profile of the PBS audience nor the fact that pre-addressed postcard ballots were available only to contributing viewer-members was seen to qualify the results of the debates. What was emphasized was the bipartisan nature of the voting audience—a pattern that was then evoked to affirm PBS's ability to produce political balance . . . "The vote swings heavily from conservative to liberal and occasionally perches in the middle of the fence," explained a PBS press release, and the majority of "liberal positions on social issues" were balanced by some "very conservative thinking on the subjects of law and order and the economy."

(Ouellette 1999, 84)

As Ouellette suggests, this "balance" simply reflects the class background of the voting population rather than public opinion in general.

Polls provide very little evidence that majorities have been persuaded to think in terms of this ideological range (or lack thereof)—most notably in the tendency of polls to show most people to the left of elites on economic or budgetary questions. But to what extent have people been taught to replicate the notion upon which this idea of ideological range rests—namely, that it is civil liberties issues (rather than broadly economic issues) that define political ideology? The following question in the 1998 and 1999 student surveys was an attempt to begin testing the power of this framework: the students were asked to identify the "litmus test" issues that best signify political ideology, choosing between two issues with significant economic implications and two more commonly identified as civil liberties issues:

Someone with a coherent liberal/left or conservative/right ideology is likely to have a clear and predictable position on a number of issues. On which one of the following issues might these ideologies be less clear or predictable (i.e., it is not so obvious what a left-wing liberal or a right-wing conservative might think)?

	SEPT. '98 N = 280	SEPT. '99 N = 201
a. Abortion	19	20
b. Gay rights	14	9
c. Redistribution of wealth	37	36
d. Health care	30	32

Although this sample is somewhat limited in class terms, the fact that two-thirds—67 percent to 68 percent—felt that it was one of the overtly *economic* issues that was less easy to place on a left/right continuum is certainly indicative of a media climate in which these issues are less often defined in those terms, while issues like abortion and gay rights (devoid of their economic underpinnings) *are* portrayed as being symptomatic of political ideology. This response is, to say the least, unhelpful in understanding political difference: elites (whether conservative Democrats or moderate Republicans) tend to be *less* clearly defined on an issue like abortion than they are on issues like healthcare and the redistribution of wealth. Thus, while there are a number of prochoice Republicans, very few would advocate a move toward a redistribution of wealth or a switch to a public healthcare system.

The focus on civil liberties also sustains a number of mythic propositions about the liberal or leftist nature of certain institutions—notably the notion of the "liberal media." If journalists are sometimes more liberal on civil liberty issues than the public as a whole—which, given their class profile, we might expect them to be—these left-leaning attitudes *do not* extend to economic questions. Indeed, on economic issues, people who work in the media are generally to the *right* of the general public—something that, given their class profile, is also fairly predictable—a point admirably demonstrated by David Croteau's comprehensive survey of reporters' practices and beliefs (Croteau 1998). The exclusion of economic issues also allows members of the Republican Party to rail against what they identify as a "liberal elite"—an invocation that allows them to stand for "the people" against the "power bloc" (Hall 1988). Polling data suggest that on economic issues the "liberal elite" coupling is almost a contradiction in terms—one that would appear ludicrous if it were not for the suppression of economic issues as political indicators. It is precisely the *absence* of such indicators that gives the notion of a "liberal elite" its discursive coherence.

The power of this discourse is clearly manifested in the opinion research data. Thus it is that, as John Harrigan points out, while poorer people are likely to hold fairly left-wing views on economic policy issues, "they do not feel very positive about liberals generally" (Harrigan 1993, 143), because the term "liberal" is more likely to be articulated with progressive positions on civil liberties than with a progressive economic platform. The phrase "liberal elite," in this context, has a certain resonance.

THE NOTION THAT THE UNITED STATES IS A MODEL OF A FREE AND DEMOCRATIC SOCIETY

American exceptionalism takes many forms, but the idea of the United States as an exemplar of democracy rests upon the negation of alternatives (i.e., other countries with greater protection against business influence in the democratic process). The invocation of this discourse in political rhetoric is well known: the United States is characterized as a "beacon of democracy" in an unstable world, "a city on a hill" for others to emulate. It is also a notion that underpins democratic theory and analysis in the United States to an extent not found elsewhere. In their book on education and democratic citizenship in America, for example, Nie, Junn, and Stehlik-Barry begin their analysis with the observation: "While Americans today may not live up to Tocqueville's nineteenth-century characterization of us as continuously engaged and active citizens, we are, nevertheless, among the most active citizens of democracy anywhere in the world" (Nie, Junn, and Stehlik-Barry 1996, 2). To an outside observer, this may seem a strange claim to make about a country whose rate of electoral participation is conspicuously lower than that of most other countries, and where involvement in campaigns is far less evenly distributed among the population than elsewhere (Hellinger and Judd 1991). It is even more surprising in a book that argues *against* the notion that the only problem with American democracy is an insufficiently educated citizenry, and *for* the idea of structural inequalities in the U.S. system. The fact that such a claim is made in such an unlikely context speaks to the power of a discourse in which the U.S. model is regarded as the ideal type.

In media representations, the certainty of American exceptionalism can lead to some extraordinary pronouncements. So, for example, CBS news anchor Mark McEwen, pitching a question about low voter turnout, stated:

This is one of the few countries in the world where the government actually says, "You have a choice. You can vote." How come the turnout is so low?

(*CBS This Morning*, November 4, 1996)

With a blithe disregard for dozens of democratic (or, at least, equally democratic) countries in all directions, the viewer is encouraged to see themselves as part of this "happy few."

While the development of this discourse in the United States during the cold war melded the idea of democracy to a form of free enterprise, it also took a particularly isolationist form. The U.S. role as self-proclaimed "leader of the free world" was a function of economic and military power, and yet the phrase worked rhetorically to imply that the U.S. democratic model was, in some way, superior. Indeed, the very idea of the "free world" became an appendage to the U.S. model rather than a category that defined it alongside equivalent others. Thus in the U.S. the rest of the world is regarded as either totalitarian or—in some indistinct way—less democratic or less secure in its democratic traditions. This discourse has been undeniably powerful in discouraging comparisons with other systems. A series of polls taken in the 1980s, for example, found that only a third of respondents identified Japan as a democracy—as opposed to a monarchy or military dictatorship (Popkin 1991).

In order to begin to test this notion (that democracy is less widespread outside the United States), the 1998 and 1999 student surveys included the following question:

What percentage of the following twenty countries do not have a democratic system of government (with regular free elections; one person, one vote; and a secret ballot): Austria, Costa Rica, France, Finland, Germany, Great Britain, Greece, Iceland, Ireland, Jamaica, Japan, Lithuania, Luxembourg, New Zealand, Nicaragua, Mauritius, Norway, Slovakia, Spain, South Africa?

	SEPT. '98	SEPT. '99
	N = 280	N = 201
a. 0%	18	21
b. 30%	50	45
c. 50%	4	4
d. 60%	18	19
e. 100%	8	9

While the results tend to be skewed correctly toward the lower percentages, even though most of the countries on this list are well-known European democracies, and all of them have a democratic system of government (insofar as the United States can be described as democratic), more than four out of five students assumed that at least some of them were not, while a quarter assumed that most (or all) of them were not.

It is a discourse made possible, in part, by a cultural and information system that is distinctively inward looking. The size of the U.S. domestic market means not only that its cultural products are cheap and plentiful on the world market, but that it does not rely on cultural imports. The discourse of news reflects this lack of interest in the rest of the world. Other democratic models or institutions—whether they are broadcasting systems or political/economic structures—are rarely seriously considered. On the contrary, practices and institutions in the United States are made to seem natural by the absence of any clear points of comparison. This point is suggested by the various misconceptions discussed in the previous two chapters about the position of the United States in relation to the rest of the world. For example, in a series of student surveys, the following responses suggest that it is assumed that the commercial system the students have grown up with is the most typical form of media system:

Among the world's broadcasting systems, most are:

	FEB. '96	SEPT. '96	SEPT. '98	SEPT. '99
	N = 120	N = 121	N = 280	N = 201
Commercial, privately owned systems (like ABC, NBC, MTV, CNN, etc.)	77	76	71	78
Public or government-run systems (like PBS)	21	23	24	17

Despite the intrusions of satellite broadcasting, purely commercial systems are in a minority (Head and Stirling 1990), and yet students overwhelmingly choose the commercial option. This is all the more notable among a group who have, in their classes, been introduced to a comparative analysis of media systems. Thus it is that the absence of points of comparison in media discourse comes to signify a more general absence.

The lack of alternatives makes any sustained critical analysis much more difficult. In this discursive climate, it is easy to resort to a defeatist assumption that certain problems are inevitable *because it is difficult to imagine how else things could be.* Existing structures are naturalized rather than scrutinized. The easiest and most practical response in this instance is to shrug the shoulders and abstain from the whole process. And, while there are many reasons for not voting (such as being unable to get a baby-sitter or time off work, or actively deciding to abstain), the socioeconomic profile of the high percentage of nonvoters in the United States suggests that apathy or disillusionment tends to exclude those most at odds with the interests of the "donor class." It is traditional to blame nonvoters for this failure, but it is inertia born of a system whose political economy is, in very concrete ways, stacked against them.

Sustaining the Appearance of Plurality

As I have suggested, these three discursive elements are part of a larger discourse casting a veil of legitimacy over the political system, a discourse in which political representation is seen as more or less representative of the ideological range of public opinion. But to what extent is this discourse manifested in opinion surveys themselves (even while the data from those surveys contradict it)? One way to answer this question is to explore one of the central manifestations of this discourse: Are those designated as representing the left side of the political spectrum actually seen as being farther to the left than their record would indicate? Has this discourse, in short, created an imaginary left in Washington?

These questions were explored in the 1998 general population survey (see appendix). The survey focused on Bill Clinton, who, as a Democratic president, is the principal standard bearer for a liberal/left politics in the dominant media framework—all the more so when the central political conflict in media discourse is between a Democratic president and a Republican Congress. The questions asked people to place Clinton on a political spectrum, not merely in general terms but in relation to specific aspects of his political predilections and background. This is typically unfamiliar ground for most opinion surveys—many of which tend to ask questions that assume knowledge of such things. For example, in light of the Monica Lewinsky scandal, polls by the Pew Research Center in 1998 asked respondents how much they liked President Clinton as a person, and how much they liked his policies. The survey—very much in tune with the conventional wisdom at the time—suggested that while only a minority like both Clinton and his policies (39 percent in February, dropping to 29 percent in October), a sizeable group disliked Clinton but claimed to like his policies (30 percent in February, rising to 41 percent in October). Thus, while his personal popularity was fairly low, more than two-thirds suggested they like Clinton's politics—a distinction that allowed pundits to explain the high approval ratings of an apparently scandal-ridden administration.

If the meaning of such responses seems self-evident, it is contingent upon an assumption that Clinton's politics are generally understood. While such an assumption fits neatly within a functional democratic model, answers to these kinds of questions tell us very little on their own. Most importantly, if we assume that it is *not* clear that most people know what Clinton's politics are, we cannot assume that a declaration that one approves of his policies is an endorsement of them. Indeed, if the ideological mechanism I have described does, in fact, inform public opinion, we would expect people to ascribe to a Democratic president a series of liberal or left-leaning political positions, even as that president is pursuing a more procorporate, right-wing agenda.

The presence of precisely this assumption was suggested by the 1992 election study, in which people were asked a series of questions about Clinton's past or current policy positions. Most respondents consistently assumed Clinton's gubernatorial experience in Arkansas was more progressive than the record suggested, while his conservative positions were largely unknown (Lewis, Morgan, and Ruddock 1992). The survey also asked a series of questions based on the following premise:

I'm going to read you some statements about the presidential candidates. For each one, please tell me whether the statement applies to George Bush, to Bill Clinton, to both Bush and Clinton, or to neither one. If you're not sure, please take a guess, based on what you know of the candidates.

A number of the statements that followed involved instances in which the more conservative possibilities could be attributed to both Clinton and Bush, and yet in all of these cases, comparatively few people associated both the Democrat and Republican standard bearers with these conservative positions. As the following responses indicate, people tended to assume Clinton had endorsed more progressive positions and Bush the more conservative positions.

Which candidate has proposed reducing military spending by more than 50 percent over the next five years?

George Bush	19.0%
Bill Clinton	67.1%
Both	5.5%
Neither	3.2%
Don't know	5.3%

Which candidate supports the death penalty?

George Bush	35.4%
Bill Clinton	25.5%
Both	11.8%
Neither	8.0%
Don't know	19.3%

Which candidate supports "right to work" laws opposed by labor unions?

George Bush	43.1%
Bill Clinton	32.3%
Both	5.0%
Neither	3.0%
Don't know	16.6%

In the first case, only 3 percent were aware or guessed that neither Clinton nor Bush proposed major cuts to the military budget (although Clinton did appear to favor a somewhat less extravagant military budget than Bush), only 12 percent stated that both favored the death penalty (an issue on which both candidates were unambiguous), and only 5 percent saw them both as adopting an antilabor position on "right to work" laws. Responses, in other words, appeared

to support the widespread assumption that associated a Democrat with positions on the left regardless of a more conservative record.

The student surveys suggested that this impression endured throughout the
Clinton presidency, as responses to the following question suggest.

Which of the following policies does Bill Clinton support?

	SEPT. '95	FEB. '96	SEPT. '96	SEPT. '98	SEPT. '99
	N = 125	N = 120	N = 121	N = 280	N = 201
a. Making significant savings in the military budget	3	3	6	13	8
b. A Canadian-style national health care system	8	6	10	11	11
c. Reversing Reagan/Bush cuts in capital gains taxes	3	7	9	13	6
d. The death penalty	3	7	5	4	6
e. a, b, and c	81	76	69	59	67

Very few students associate Clinton with the only conservative position on the
list, while the dominant response (albeit one that appears to have perhaps
declined a little over time) is to assume he had endorsed *all* the more liberal
positions—none of which, certainly from 1995 onward, he had. In short, the
proportion giving the correct answer never rises above 6 percent.

In order to explore this perception further, a series of nine questions in the
1998 General Population Survey were intended to provide an indication of
where people placed President Clinton on a left/right political map—questions linked to documented, verifiable aspects of Clinton's background and
record. Respondents were then asked to choose between responses that placed
Clinton, in very general terms, either on the right or the left. Correct answers
to two of the nine questions were designed to place Clinton in accord with the
more liberal response offered to respondents. These questions involved his
position on abortion and a State of the Union speech in which he prioritized
Social Security over tax cuts. The other seven questions involve instances
where, in terms of the options available, Clinton's record, positions, or actions
place him on the right. These questions dealt with his signing of the Welfare
Bill, healthcare reform, the international treaty to ban land mines, the death
penalty, the deregulation of telecommunications, sources of campaign funding (labor versus big business), and a general question asking respondents to

place Clinton within the Democratic Party. Table 8.1 lists the responses (see appendix for details).

It is, of course, difficult to be precise in attaching positions to specific candidates, particularly when political rhetoric and political actions do not always flow in exactly the same direction. The questions therefore reflect fairly well-documented and verifiable aspects of the record, such as the signing of (or refusal to sign) bills or treaties, or the source of campaign contributions. The seven questions in which the correct response places Clinton on the right reflect positions on which the more left-wing members of his own party have criticized Clinton—such as his signing of the Welfare Reform Bill, or his advocacy of a healthcare reform package that maintained the centrality of private insurance and failed to adopt a national and universal public or single-payer system (Canham-Clyne 1996). The least precise question simply asks people to place Clinton within a Democratic Party spectrum: since running for the presidency in 1992, Clinton has been close to the more conservative wing of the Democratic Party and *at no point* on a major area of policy—even with a Democratic majority in Congress—has he sided with liberal Democrats against that more conservative or "moderate" group.

TABLE 8.1

Percent Who Have Liberal and Conservative Views of Bill Clinton's Policies

(N = 600; ROWS = 100%)

	PERCENT WHO VIEW CLINTON AS:		
ISSUE	"CONSERVATIVE"	"LIBERAL"	DON'T KNOW
Welfare reform Bill	13.0*	53.9	33.1
Healthcare	26.2*	58.8	15.0
Land mines	23.5*	43.7	32.8
Campaign funds	29.2*	50.3	20.5
Telecomm Act	23.0*	28.2	48.8
Death penalty	27.7*	21.0	51.3
Abortion	14.8	69.0*	16.2
Budget surplus	7.8	73.7*	18.5
In general, within the Democratic Party	31.0*	51.3	9.5

* Correct response

The table suggests that the two instances in which the more left-wing option is correct are also the only two cases in which most people get the answer right. Indeed, the difference between these instances and the others (where the more conservative option is correct) is fairly dramatic. Thus most respondents (69%) either knew or were able to guess that he favored keeping abortion legal and most (74%) stated that he prioritized Social Security over tax cuts in his 1998 state of the union address. By contrast, the numbers correctly identifying him with conservative options are uniformly low: only 13 percent said he signed the Welfare Reform Bill; only 26 percent said that he favors making the existing private insurance system available to more people rather than replacing it with a national, universal system; only 24 percent said that he was against signing the land mine treaty; only 28 percent said that he supports the death penalty; only 23 percent said that he signed the deregulatory Telecommunications Bill; only 29 percent said that his 1996 campaign—and Democratic campaigns generally—received more money from business than it did from labor; and only 31 percent said that he is on the more conservative (rather than the liberal) wing of the Democratic Party.

What is especially striking is that respondents were, on the whole, *much more likely* to choose "liberal" options to questions, regardless of the record. For example, 54 percent said that he refused to sign the Republican Welfare Reform Bill, 59 percent said he favored a national and universal healthcare system, and 51 percent placed him on the liberal wing of the Democratic Party.

The only case in which this pattern was not repeated involved his position on the death penalty. In this instance, over half of the respondents (51%) stated that they did not know—which may suggest that people are less confident that this issue is emblematic of party political ideology. Nevertheless, for five of these seven questions, even if we make the unlikely assumption that no one actually knew the correct response, the proportion who identified Clinton's rightward tilt is *lower* than it would have been if the response had been made completely at random. Since it is likely that a small percentage knew the answers, the remaining guesses are clearly moving disproportionately toward the "liberal Clinton" responses.

If we look at the questions individually, it would be hard to claim that the source of incorrect assumptions has any *direct* relationship to media content. Although media coverage of politics is often muddled and vague on detail, it would be difficult to argue, for example, that the news media did not report President Clinton's signing of the Welfare Bill in his first term. Indeed, most commentators regarded it—erroneously, these results would suggest—as a pivotal moment in his reelection bid. In his memoir *Behind the Oval Office: Winning the Presidency in the Nineties*, self-described Machiavellian presidential advisor and pollster Dick Morris triumphantly records his successful efforts to persuade Clinton to sign the Welfare Bill, representing it as a watershed in the successful reelection campaign (Morris 1997). While Morris is often represented as the apotheosis of "poll-driven politics," one can also read his book as an exercise in the skillful and selective use of polls to advance a center-right ideology.

At most, one could argue that many of these events—notably the Telecommunications Act—received less critical attention than they might. But, while this may explain a random spray of uninformed responses, it does not explain the pattern of mistaken assumptions revealed in the survey. Rather, the "right versus left" framework described earlier would seem, for many, to have a significant ideological influence on the perception of contemporary politics. As a consequence, it is difficult for many people to associate a Democratic president with anything other than left-leaning positions.

When this rather skewed perception is discussed at all in mainstream news, it is often to reinforce the frame. So, for example, a CBS report from the Democratic National Convention on August 29, 1996, used the "liberal Clinton" perception to *inform* "Republican attacks" on his liberalism. As Dan Rather put it:

> President Clinton has been under attack by Republicans trying to paint him as a, quote, "liberal." And, in fact, our latest CBS News poll indicates that some 43 percent of those questioned do perceive President Clinton as liberal. But he's apparently not nearly liberal enough for some. He is also under attack from the left, including Jesse Jackson, for signing welfare reform legislation.

While Rather points out that he is also "under attack from the left" and "not nearly liberal enough for some," the framework being used here suggests that this is essentially a question of degree. The dispute between Jackson and Clinton is thus represented as a dispute *within* the left side of the political ledger. As reporter Bob Schieffer explained to Rather in a subsequent exchange: "My sense of it is that the president was glad to see that because all politicians like to have someone to the left, someone that the public can look at and say, 'He's not as liberal as Jesse Jackson.' " This statement not only maintains Clinton on the left side of the spectrum (albeit more moderate than the likes of Jesse Jackson), it also assumes that being on the left is, in terms of public opinion, a problem.

Who Believes in Representational Democracy?

In some respects, these responses are not surprising: they suggest the widespread presumption that a Democratic president will be associated with a generally left-leaning record: someone who will be closer to labor than to business, who believes in activist government, protecting the poor, and a humane foreign policy. This is, after all, the assumption that informs much mainstream political science. In data analyzed by Brians and Wattenberg (1996), for example, respondents were asked (during the 1992 election) a series of scaled questions about Clinton's support for various types of government spending. Those who put him at the extreme left end of these scales (e.g., giving him in the maximum score on notions such as "government should provide many more services, increase spending a lot") were coded as "correct," while those who placed him in the middle were coded as "wrong." Because these are rather free-floating categories, it is difficult to be precise. Nonetheless, even within the confines of the Washington political spectrum, it seems remarkable that the assumption that President Clinton was liberal or left-leaning rather than a centrist (let alone a conservative) is so well entrenched that one can be categorized as "wrong" for believing so.

The most plausible explanation for this pattern of responses is that it signifies the extent to which the frameworks I have described seep into many people's assumptions about the world. The other explanation for assumptions of a "left-wing Clinton" involves two pressures that might push certain people toward "left-wing Clinton" responses: people who like Clinton are more likely to hold liberal views and therefore project those views onto him (assimilation), while those who dislike him will do the same for the opposite reason (contrast). The presence of the pulls and pushes of assimilation and contrast would reveal itself by dividing partisans (Democrats and Republicans) from nonpartisans. However, in this survey there is *no* significant difference in response on these questions between independents and more traditionally partisan respondents (Democrats and Republicans). Regardless of whether someone is for, against, or uncommitted, they are all more likely to suppose that Clinton is on the left than the record would imply.

The pattern of responses in this survey also throws up an issue that has been the subject of much discussion and analysis in political science: the extent to which people use the forms of ideologically consistent reasoning suggested by these data (Converse and Markus 1979; Feldman 1988). For example, Iyengar's work suggests that patterns of understanding news and politics tend to be issue-specific, a response to an episodic form of coverage in which any one issue may bear little apparent relation to another. Iyengar contextualizes this finding with reference to "the much documented absence of general 'ideological' reasoning by ordinary citizens" (Iyengar 1991, 136). There is, nonetheless, evidence that people employ various ideological or "partisan schemas" that enable them to identify, on a general level, differences between political parties (Lau and Sears

1986; Hamill and Lodge 1986; Lodge and Hamill 1986). These studies suggest that most people are able to correctly place Democrats on the left and Republicans on the right for issues on which the parties manifest a left/right split. These two sets of findings are not entirely contradictory: it may be that while many people have political beliefs that defy a traditional left/right framework, they understand the basic parameters of that framework and then apply that understanding to party politics. Or, as Erikson, Luttbeg, and Tedin put it, "a greater porportion of the electorate can utilize the ideological language than can be classified as ideologues" (Erikson, Luttbeg, and Tedin 1991, 84).

I also suggested earlier that there is not a clear correspondence between the labels conventionally used in the news media—notably "liberal" and "conservative"—and the series of positions on the left or right that these labels are intended to refer to. Thus the number of self-declared liberals tends to be smaller than the number of people who hold a series of positions on the left, while working-class people—who are likely to be on the left on a range of economic issues—express a degree of suspicion and hostility toward the label (Harrigan 1993). This hostility, I suggested in chapter four, may be partly informed by the media's tendency to use the phrase "liberal" in conjunction with privileged groups (such as "the liberal media" or "liberal elites") rather than with working-class people. This means that in media discourse, the term "liberal" has a contradictory set of associations, being simultaneously connected to (and disconnected from) the interests of groups like the poor or labor unions and with privileged elites. Thus the labels "liberal" and "conservative" may, for many people, form part of what Erikson, Luttbeg, and Tedin describe as a "confusion of background noise" (Erikson, Luttbeg, and Tedin 1991, 84–90).

Both these points are illuminated by analysis of the data. On the one hand, a factor analysis indicates that six of the incorrect "left-wing Clinton" responses do line up along a unidimensional axis (if not very powerfully—eigenvalue = 1.71, explaining 28.5 percent of the variance), suggesting a degree of ideological consistency in the responses. However, a regression analysis of these items indicates that the odd one out here is the one question that conventional wisdom would lead us to expect *would* be associated with the tendency to assume Clinton has taken positions on the left, namely whether people see him as a "liberal," "moderate," or "conservative" Democrat. In other words, saying Clinton is a "liberal Democrat" is *not* linked with the tendency to incorrectly attribute to him left-leaning positions (in the regression, beta = .043, 32). This indicates that many people *do* understand the basic parameters of a classic left/right dichotomy but *not* in any clear relation to the liberal/conservative labels.

This point can be developed by breaking down the sample in terms of education, since the ability to replicate the classic left/right schema used by political elites is most clearly manifested by the demographic groups closest to those elites (Zaller 1992). Surveys therefore suggest that those with more years of formal education tend to score higher on tests of political knowledge and to exhibit a more straightforward understanding of ideological frames. They are also more likely to adopt those frames themselves. As Delli Carpini and Keeter found: "A unidimensional liberal-conservative axis underlies the attitudes of the well informed . . . whereas the pattern for the less well informed is much more ambiguous. . . . Better-informed citizens . . . have opinions that are more internally consistent with each other and with the basic ideological alignments that define American politics" (Delli Carpini and Keeter 1996, 238).

Most studies of the use of ideological frames tend to be premised upon a functionalist view of democracy, whereby the ability to use or apply conventional ideological frameworks is treated as *useful political knowledge*. The study analyzed here is founded on a very different notion: namely, that assumptions about these "partisan schemas" can have an ideological function, one that works to preserve a belief in representative democracy in spite of the system's built-in bias. In this instance, the ability to use ideological frames may *not* be useful for citizens. On the contrary, it may work as an "information short-cut" that leads people to a series of incorrect assumptions.

For the more educated group, we therefore have two tendencies pulling in opposite directions. On the one hand, those with more formal education are more likely to know the details of contemporary politics (see chapter five)—to know, for example, that President Clinton signed the Welfare Bill and the Telecommunications Bill but refused to sign the treaty to ban land mines. On the other hand, their ability to use ideological frames may potentially make them more susceptible to the inappropriate use of those frames—to assume, for example, that a left-leaning Democrat might have been inclined to veto the Republican Welfare Reform Bill or to have been suspicious of the policy of corporate deregulation that informed the 1996 Telecommunications Bill (the deregulatory nature of which was spelled out in the questionnaire).

This, of course, points to the limits of these kinds of quantitative data—the presence of two contradictory tendencies may simply cancel each other out in a series of unrevealing figures. Nevertheless, if the responses of the more formally educated half of the sample (those with at least some college) are compared with those with less formal education (those with no college), there are signs of these competing determinations.

Table 8.2
Perceptions of Clinton as Liberal, by Education

		NO COLLEGE	AT LEAST SOME COLLEGE	SIGNIFICANCE
Welfare	Signed Republican bill*	13.7%	12.1%	p = .014
	Had own plan	37.9%	51.5%	
	Was antireform	10.0%	7.2%	
	Don't know	38.4%	29.2%	
Healthcare	Wanted national system	50.7%	64.5%	p = .003
	Wanted to keep private*	30.1%	23.7%	
	Don't know	19.2%	11.8%	
Mines	Ban mines	41.6%	44.9%	p = .022
	No ban*	17.8%	27.3%	
	Don't know	40.6%	27.8%	
Death penalty	Supports*	22.4%	30.6%	p = .10
	Opposed	3.3%	19.8%	
	Don't know	54.3%	49.6%	
Abortion	Prochoice*	58.4%	74.9%	p = .000
	Prolife	19.6%	12.4%	
	Don't know	21.9%	12.7%	
Telecomm act	Signed bill*	20.1%	25.3%	p = .22
	Favored regulation	27.4%	28.9%	
	Don't know	52.5%	45.7%	
Campaign funds	From labor	20.1%	31.4%	p = .02
	From business*	33.3%	26.4%	
	About the same	23.7%	23.4%	
	Don't know	22.8%	18.7%	
Budget surplus	Use for tax cuts	9.6%	6.9%	p = .03
	Fix social security*	67.6%	77.4%	
	Don't know	22.8%	15.7%	
Overall perception	Liberal	44.7%	55.1%	p = .000
	Moderate/conservative*	37.9%	40.7%	
	Don't know	17.4%	4.1%	

Significance based on Chi-square test.

* Correct response.

As we might expect, in those instances where a left-leaning ideology is associated with a correct response (the abortion and budget surplus questions), the
more educated respondents respond in traditional fashion, being more inclined
to display their knowledge of contemporary politics. But, if the respondents in
the more educated group are being pulled simultaneously in *opposite* directions, we would expect them to end up in roughly the same place as the less educated group—hence the difference between them is sometimes not that significant. Nevertheless, a pattern emerges across these responses: in every case,
those in the more educated group are more likely to give an answer rather than
acknowledge they don't know; in some instances, members of this group are
pulled more toward the left-leaning (and wrong) response (welfare, healthcare,
campaign funding, and overall perception of Clinton); in other cases, those in
the more educated group are more likely to give the correct response (land
mines, death penalty, and media deregulation). In answer to the welfare question, those with more education are pulled toward the option that is closest to
the correct response (they are more likely to say that he had declined to sign the
bill and presented his own plan rather than that he rejected the bill and offered
nothing in its place). In the case of the campaign-funding question, they are
more likely to give the least accurate response (that Clinton and the democrats
receive more money from labor than from business).

Overall, the stronger of the two tendencies would appear to be the (incorrect) use of an ideological frame associating a Democratic president with left-
leaning positions. If we exclude the two questions in which the correct response
is the left-leaning response (the abortion and budget surplus questions), this
group is more likely to be right in four out seven instances. And yet they are
more likely to choose the left-wing response *in every instance but one* (the death
penalty question). The tendency of the more educated group to assume that,
given a choice, Clinton is more likely to be on the left would therefore seem to
strongly interfere with their tendency to know (or guess) the answer. In the four
instances where they are more likely to get the answer right, it is by fairly small
proportions (3 percent, 3 percent, 5 percent, and 8 percent—compared with the
10 percent and 17 percent difference in the two instances where the correct
answer is the left-leaning response), while in three instances (welfare, health
care, and campaign funding) they are *less* likely to get the answer right than
those with less formal education, a finding that goes against the norm of most
knowledge surveys (with some interesting exceptions [Delli Carpini and Keeter
1996]).

While it is always difficult to invoke the power of the news media in these
kinds of data, the pull of the "left-leaning Clinton" framework on the more edu-

cated group is suggestive. As I have indicated, it may be partly a function of the ability of the more educated people to use ideological frames in understanding the world. Nonetheless, it is unlikely that the use of these ideological frames would take place in a media landscape that deemed them inappropriate. As Zaller points out (1992, 1994), those with more education tend to be more likely to follow the news and hence are more likely to replicate elite-informed media frameworks. Thus the tendency of those with more formal education to assume a left-leaning Clinton is an important piece of evidence to support the notion that *this assumption is informed by the news media.*

If, as Nie, Junn, and Stehlik-Barry argue, more education leads people to be closer to the world of contemporary mainstream politics, it may also incline people to become immersed in the forms of political mythology that encourage consent to political elites. Since this group is also more likely to vote, this becomes a particularly effective ideological mechanism for maintaining the hegemony of a political system that favors right-leaning, corporate interests.

We should not underestimate the potential significance of the popular perception that the inclination toward social democratic positions on a number of issues that we find in poll responses *is* reflected in government. Any pressure for reforming the political system to reduce the degree of bias toward wealthy interests is undoubtedly diminished if one assumes that a Democratic president will be able or inclined—as suggested in this survey—to oppose the interests of the health insurance industry, the Pentagon, the munitions industry, and the telecommunications industry.

THE REPRODUCTION OF HEGEMONY

To sum up: it is clear from the evidence provided from polling data that there are considerable pockets of resistance to the procorporate, center-right agenda that informs Washington politics. This is not something that we can attribute to the limits of polling surveys, since we should expect those limits to accentuate rather than diminish support for elite concerns. If this resistance is sometimes ameliorated by campaigns to achieve consent (such as those outlined in the previous chapter), such attempts are not always successful. The elite consensus in favor of the North American Free Trade Agreement (NAFTA), for example, may have boosted the numbers of those declaring themselves in favor of it, but it did not create a popular majority. Indeed, the fact that NAFTA was imposed and maintained without such consent indicates that political elites are often more likely to attend to the interests of major campaign donors—who were, on the whole, very supportive of NAFTA—than to public opinion.

This indicates that hegemony is sustained, in the first instance—in Hall's sense of the term (1996)—at the level of political economy: through the system of campaign finance, political advertising, and corporate interference in the legislative process. Consent is achieved at the ideological level through a series of linked discourses in which *the system itself* is represented as democratic and pluralistic. Thus we find a series of popular assumptions in which many people identify a procorporate Democratic president as someone who is consistently representative of left-leaning, liberal positions.

These assumptions are clearly manifested in polls that ask people to identify Democrats and Republicans on various ideological questions and then identify themselves in relation to (their perception of) the two parties. In response to this exercise, most people put themselves in between where they *think* the Democrats and Republicans stand (Erikson, Luttbeg, and Tedin 1991, 262; Knight and Erikson 1997, 105). This self-identification *might appear* to support the conventional notion of a generally moderate public—and yet such an interpretation assumes common knowledge of party positions. Indeed, these responses tell us almost nothing about people's political beliefs, because they are entirely contingent on an understanding of Democratic and Republican Party positions. As a consequence, in placing the Democrats farther to the left of the scale than they deserve to be, most people subsequently place themselves farther to the right than their positions on a range of specific issue would indicate.

What we see manifested here is a very particular form of hegemony (Bennett 1995; Ouellette 1999). Rather than win consent for a particular set of ideological positions, the probusiness, rightward drift of Washington politics is put in place by the political economy of governance and sustained by establishing consent—among the voting population—for *a system* of government that favors certain dominant interests.

This is, perhaps, best encapsulated by attitudes to campaign finance reform. When asked about proposals that might reform campaign finance and create a more equitable system, most people respond positively. For example, a Gallup poll in 1996 found majorities in favor of most progressive measures on changing campaign finance: 81 percent were in favor of limiting business contributions, 71 percent would limit individual contributions, 67 percent would limit a candidate's own contributions, and 79 percent were in favor of spending caps. Another Gallup poll in 1997 recorded 70 percent in favor of a "complete overhaul" or "major changes" to the system, with only 5 percent saying the system was "fine the way it is," while a majority (53%) say that campaign contributions influence elected officials "a great deal." In one sense, this is just another instance of popular majorities in polls being to the left of majorities in Washington. In terms of the hegemony of the existing, procorporate system, however, the most important piece of polling data is contextual—as Gallup's Lydia Saad puts it: "Americans tell Gallup that campaign finance is not a critical issue for them . . . less than half of Americans (41%) rated campaign finance reform as either a top or a high priority for Congress and the President to deal with. . . . Issues such as education, crime, Social Security, and even defense spending are of much greater public concern" (Saad 1999, 1).

Dissatisfaction with the current system, in other words, is widespread but, in a majority of cases, not especially urgent. While this is partly a function of media agenda-setting, it operates in the context of the ideological parameters I have outlined.

HEGEMONY AND ITS DISCONTENTS

There are occasions when a dominant culture reveals itself most clearly in moments of critical reflection. In an article on polling on the front page of its Sunday Review section (November 21, 1999), the *New York Times* made a series of well-rehearsed gestures. It began:

> President Clinton is such a devoted student of public opinion polls that his aides say he can recite, from memory, the American people's double digit tastes on a wide variety of issues. Besides using survey data to help shape some of the most important decisions of his presidency, Mr. Clinton has also consulted polls before deciding whether his family should go to the beach or the mountains on their summer vacations.

The article then proceeds to question this fealty to survey technology by revealing the "dirty little secret" of contemporary polling—this being, according to the article, the fact that "far fewer people agree to participate in surveys than ten years ago," creating a level of nonresponse that throws into question the ability of polls to accurately reflect the population as a whole. The article concludes with a quote from Senator Daniel Patrick Moynihan (a New York politician often characterized as a maverick who is prepared to question the conventional wisdom) condemning "politicians who vote according to polls rather than their consciences."

In chapter two, I referred to George Will's appeal to principled leadership in the face of polls suggesting the public was insufficiently mindful of the conservative position. NBC's political primetime drama *The West Wing* neatly captured a liberal version of this critique in an episode in which the president is persuaded to drop the phrase "the era of big government is over" from a State of the Union address. Throughout the episode, various characters remind the president that the phrase has polled well in their surveys. He is, nonetheless, moved to delete it after a principled appeal from one of his speech writers, who reminds him of the importance of "good" government in pursuit of compassionate goals. Some viewers will no doubt have recognized this as an attack on a "poll-driven" President Clinton, who used the phrase in precisely this context. This position is familiar territory for pundits on the left. In Jonathan Schell's critical review of Dick Morris's books ("Master of All He Surveys"), for example, Schell discusses Morris's Machiavellian influence on President Clinton in pursuance of a "policy that sacrifices principle to win votes," without really questioning the extent to which Morris's polls were an impartial reflection of popular attitudes (Schell 1999).

Two assumptions inform these critical gestures. First, there is an image of a body politic gorging itself on an excess of populism, abandoning the notion of principle in an attempt to advance a candidate's public appeal. It is as if the democratic project has gone too far, suffocating the wisdom we desire in our political leaders. Second, the pollster's art is questioned only on its ability to *statistically* replicate "the public mind." The complex ideological constructions contained in the discursive apparatus of poll technology are sidelined by a focus on whether samples are truly representative. The *New York Times* article thus simultaneously legitimizes polls while questioning their political value. On the one hand, it is implied that if polls are based on *representative* samples, they are indeed an authentic voice of the public. On the other hand, we are asked to question whether political leaders should be listening to that voice.

Notwithstanding the contradictory nature of this juxtaposition—if the issue is principled leadership rather than pandering populism, then the statistical problems with polling are surely irrelevant—we can see how these assumptions are both flattering and convenient to political elites. Indeed, if the only criticism being made of the body politic is that it is, in a sense, *too* democratic, then politicians are given license to pursue political objectives, in the name of principle, that disregard popular opinion.

The first part of this book is an attempt to dismantle these assumptions. Although it is true that political leaders routinely use polls, they do so selectively, whether to wrap an idea in popular imagery (thus we have "welfare reform" rather than a cut in programs for the poor, and we fight wars to stop the advance of dangerous dictators rather than to pursue certain economic and strategic goals) or to choose those issues on which they are prepared to negotiate compromises. What is particularly striking is the degree to which a whole range of apparently popular opinions can be ignored if they fall outside the general political framework advanced by political elites. In short, while the more centrist or conservative connotations of poll responses inform public debate, many of the left-leaning, social democratic inclinations suggested by opinion surveys—whether support for universal healthcare, for increases in most forms of social spending, or for limiting the power of large corporations—are generally ignored.

It is the difference between a genuine attempt to use poll technology to advance a kind of democratic ideal—as envisioned by technocrats like George Gallup—and commercial market research. For example, if market research tells car manufacturers that people want less air pollution and greater investment in public transit systems, they are unlikely to act upon these concerns. They will either ignore them—in the name of economic realism—or they will seek to use public relations strategies that alleviate or even make use of these concerns. Survey results are thus a well of ideas to draw from rather than a series of directives.

President Clinton and other Democratic Party leaders do not pursue a conservative economic agenda because the polls command them to but because they are sympathetic to a version of that agenda and to the political merits of yielding to the powerful economic interests promoting it (not least as a way to attract campaign donations). A genuinely left-leaning politics whose terms fall outside the mainstream of contemporary U.S. politics has at least as much polling research to draw upon in articulating a popular message as the politics pursued within that center-right mainstream. If the voice of principle in *The West Wing* was presented as going above the petty concerns of poll responses, this was a matter of choice rather than necessity—he might just have as easily used polling data to make his more liberal case. The abstraction "big government" may not poll well, but there is a long list of apparently popular social welfare programs that do.

The notion of a poll-driven body politic is plausible only because the media coverage of polls reflects the political agendas of elites. Polls that suggest the popularity of ideas of little interest to the leadership of the two main parties are deemed irrelevant to the day-to-day coverage of politics, while polls that tie public opinion to political elites—notably horse race polls—surface in abundance. The media thus produce a form of public opinion that is largely compatible with the elites who claim, most of the time, to represent the popular will, and it is from this narrow space that assumptions can be made about politicians drifting with the ebb and flow of the polls.

If the actual use of polls is more opportunistic, it is, in a sense, an acknowledgment of the nature of polling data. The idea that poll results are authentic expressions of a popular will has been criticized for some time, and yet the dominant manifestation of this critique in public discourse is one that turns it on its head. While the critical literature emphasizes the socially constructed quality of poll responses, the question we hear most often is, as the *New York Times* article puts it, "Who actually talks to pollsters and who does not?" In other words, all pollsters need to do is talk to the right mix of people and everything will be well. This is not to belittle the technicalities of sampling, but the size or composition of the sample does not mitigate the interpretative nature of the whole exercise. The most ambiguous forms of polling, I have suggested, are those with the largest sample. An election, after all, asks everyone a question whose meaning is highly contested and generates an answer that might spring from a variety of contradictory positions. As a consequence, general movements to the right or left in the broad mass of U.S. polling data are very poor predictors of presidential elections. As Murray Edelman argues, the meaning of elections often has less to do with opinion preference than with their broader role as rituals vindicating a political mainstream.

If the dominant meaning of polls is caught up in a set of interpretations that vivify the notion of representative democracy, an analysis of the polling data excluded from this interpretation prompts us to explore the conditions of this dominant construction. Although these conditions involve a corporate media whose interests are generally allied with the center-right preferences of political elites, the ideological practices that exclude discussion of polls to the left of a Washington consensus have their own momentum. Reporters are caught up in a set of professional ideologies that make it difficult to go beyond the confines of elite political frameworks and a set of broader ideologies that make it difficult to question the notion of representative democracy.

If polls are a form of representation, then the image of a moderate-to-conservative public reflecting the political range of its political leaders is a highly selective representation of those representations. My point here is not so much that the media misrepresent the "true" nature of a more left-leaning public, but that they *limit the possibilities* that the polling data offer us. This, of course, raises the question of what the opinions produced by polls really *do* mean, and it is this issue that is the subject of the second part of this book.

The meaning of poll responses is contingent upon a complex array of discursive conditions—conditions in which a proffered opinion will be plausible or implausible. These conditions involve the particular narratives or associations conjured up by the pollster's question. For example, if "big government" is understood as referring to a cluster of negative images—snooping
tax inspectors, uncaring bureaucrats, and so on—we might well be against it.
Spending public money on education, heathcare, the environment, or home-
less shelters may well be an idea that triggers more positive associations of
social justice and civilized society, and may therefore be something we want to
see more of. Either way, in modern (or postmodern) democracies, the media
have a significant role in the construction of these discursive conditions.

While the weight of research into the ideological drift of mass media (and
the news media in particular) sees media institutions as operating within an
elite, dominant framework, viewer or citizen subjectivity means that there are
no guarantees that elite views of the world will become popular conceptions.
Our understanding of this uncertainty has been informed by the entry of semiotics into the study of media reception: whereby meaning is seen as a complex
social construction rather than something that can be assumed (Hall 1980;
Morley 1980). The potential gap between "encoding" and "decoding" has been
the subject of much debate—one amplified by the postmodernist stress on the
instability of meaning in what Ien Ang has called the "age of uncertainty" (Ang
1996). If this debate, for some, threatens to become rather tiresome, the central
question it addresses could hardly be more significant. How and to what extent
do media discourses play a role in creating *popular consent* for dominant systems of power? Or, to put it another way, how does hegemony work in the
struggle between different ideologies and meanings?

I have argued against two straightforward accounts of this process. The
first account is one in which the media consistently persuade a voting majority of the value or necessity of policies advocated by elites. The second tends
to focus on evidence of popular resistance as indicative of a failure of media
influence and of hegemony in general. There is undoubtedly evidence that
might support both positions, but on the substantial question of investigating
the ideological conditions that sustain the center-right hegemony of the U.S.
political system, opinion polls offer us glimpses of moments of consent and
moments of opposition. As it stands, this is not a terribly surprising conclusion (it is one arrived at in different contexts by many others [Morley 1992;
Press 1991]). I have tried to show how these moments inform—or fail to
inform—political power, and to explore ways in which some of the preferences recorded by opinion polls become connected to mainstream political

discourse and policy, while others are left to gather dust in the vast archives of unfulfilled ideas.

This is not a matter of transferring opinions from one place—the media—onto another—the citizenry—but a more complex interplay of information patterns. Moreover, understanding these information patterns is not something that can be read from a straightforward analysis of media content. This is particularly the case with news media, which most people consume selectively and without a great deal of attention. What slips through are oft-repeated narratives or associations.

Perhaps the most basic of these connections, in the U.S. context, is the way in which the more moderate or conservative ideas produced by polling technology are articulated with the notion of "America" and its people—in ways that more progressive ideas tend not to be. In chapters seven and eight, I also consider two broad questions in detail: first, the degree or nature of support for a cold-war military budget and the maintenance of the military industrial complex; second, the ways in which a political system whose political economy pushes it to the right is sustained ideologically. In both cases, the polling data suggest limited but precise forms of what Murrey Edelman (1964) calls "quiescence."

In recent decades support for military spending has, by comparison with other priorities, been generally weak. Indeed, it would be hard to make a case based on these polling data for maintaining a military over five times the size of the second biggest spender. Instead, I have argued that public support—in as much as it exists—is gleaned in other ways: first by the establishment of an informational climate that associates the military budget with moderation rather than excess; second, by the construction of various narratives in which the use of military force is seen as necessary to deter the advance of dangerous dictators. Support for the *use* of a global military is thereby recuperated by political elites into support for high levels of military spending. Alarmingly, in the post–cold war period, there is a real sense in which fighting "necessary" wars has, in terms of generating public support, become the political raison d'être of the military industrial complex. Without such periodic intervention, even in a climate in which military spending is generally underestimated, it is hard to see what would prevent support for *cuts* in military spending from rising above 50 percent, as they threatened to do before the Gulf war.

Political elites are, of course, more than capable of ignoring public opinion polls to carry on spending vast resources on the military, regardless of the lack of visible public support. This is, after all, done in many areas of policy as a matter of quiet routine. In this context, perhaps the most significant ideological platform that sustains the center-right hegemony in Washington is to establish support for what Tony Bennett (1995) calls the "political rationality" of the system as a whole, or what his namesake Lance Bennett (1989) refers to as the conditioning of public opinion to accept a "managerial democracy."

This is achieved in the face of fairly high levels of cynicism about the role of money in politics. It relies partly upon the oft-repeated celebration of the United States as the apotheosis of democracy, and partly upon a media framework in which the range of opinion in Washington is represented as broader than it really is. The left may be poorly represented among power brokers in the body politic, but it is well represented in the symbolic structure of news reporting. This structure tends to override the coverage of specific events — thus it is that most people associate President Clinton (or Democrats in general) with liberal or left-leaning positions, even when the record suggests otherwise. In this symbolic world, left battles right in ways that encompass the broad range of views we might find in public opinion.

The beauty of this strategy from a hegemonic perspective is that it means political power does not depend on the continual need to persuade popular opinion — a series of struggles in which the outcome cannot be guaranteed. Instead, it survives on the perception that the system of representation, for all its flaws, is generally a fair reflection of popular opinion. It is a hegemonic structure that can absorb inconsistencies, contradictions, and resistance in ways that more overt forms of power might not.

A metaphor for the processes I have described in the second half of this book would be a series of devices — intricate without being elegant, sometimes constructed with deliberation, sometimes not — whose piecemeal, complex appearance conceals a certain solidity. Unraveling these devices — and the media's role in their construction — is to explore a kind of guided forgetfulness.

For those who, like me, believe in much of what gets forgotten, the research presented in this book paints a fairly depressing picture. And yet there is something hopeful in the idea that change, if it is to occur, is more a process of reminding than of persuading, of making connections rather than speaking anew.

APPENDIX

THE GENERAL POPULATION SURVEYS

All three samples were gathered by random-digit dialing procedures. In all cases this produced samples that were, in terms of age, gender, race, education, income, and political orientation, broadly representative of the population on which they were based. Apart from the Gulf war study, samples were also drawn from a representative geographical range within the United States. The findings were tested for standard measurements of statistical significance (based on the universally accepted figure of .05, which means there is only a one in twenty probability that the relationship is based on chance), and the relationships explored were isolated after running controls for other explanatory variables.

Some questions in the the surveys were open-ended (in these instances, respondents could not choose from a list of possible responses), others provided options for respondents to choose from. The open-ended questions are indicated in the list of questions and frequencies.

The Gulf war study was based upon telephone interviews, carried out between February 2 and February 4, 1991, with 250 randomly selected adults living in the Metropolitan Denver area.

The 1992 Election study was based on a nationwide telephone survey of 726 randomly selected adults in the United States, from which a sample of 601 "likely voters" was derived (i.e., those of the 726 who said they would definitely or probably vote). The survey was conducted during the first week of October. This was supplemented by a series of six focus groups conducted in Springfield, Massachusetts, in August and September.

The 1998 study of policy knowledge and President Clinton was based on a nationwide telephone survey of 601 randomly selected people in the United States, conducted on February 3–5, 1998.

THE STUDENT SURVEYS

A series of student surveys were conducted between 1992 and 1998. The 1992 survey involved students interviewed in a random selection of classes and student dormitories at the University of Massachusetts. The surveys conducted between 1995 and 1998 involved students enrolled in an introductory large-lecture class (entitled the "Social Impact of Mass Media"). The survey was conducted at the beginning of the course, based on written responses to a questionnaire. In some cases, the results were the subject of a subsequent discussion. The dates and number of responses were as follows:

April 1992:   N = 550
Sept. 1995:   N = 125
Feb. 1996:   N = 120
Sept. 1996:   N = 121
Sept. 1998:   N = 300
Sept. 1999:   N = 201

The student surveys were also structured like a quiz, and did not therefore offer the possibility of a "don't know" response, the students being encouraged to make an informed guess.

QUESTIONS AND FREQUENCIES

Listed below are the questions (relevant to the areas discussed) and frequencies in the 1991, 1992, and 1998 surveys. Where appropriate, the correct response is marked thus: *.

The 1991 Study

1. Do you support President Bush's decision to use military force against Iraq?

Yes	83.6%
No	13.2%
Don't know/not sure	3.2%

2. In July 1990, just before he invaded, Saddam Hussein indicated he may use force against Kuwait. How did the United States respond? (please state whether the following statements are true or false)

a. The United States said it would impose sanctions against him.
True 73.6%
False* 26.4%
b. The Unites States said it would regard it as a threat to the United States.
True 46.8%
False* 53.2%
c. The United States said it would take no action.
True* 13.2%
False 86.8%
d. The Unites States said it would support Kuwait with the use of force.
True 65.2%
False* 34.8%

3. Do you recall why Saddam Hussein invaded Kuwait? (open-ended)

Because Kuwait was forcing down the price of oil	2.4%
To control Kuwait's oil fields	24.8%
Other	40.8%
Don't know	26.4%

4. There have been conflicting reports about the number of people who have lost their lives in the war to date.

a. How many American lives would you estimate
have been lost? (open-ended)   45 (mean)
b. How many Iraqi lives would you estimate
have been lost? (open-ended)   4,870 (mean)

5. Do you know what religion Saddam Hussein practices? (open-ended)

Moslem/Islamic*	74.0%
Hindu	0.8%
Other	2.8%
Don't know	22.0%

6. I am now going to describe three possible situations. Please tell me whether you feel the United States should intervene with the use of military force in each case.

a. A guerrilla army takes power in a country and proceeds to slaughter hundreds of thousands of civilians. Should the United States intervene with force to protect human rights?

Yes	58.0%
No	26.8%
Don't know/not sure	15.2%

b. A previously friendly oil-producing country adopts new policies antagonistic toward the United States. Should the United States intervene to protect its interests?

Yes	18.0%
No	72.8%
Don't know/not sure	9.2%

c. One country violently invades and occupies another, setting up an illegal government against the wishes of the people. Should the United States intervene to restore the sovereignty of the occupied country?

Yes	52.8%
No	32.0%
Don't know/not sure	13.2%

7. Last year, President Bush ordered Operation Just Cause, in which the United States successfully captured the Panamanian dictator. Do you know his name? (open-ended)

Manuel Noriega.*	70.8%
Other	1.6%
Don't know	27.6%

8. How would you compare the number of civilian casualties in the U.S. action in Panama and the Iraqi invasion of Kuwait? (prompt on whether there were more civilian casualties in Kuwait or Panama)

More civilian deaths in Kuwait	57.2%
About the same	4.8%
More civilian deaths in the invasion of Panama	20.4%
Other	1.2%
Don't know	16.4%

9. I'm now going to read you a list of three countries. I want you to tell me whether you would describe the following countries as democracies (yes, it is a democracy, or no, it is not a democracy). The three countries are Iraq, Kuwait, and Saudi Arabia.

a. Iraq

Yes	4.8%
No*	92.0%
Don't know/not sure	3.2%

b. Kuwait (before the invasion)

Yes	23.2%
No*	66.8%
Don't know/not sure	10.0%

c. Saudi Arabia

Yes	21.6%
No*	69.2%
Don't know/not sure	9.2%

10. *Iraq has been using Scud missiles against Israel and the allied forces. Do you know the name of the missile the Allies have used to intercept them? (open-ended)*

Patriot*	80.8%
Other	2.0%
Don't know	17.2%

11. *The United Nations has had a number of votes on attempting to reach a political settlement to the Arab/Israeli conflict. The most recent vote was 153 to three in favor of trying to reach a settlement. Can you name any of the of three countries that voted against it? (To interviewer: may need to repeat this question. Prompt them to take a guess.) (open-ended)*

Cuba	7.6%
Dominica*	0.8%
Iran	9.6%
Iraq	11.6%
Israel*	16.4%
Libya	4.0%
Soviet Union.	3.6%
United States*	13.6%
Other	34.4%
Don't know	56.0%

12. *In addition to the occupation of Kuwait, are there, to your knowledge, any other lands in the Middle East under occupation?*

Yes*	46.0%
No	36.0%
Don't know/not sure	18.0%

13. *If yes, which countries are occupying foreign land? (open-ended)*

Israel*	30.8%
Syria*	3.2%
Other	10.4%
Don't know	4.0%

14. *Have you ever heard of the Intifada? (To interviewer: if yes, ask: Do you know what it refers to?) (open-ended)*

Palestinian uprising in the West Bank*	15.2%
Other	6.8%
Don't know	78.0%

15. *Before the war began, had Saddam Hussein, to your knowledge, ever used chemical weapons? If yes: Do you know who he has used them against? (open-ended)*

Iran	22.8%
The Kurdish population of Iraq	16.0%
His own people	14.4%
Other	2.4%
Don't know	18.0%

16. *President Bush has described the American forces during the Vietnam War as "fighting with one hand tied behind their back." Do you think this is a fair assessment?*

Yes	79.2%
No	15.2%
Don't know/not sure	5.6%

17. *Can you tell me what the initials MIA/POW stand for? (open-ended)*

Missing in Action/Prisoner of War*	90.0%
Other	2.0%
Don't know	8.0%

18. *It has been stated that Vietnam is still holding American prisoners of war. Would you agree with this statement?*

Yes	69.6%
No	16.0%
Don't know/not sure	14.4%

19. *During the Vietnam War, approximately 55 thousand U.S. servicemen lost their lives. How many Vietnamese deaths, roughly, would you estimate there were? (open-ended)*

100,000 (median)   286,955 (mean)

20. *There has been some discussion that, if the war in the Gulf continues for more than a month, a war tax may be introduced. Would you support an increase in your taxes to pay for the war?*

Yes	57.6%
No	36.4%
Don't know/not sure	6.0%

THE 1992 STUDY

1. There has been some debate about the role of the media in politics. Overall, in recent presidential elections, would you say more newspapers have endorsed:

The more liberal candidates	40.9%
The more conservative candidates*	19.1%
Both equally	11.5%
Don't know/can't answer	28.5%

2. On the whole, would you say that the media tend to be biased in a liberal direction or in a conservative direction, or are the media pretty balanced?

Liberal	34.3%
Conservative	8.2%
Pretty balanced	45.4%
Don't know/other	12.1%

3. During the campaign, much has been said about the influence of "special interests" on the candidates. When you hear about "special interests," who do you think of? (open-ended)

Women/feminists	5.8%
Blacks or (other) minorities	3.7%
Prochoice/abortion groups	7.0%
Antiabortion/prolife groups	7.3%
Labor unions	8.0%
Gays/homosexuals	5.0%
Environmentalists	7.7%
Lawyers and/or doctors	2.8%
Big business/corporations (general or specific, e.g., the oil industry, insurance companies, etc.)	28.0%
Liberals	2.0%
Religious groups	1.3%
The elderly	2.3%
The disabled	0.8%
Don't know/cannot answer	32.4%
Other responses	28.6%

4. Thinking of the presidential candidates and their running mates, which of them comes from a family that owns a chain of newspapers? (open-ended)

George Bush	3.3%
Bill Clinton	3.5%
Al Gore	3.8%
Dan Quayle*	23.6%
Other response	1.8%
Don't know	63.9%

5. *Of the four candidates for president and vice president, have any been accused of using family influence to avoid being sent to Vietnam? (open-ended)*

George Bush	1.0%
Dan Quayle	15.1%
Bill Clinton	41.3%
Quayle *and* Clinton*	23.0%
Al Gore	0.5%
Other	3.7%
Don't know	15.5%

6. *Candidates for president raise money from various sources. One source is big business and corporate interests, and another is organized labor. In this election, which of these two do you think gives more money to George Bush and the Republican campaign: big business or labor?*

Big business*	86.9%
Labor	5.2%
Both equal	1.2%
Don't know	6.8%

7. *And which do you think gives more money to Bill Clinton and the Democratic campaign?*

Big business*	15.5%
Labor	68.7%
Both equal	3.2%
Don't know	12.6%

8. *Each year the president proposes a budget, and then Congress decides how much to actually spend. Which do you think was greater last year: the amount of money President Bush proposed spending on the federal budget or the amount Congress actually spent?*

The amount Bush proposed*	21.8%
The amount Congress passed	65.7%
Equal	2.0%
Don't know	10.5%

9. *Which of the following do you think the federal government will spend more money on in 1992: foreign aid, the military, or welfare?*

Foreign aid	42.3%
The military*	22.0%
Welfare	29.8%
Don't know	6.0%

10. *How many children, on the average, would you say women on welfare have? (open-ended)*

Mean = 3.25 (standard deviation = 1.14)
(No response/uncodable = 8.5%)

11. *Which income group would you say pays the highest percentage of its income in state and local taxes?*

The richest 1%	3.2%
The middle 20%	84.7%
The poorest 20%*	11.1%
Don't know	1.0%

12. *Many employers have adopted affirmative action policies for minorities in recent years. I'm going to read to you three statements about affirmative action; please tell me which one is closest to your own view.*

Affirmative action was needed in the past, but now it's done its job to give minorities more opportunities and is no longer necessary.	37.6%
Affirmative action is still needed to narrow the gap between whites and minorities.	49.1%
Affirmative action was never needed.	8.8%
Other/don't know	4.5%

13. *Please tell me whether the statement applies to George Bush, to Bill Clinton, to both Bush and Clinton, or to neither one. If you're not sure, please take a guess, based on what you know of the candidates. First, which candidate supports cuts in capital gains taxes?*

George Bush	61.7%
Bill Clinton	27.0%
Both*	4.5%
Neither	1.3%
Don't know	5.5%

14. *Which candidate's family has a dog named Millie?*

George Bush*	86.2%
Bill Clinton	4.3%
Both	0.0%
Neither	6.8%
Don't know	8.7%

15. *Which candidate has proposed reducing military spending by more than 50 percent over the next five years?*

George Bush	19.0%
Bill Clinton	67.1%
Both	5.5%
Neither*	3.2%
Don't know	5.3%

16. *Which candidate supports the death penalty?*

George Bush	35.4%
Bill Clinton	25.5%
Both*	11.8%
Neither	8.0%
Don't know	19.3%

17. *Which candidate supports "right to work" laws opposed by labor unions?*

George Bush	43.1%
Bill Clinton	32.3%
Both*	5.0%
Neither	3.0%
Don't know	16.6%

18. *Which candidate attended an Ivy League University?*

George Bush	43.1%
Bill Clinton	30.0%
Both*	14.1%
Neither	1.0%
Don't know	11.8%

19. *Many people say that wetlands are a vital part of America's natural environment. What has the Bush administration's policy been on the protection of Americas wetlands?*

Reduce the amount under protection*	37.9%
Increase the amount under protection	16.1%
Maintain the same levels	33.6%
Don't know/no answer	12.3%

20. *After the violent crackdown on prodemocracy protesters in Tiananmen Square, in China, the Bush administration:*

Imposed strong economic sanctions on China	13.8%
Imposed some selected economic sanctions on China	28.8%
Retained China's "most favored nation" trading status*	44.3%
Don't know/no answer	13.1%

21. *To your knowledge, have Arkansas state taxes been: among the highest in the nation, about average, or among the lowest in the nation during Bill Clinton's term as Governor?*

Among the highest	31.8%
About average	22.8%
Among the lowest*	21.1%
Don't know/no answer	24.3%

22. *How has Governor Clinton's record on the environment been rated by an independent monitoring group — have they found Bill Clinton's environmental record to be:*

Among the best in the nation	6.8%
About average for the nation	52.2%
Among the worst in the nation*	19.0%
Don't know/no answer	22.0%

23. *Do you recall which TV character Dan Quayle criticized for setting a poor example of family values? (open-ended)*

Murphy Brown*	89.2
Don't know/other	10.8%

24. *Do you recall which cabinet member of the Reagan–Bush administration was recently indicted for his role in the Iran–Contra scandal? (open-ended)*

Casper Weinberger*	19.1%
Don't recall/other	80.9%

THE 1998 STUDY

1. *There have been recent allegations that President Clinton had an affair with a White House intern. What was the name of this woman? Was it: Monica Lewinsky, Paula Jones, or Madeleine Albright?*

Monica Lewinsky*	93.2%
Paula Jones	2.7%
Madeleine Albright	0.5%
Other, etc.	3.7%

2. *Do you think the allegations that the president had a sexual relationship with this woman are true? (open-ended)*

Yes	37.0%
No	27.7%
Maybe, possibly	12.2%
Don't know, no answer	17.0%
Don't care	6.2%

3. *In connection with this alleged affair, there has been talk that the president acted illegally. Can you recall what he is accused of doing? (open-ended)*

He encouraged her to lie/commit perjury/not reveal the affair, etc.*	63.0%
Response implying something of a sexual nature (apart from lying)	12.8%
Other	6.8%
Can't recall, don't know, no answer, etc.	17.3%

4. *If it turns out that the president lied about his relationship with this woman, do you think he should resign?*

Yes	39.5%
No	52.8%
Not sure, don't know, no answer, etc.	7.7%

5. *A woman named Linda Tripp is a key witness in these events. Can you recall how she is involved? (open-ended)*

She is a friend of Monica Lewinsky, taped (phone) conversations with her, encouraged her to tell what happened, etc.	75.0%
She had a sexual affair with the president.	0.8%
She is part of right-wing plot to discredit Clinton.	0.2%
She is charging the president with sexual harassment.	0.2%
Part of special prosecutor/independent counsel investigation team, working with Starr, FBI, etc.	0.5%
Other	3.3%
Can't recall, don't know, no answer, etc.	20.0%

6. *These allegations against the president have been linked to a different case in which a woman is charging that the president sexually harassed her when he was governor of Arkansas. Can you recall the name of the woman in this case? Was it Susan Smith, Zoe Baird, or Paula Jones?*

Susan Smith	2.0%
Zoe Baird	0.2%
Paula Jones*	89.2%
Other, etc.	8.7%

7. *When Bill Clinton first ran for president in 1992, a woman claimed to have had a long-running affair with him. Can you recall the name of this woman? Was it: Donna Rice, Susan MacDonald, or Gennifer Flowers?*

Donna Rice	1.7%
Susan MacDonald	1.8%
Gennifer Flowers*	81.3%
Other, etc.	15.2%

8. *Independent Counsel Kenneth Starr is investigating these allegations. Can you recall the name of the case he was originally appointed to investigate? (open-ended)*

Whitewater (or private land or real estate deal in Arkansas, involving the
  Clintons' investments, bank deals, stocks, etc.; anything related)*   51.3%
Watergate   5.0%
Other (for example, "Something-gate")   3.3%
Can't recall   40.3%

9. *Are you aware of Independent Counsel Kenneth Starr's political affiliation? Is he a Democrat, a Republican, or an Independent?*

A Democrat   5.5%
A Republican*   38.5%
An Independent   8.3%
Other, don't know, etc.   47.7%

10. *In general, do you think the media have spent too much time on recent scandals in the White House, or have they got it about right?*

Too much time on scandals   77.0%
About right   18.5%
Other, etc.   4.5%

11. *In President Clinton's first term, Republicans were trying to make cuts in Welfare. Did President Clinton: (a) sign the Republicans' bill, (b) refuse to sign the bill and present a plan of his own with smaller cuts in welfare?, or (c) reject the idea of any welfare reform at all?*

Signed the Republicans' Bill*   13.0%
Refused to sign and offer a plan of his own   45.7%
Rejected the idea of any welfare reform at all   8.2%
Other, don't know, no answer, etc.   33.2%

12. *President Clinton tried without success to reform the healthcare system in his first term. Would you say he favored: (a) moving to a national health-insurance system that covers everyone, or (b) making our current private insurance system available to more people?*

Moving to a national health insurance system that covers everyone   58.8%
Making our current private insurance system available to
    more people*   26.2%
Other, don't know, no answer, etc.   15.0%

13. *The late Princess Diana was working for an international treaty to ban land mines because so many civilians are killed or injured by them in peacetime. Does President Clinton also think they should be banned?*

Yes, he thinks land mines should be banned.   43.7%
No, he does not think land mines should be banned.*   23.5%
Not sure, no answer, don't know, etc.   32.8%

14. *Many people disagree about the death penalty. What is President Clinton's' attitude? Is he: in favor of the death penalty, or is he against it?*

He is in favor of it.*   27.7%
He is against it.   21.0%
Don't know, etc.   51.3%

15. *Many people also disagree about abortion. Does President Clinton generally favor keeping abortion legal, or does he think abortion should be illegal?*

He is in favor of legal abortion.*   69.0%
He is against legal abortion.   14.8%
Don't know, no answer, etc.   16.2%

16. *In 1996 the Republican-led Congress proposed a Telecommunications bill that substantially deregulated the communications industry, so that there were fewer government restrictions on big corporations. What was President Clinton's response? Did he (a) sign the bill, or (b) refuse to sign the bill because he favors more government regulation?*

Sign the bill*   23.0%
Refuse to sign bill, favors government regulation   28.2%
Don't know, no answer, etc.   48.8%

17. *The Republicans and Democrats raise money for their campaigns from big business and from organized labor. During the previous presidential campaign, who gave more to the Democratic party—was it labor or big business? Or was it about the same?*

Labor   26.8%
Big business*   29.2%
About the same   23.5%
Don't know, etc.   20.5%

18. *In his recent State of the Union address, President Clinton projected a budget surplus. Did he propose to use the surplus for (a) tax cuts, or (b) to strengthen Social Security?*

Tax cuts   7.8%
Strengthen Social Security*   73.7%
Don't know, not sure   18.5%

19. *On which side of the Democratic Party would you put Bill Clinton, on the liberal wing or on the more conservative wing?*

Liberal wing	51.3%
Conservative wing*	31.0%
Neither/moderate	8.2%
Don't know, etc.	9.5%

REFERENCES

Adams, J. 1971. *The Works of John Adams.* Vol. 6. New York: AMS Press.

Adorno, T. and M. Horkheimer. 1979. "The Culture Industry as Mass Deception." *The Dialectic of Enlightenment.* London: Verso.

Althusser, L. 1971. "Ideology and Ideological State Apparatuses." In *Lenin and Philosophy.* London: New Left Books.

Alterman, E. 1992. *Sound and Fury: The Washington Punditocracy and the Collapse of American Politics.* New York: HarperCollins.

Ang, I. 1985. *Watching Dallas: Soap Opera and the Melodramatic Imagination.* London: Routledge.

———. 1991. *Desperately Seeking the Audience.* London: Routledge.

———. 1996. *Living Room Wars: Rethinking Media Audiences for a Postmodern World.* New York: Routledge.

Aristotle. 1962. *The Politics.* Baltimore: Pengin Books.

Asher, H. 1998. *Polling and the Public.* Washington: Congressional Quarterly Press.

Baker, K. 1987. "Politics and Public Opinion Under the Old Regime." In *Press and Politics Under the Old Regime.* Edited by J. Censer and J. Popkin. Berkeley: University of California Press.

Bartels, L. 1996. "Uninformed Voters: Information Effects in Presidential Elections." *American Journal of Political Science* 40 (1): 194–230.

Barthes, R. 1974. *S/Z.* New York: Hill and Wang.

———. 1975. *The Pleasure of the Text.* London: Jonathan Cape.

——. 1988. *Mythologies*. New York: Noonday Press.

Behr, R. and S. Iyengar. 1985. "Television News, Real World Cues, and Changes in the Public Agenda." *Public Opinion Quarterly* 46:38–57.

Beniger, J. R. 1987. "Toward an Old New Paradigm: The Half-Century Flirtation with Mass Society." *Public Opinion Quarterly* 51:46–66.

——. 1992. "The Impact of Polling on Public Opinion: Reconciling Foucault, Habermas, and Bourdieu." *International Journal of Public Opinion Research* 4 (3): 204–219.

Benjamin, W. 1985. *Illuminations*. New York: Schocken Books.

Bennett, L. 1989. "Marginalizing the Majority: Conditioning Public Opinion to Accept Managerial Democracy." In *Manipulating Public Opinion*. Edited by M. Margolis and G. Mauser. Pacific Grove, CA: Brooks/Cole.

Bennett, L. and D. Paletz. 1994. *Taken by Storm: The Media Public Opinion and U.S. Foreign Policy in the Gulf War*. Chicago: University of Chicago Press.

Bennett, T. 1995. *The Birth of the Museum*. London: Routledge.

Berelson, B., P. Lazarsfeld, and W. McPhee. 1954. *Voting: A Study of Opinion Formation in a Presidential Campaign*. Chicago: University of Chicago Press.

Blumer, H. 1948. "Public Opinion and Public Opinion Polling." *American Sociological Review* 13:542–47.

Blumler, J. and E. Katz, eds. 1974. *The Uses of Mass Communications*. Thousand Oaks, CA: Sage.

Blumler, J. and D. McQuail. 1970. "The Audience for Election Television." In *Media Sociology*. Edited by J. Tunstall. London: Constable.

Bogart, L. 1972. *Silent Politics: Polls and the Awareness of Public Opinion*. New York: Wiley-Interscience.

Bourdieu, P. 1979. "Public Opinion Does Not Exist." In *Communication and Class Struggle*. Edited by A. Mattelart and S. Siegelaub. New York: International General.

——. 1984. *Distinction: A Social Critique of the Judgment of Taste*. Cambridge: Harvard University Press.

Brady, H. E. and G. R. Orren. 1992. "Polling Pitfalls: Sources of Error in Public Opinion Surveys." In *Media Polls in American Politics*. Edited by T. E. Mann and G. R. Orren. Washington, DC: Brookings Institution.

Brians, C. and M. Wattenberg. 1996. "Campaign Issue Knowledge and Salience: Comparing Reception from TV Commercials, TV News, and Newspapers." *American Journal of Political Science* 40 (1): 172–193.

Brody, R. 1991. *Assessing Presidential Character: The Media, Elite Opinion, and Public Support*. Stanford, CA: Stanford University Press.

Brule, M. and P. Giacometti. 1990. "Opinion Polling in France at the End of the '80s." *Public Perspective* (March–April).

Brunsden, C. and D. Morley. 1979. *Everyday Television—Nationwide*. London: BFI.

Bryce, J. 1895. *The American Commonwealth*. New York: Macmillan.

Canham-Clyne, J. 1996. "When Both Sides Aren't Enough: The Restricted Debate Over Health Care Reform." In *The FAIR Reader: An Extra Review of Press and Politics*. Edited by J. Naureckas and J. Jackson. Boulder: Westview.

Carey, J. 1992. "The Press and Public Discourse." *Kettering Review* (Winter 1992): 9–23.

Carragee, K. 1990. "Interpretive Media Study." *Critical Studies in Mass Communication* 7 (2): 81–96.

Christians, C. and J. Carey. 1989. "The Logic and Aims of Qualitative Research." In *Research Methods in Mass Communications*. Edited by G. H. Stempel and B. H. Westley. Englewood Cliffs, NJ: Prentice-Hall.

Cohen, B. 1963. *The Press and Foreign Policy*. Princeton, NJ: Princeton University Press.

Cohen, S. 1972. *Folk Devils and Moral Panics: The Creation of the Mods and Rockers*. London: MacGibbon and Lee.

Cohen, S. and J. Young. 1983. *The Manufacture of News*. London: Constable.

Condit, C. 1989. "The Rhetorical Limits of Polysemy." *Critical Studies in Mass Communication* 6 (2): 103–122.

Converse, P. 1964. "The Nature of Belief Systems in Mass Publics." In *Ideology and Discontent*. Edited by D. Apter. New York: Free Press.

Converse, P. and G. Markus. 1979. "Plus ca change. . . . The New CPS Election Study Panel." *American Political Science Review* (73): 32–49.

Cook, M. and J. Cohen. 1996. "The Media Go to War: How Television Sold the Panama Invasion." *The FAIR Reader: An Extra Review of Press and Politics*. Edited by J. Naureckas and J. Jackson. Boulder: Westview.

Cook, T. 1994. "Washington Newsbeats and Network News After the Iraqi Invasion of Kuwait." In *Taken by Storm: The Media, Public Opinion and U.S. Foreign Policy in the Gulf War*. Edited by W. Bennett and D. Paletz. Chicago: University of Chicago Press.

Corner, J. 1991. "Meaning, Genre, and Context: The Problematics of Public Knowledge in the New Audience Studies." In *Mass Media and Society*. Edited by J. Curren and M. Gurevitch. London: Edward Arnold.

Corner, J., K. Richardson, and N. Fenton. 1990. *Nuclear Reactions*. London: John Libbey.

Croteau, D. 1998. "Examining the Liberal Media Claim." Virginia Commonwealth University, Dept. of Sociology and Anthropology.

Croteau, D and W. Hoynes. 1997. *Media/Society: Industries, Images and Audiences*. Thousand Oaks, CA: Pine Forge Press.

Curran, J. 1990. "The New Revisionism in Mass Communications Research." *European Journal of Communications* 5 (2–3): 135–164.

Defleur, M. 1998. "Where Have All the Milestones Gone? The Decline of Significant Research on the Process and Effects of Mass Communications." *Mass Communication and Society* 1 (1–2): 85–98.

Delli Carpini, M. X. and S. Keeter. 1992. "The Public's Knowledge of Politics." In *Public Opinion, the Press, and Public Policy.* Edited by J. Kennamer, 19–30. Westport, NY: Praeger.

———. 1996. *What Americans Know About Politics and Why It Matters.* New Haven, CT: Yale University Press.

DeLuca, T. 1995. *The Two Faces of Political Apathy.* Philadelphia: Temple University Press.

Diamond, E. and G. Geller. 1995. "Campaign '96: Never Have So Many Written So Much About So Little." *The National Journal* April 29, 1995.

Dolny, M. 1998. "What's in a Label? Right-Wing Think Tanks Are Often Quoted, Rarely Labeled." *Extra* (May/June).

Dorman, W. and S. Livingston. 1994. " The Establishing Phase of the Persian Gulf Policy Debate." *Taken by Storm: The Media Public Opinion and U.S. Foreign Policy in the Gulf War.* Edited by W. Bennett and D. Paletz. Chicago: University of Chicago Press.

Douglas, S. 1994. *Where the Girls Are.* New York: Times Books.

Easter, D. 1996. "Recapturing the Audience: An Encoding/Decoding Analysis of the Social Uses of Channel One." Ph.D. dissertation, University of Massachusetts at Amherst.

Edelman, M. 1964. *The Symbolic Uses of Politics.* Urbana: University of Illinois Press.

———. 1988. *Constructing the Political Spectacle.* Chicago: University of Chicago Press.

———. 1995a. *From Art to Politics.* Chicago: University of Chicago Press.

———. 1995b. "The Influence of Rationality Claims on Public Opinion and Policy." In *Public Opinion and the Communication of Consent.* Edited by C. Salmon and T. Glasser. New York: Guilford Press.

Edy, J. 1999. "The Content of Our Attitudes: Public Opinion in the Contemporary United States." In *Public Opinion.* Edited by C. Glynn, S. Herbst, G. O'Keefe, and R. Shapiro. Boulder: Westview Press.

Ehrenreich, B. and J. Ehrenreich. 1979. "The Professional-Managerial Class" In *Between Labor and Capital.* Edited by P. Walker. Boston: South End Press.

Eisenstein, E. 1979. *The Printing Press as an Agent of Change: Communications and Cultural Transfomations in Early-Modern Europe.* Cambridge: Cambridge University Press.

Entman, R. 1989. *Democracy Without Citizens: Media and the Decay of Amercian Politics.* New York: Oxford University Press.

Entman, R. and B. Page. 1994. "The Iraq War Debate and the Limits to Media Independence." In *Taken by Storm: The Media Public Opinion and U.S. Foreign Policy in the Gulf War.* Edited by W. Bennett and D. Paletz. Chicago: University of Chicago Press.

Erikson, R., N. Luttbeg, and K. Tedin. 1991. *American Public Opinion: Its Origins, Content, and Impact.* New York: Macmillan.

Erskine, H. G. 1963. "The Polls: Textbook Knowledge." *Public Opinion Quarterly* 27:133–41.

Feldman, S. 1988. "Structure and Consistency in Public Opinion: The Role of Core Beliefs and Values." *American Journal of Political Science* 32:416–38.

Ferguson, T. and J. Rogers. 1986. *Right Turn: The Decline of the Democrats and the Future of American Politics.* New York: Farrar, Straus and Giroux

Fiske, J. 1987. *Television Culture.* London: Methuen.

——. 1989. *Understanding Popular Culture.* Boston: Unwin Hyman.

Foucault, M. 1977. *Discipline and Punish: The Birth of the Prison.* New York: Pantheon.

Frankovic, K. 1992. "Technology and the Changing Landscape of Media Polls." In *Media Polls in American Politics.* Edited by T. E. Mann and G. R. Orren. Washington, DC: Brookings Institution.

Free, L. and H. Cantril. 1967. *The Political Beliefs of Americans: A Study of Public Opinion.* New Brunswick, NJ: Rutgers University Press.

Funkhouser, G. R. 1973. "The Issues of the Sixties: An Exploratory Study in the Dynamics of Public Opinion." *Public Opinion Quarterly* 37:62–75.

Gallup, G. 1966. "Polls and the Political Process—Past, Present, and Future." *Public Opinion Quarterly* 29:544–49.

Gallup, G. Jr. 1990–1996. *The Gallup Poll: 1990–1996.* Wilmington, DE: Scholarly Resources.

Galtung, J. and M. Ruge. 1973. "Structuring and Selecting News." *The Manufacture of News.* Edited by S. Cohen and J. Young. London: Constable.

Gamson, W. 1989. "News as Framing." *American Behavioral Scientist* 33:157–61.

——. 1992. *Talking Politics.* Cambridge: Cambridge Universtiy Press.

Gans, H. 1979. *Deciding What's News.* New York: Vintage.

——. 1985. "Are U.S. Journalists Dangerously Liberal?" *Columbia Journalism Review* (November/December).

Garnham, N. and R. Williams. 1980. "Pierre Bourdieu and the Sociology of Culture: An Introduction." *Media, Culture and Society* 2 (3): 209–223.

Gauntlett, D. 1998. "Ten Things Wrong with the 'Effects' Model." In *Approaches to Audiences,* Edited by R. Dickinson, R. Harindranath, and O. Linne. London: Arnold.

Gerbner, G. and L. Gross. 1976. "Living with Television: The Violence Profile." *Journal of Communication* 28 (3): 173–199.

Gerbner, G., L. Gross, M. Morgan, and N. Signorielli. 1980. "The Mainstreaming of America." *Journal of Communication* 30: 10–29.

Gerbner, G., L. Gross, M. Morgan, and N. Signorielli. 1986. "The Dynamics of the Cultivation Process." *Perspectives on Media Effects.* Edited by J. Bryant and D. Zillman. Hillsdale, NJ: Erlbaum.

Gillespie, M. 1999. "Kosovo May Be Causing Amercians to Rethink Military Spending." Princeton: Gallup, May 19th.

Ginsberg, B. 1986. *The Captive Public: How Mass Opinion Promotes State Power.* New York: Basic Books.

Gitlin, T. 1980. *The Whole World Is Watching.* Berkeley: University of California Press.

Glasgow Media Group. 1976. *Bad News.* London: Routledge and Kegan Paul.

———. 1980. *More Bad News.* London: Routledge and Kegan Paul.

———. 1982. *Really Bad News.* London: Writers and Readers.

Glynn, C., S. Herbst, G. O'Keefe, and R. Shapiro. 1999. *Public Opinion.* Boulder: Westview Press.

Gramsci, A. 1971. *Selections from the Prison Notebooks.* London: Lawrence and Wishart.

Gray, A. 1987. "Reading the Audience." *Screen* 28 (3): 25–34.

Gray, H. 1995. *Watching Race: Television and the Struggle for Blackness.* Minneapolis: University of Minnesota Press.

Green, J., P. Herrnson, L. Powell, and C. Wilcox. 1988. *Why Donors Give.* Washington, DC: The Center for Responsive Politics.

Grossberg, L. 1992. *We Gotta Get Out of This Place: Popular Conservatism and Postmodern Culture.* New York: Routledge.

Habermas, J. 1974. "The Public Sphere: An Encyclopedia Article (1964)." *New German Critique* 1 (Fall): 49–55.

———. 1989. *The Structural Transformation of the Public Sphere: An Inquiry Into a Category of Bourgeois Society.* Cambridge: MIT Press.

Hall, S. 1980. "Encoding/Decoding." In *Culture, Media, Language.* Edited by S. Hall et al. London: Hutchinson.

———. 1982. "The Rediscovery of Ideology: Return of the Repressed in Media Studies." In *Culture, Society, and the Media.* Edited by M. Gurevitch et al. London: Methuen.

———. 1986. "Popular Culture and the State." In *Popular Culture and Social Relations.* Edited by T. Bennett, C. Mercer, and J. Woollacott. Milton Keynes, UK: Open University Press.

———. 1988. *The Hard Road to Renewal.* London: Verso.

———. 1994. "Reflections Upon the Encoding/Decoding Model: An Interview with Stuart Hall." In *Reading, Viewing, Listening,* Edited by J. Cruz and J. Lewis, 253–74. Boulder: Westview.

———. 1996. "The Problem of Ideology: Marxism Without Guarantees." In *Stuart Hall, Critical Developments in Cultural Studies.* Edited by D. Morley and K-H Chen. London: Routledge.

———. Hall, S. 1996. "On Postmodernism and Articulation: An Interview." In *Stuart Hall, Critical Developments in Cultural Studies.* Edited by D. Morley and K-H Chen. London: Routledge.

Hall, S. and T. Jefferson, eds. 1978. *Resistance Through Rituals.* London: Hutchinson.

Hall, S., C. Critcher, T. Jefferson, J. Clarke, and B. Roberts. 1978. *Policing the Crisis: Mugging, the State, and Law and Order.* London: Macmillan.

Hallin, D. and T. Gitlin. 1994. "The Gulf War as Popular Culture and Television Drama." In *Taken by Storm: The Media Public Opinion and U.S. Foreign Policy in the Gulf War.* Edited by W. Bennett and D. Paletz. Chicago: University of Chicago Press

Hamill, R. and M. Lodge. 1986. "Cognitive Consequences of Political Sophistication." In *Political Cognition.* Edited by R. Lau and D. Sears. Hillsdale, NJ: Erlbaum.

Harrigan, J. 1993. *Empty Dreams, Empty Pockets: Class and Bias in American Politics.* New York: Macmillan.

Head, S. and C. Sterling. 1990. *Broadcasting in America,* 6th ed. Boston: Houghton Mifflin.

Hebdige, D. 1979. *Subculture: The Meaning of Style.* London: Methuen.

Heide, M. 1995. *Television, Culture, and Women's Lives: Thirtysomething and the Contradictions of Gender.* Philadelphia: University of Pennsylvania Press.

Heith, D. J. 1998. "Staffing the White House Public Opinion Apparatus." *Public Opinion Quarterly,* 62 (2): 165–190.

Hellman, C. 1997. *Last of the Big Time Spenders.* Washington, DC: Center for Defense Information.

Hellinger, D. and D. Judd. 1991. *The Democratic Façade.* Pacific Grove, CA: Brooks/Cole.

Herbst, S. 1993a. *Numbered Voices.* Chicago: University of Chicago Press.

——. 1993b. "The Meaning of Public Opinion." *Media, Culture, and Society* 15 (3): 437–454.

——. 1998. *Reading Public Opinion.* Chicago: University of Chicago Press.

Herman, E. 1994. "David Broder and the Limits of Mainstream Liberalism." *Extra* (December).

——. 1999. *The Myth of the Liberal Media.* New York: Peter Lang.

Herman, E. and N. Chomsky. 1988. *The Manufacture of Consent.* New York: Pantheon.

Hertsgaard, M. 1989. *On Bended Knee: The Press and the Reagan Presidency.* New York: Farrar, Straus and Giroux.

Hirsch, P. M. 1980. "The 'Scary World' of the Non-Viewer and Other Anomalies— A Re-Analysis of Gerbner et al.'s Findings in Cultivation Analysis, Part 1." *Communication Research* 7 (4): 403–456.

Hobson, D. 1980. "Housewives and the Mass Media." In *Culture, Media, Language.* Edited by S. Hall et al. London: Hutchinson.

——. 1982. *Crossroads: The Drama of a Soap Opera.* London: Methuen.

Hodge, B. and D. Tripp. 1986. *Children and Television.* Cambridge: Polity Press.

Hovland, C. 1959. "Reconciling Conflicting Results Derived from Experimental and Survey Studies of Attitude Change." *The American Psychologist* 14:8–17.

Hume, D. 1963. *Essays Moral, Political, and Literary.* London: Oxford University Press.

Huntemann, N. 1999. "Corporate Interference: The Commercialization and Concentration of Radio Post the 1996 Telecommunications Act." Paper delivered at 49th annual conference of the International Communication Association, San Francisco, May, 1999.

Iyengar, S. 1991. *Is Anyone Responsible?* Chicago: University of Chicago Press.

Iyengar, S., M. Peters, and D. Kinder. 1982. "Demonstrations of the 'Not-So-Minimal' Consequences of Television News Programs." *American Political Science Review* 81:815–32.

Iyengar, S and D. Kinder. 1987. *News That Matters.* Chicago: University of Chicago Press.

Jackson, J. 1996. "Sex, Polls and Campaign Strategy: How the Press Missed the Issues of the 1992 Election." In *The Fair Reader: A Review of Press and Politics.* Edited by J. Jackson, and J. Naureckas. Boulder: Westview.

Jackson, J. and J. Naureckas. 1996. "Crime Contradictions." In *The FAIR Reader: An Extra Review of Press and Politics.* Edited by J. Naureckas and J. Jackson. Boulder: Westview.

Jenkins, H. 1992. *Textual Poachers: Television Fans and Participatory Culture.* New York: Routledge.

———. 1995. "Out of the Closet and Into the Universe." In *Science Fiction Audiences.* Edited by J. Tulloch and H. Jenkins. London: Routledge.

Jensen, K. B. 1987a. "Qualitative Audience Research: Toward an Integrative Approach to Reception." *Critical Studies in Mass Communication* 4:8–17.

———. 1987b. "News as Ideology: Economic Statistics and Political Ritual in Television Network News." *Journal of Communication* (Winter): 8–27.

Jhally, S. and J. Lewis. 1992. *Enlightened Racism: The Cosby Show, Audiences, and the Myth of the American Dream.* Boulder: Westview.

Kellner, D. 1990. *Television and the Crisis of Democracy.* Boulder: Westview.

———. 1992. *The Persian Gulf TV War.* Boulder: Westview.

———. 1995. *Media Culture: Cultural Studies, Identity, and Politics Between the Modern and the Postmodern.* Boulder: Westview.

Kennamer, J. 1992. *Public Opinion, the Press, and Public Policy.* Westport, NY: Praeger.

King, E. and M. Schudson. 1995. "The Press and the Illusion of Public Opinion." In *Public Opinion and the Communication of Consent.* Edited by C. Salmon and T. Glasser. New York: Guilford Press.

Knight, K. and R. Erikson. 1997. "Ideology in the 1990s." In *Understanding Public Opinion.* Edited by B. Narrander and C. Wilcox. Washington DC: CQ Press.

Kritzer, H. 1996. "The Data Puzzle: The Nature of Interpretation in Quantitative Research." *American Journal of Political Science* 40 (1): 1–32.

Kronsnik, J. 1989. "Question Wording and Reports of Survey Results: The Case of Louis Harris and Associates and Aetna Life and Casualty." *Public Opinion Quaterly* 53 (spring): 107–13.

Kubey, R., R. Larson, and M. Csikszentmihalyi. 1996. "Experience Sampling Method Applications to Communication Research." *Journal of Communication* 46 (2): 99–120.

Kuklinski, J. and P. Quirk. 1997. "Political Facts and Public Opinion." Paper presented at *The Future of Fact* conference, University of Philadelphia (February).

Laclau, E. and C. Mouffe. 1985. *Hegemony and Socialist Strategy.* London: Verso.

Ladd, E. C. and J. Benson. 1992. "The Growth of News Polls in American Politics." In *Media Polls in American Politics.* Edited by T. E. Mann and G. R. Orren. Washington DC: Brookings Institution.

Lake, C. and P. Callbeck Harper. 1987. *Public Opinion Polling: A Handbook for Public Interest and Citizen Advocacy Groups.* Washington DC: Island Press.

Lasorsa, D. and W. Wanta. 1990. "The Effects of Personal, Interpersonal, and Media Experience of Issue Salience." *Journalism Quarterly* 67:804–13.

Lau, R. and D. Sears. 1986. "Social Cognition and Political Cognition: The Past, the Present, and the Future." In *Political Cognition.* Edited by R. Lau and D. Sears. Hillsdale, NJ: Erlbaum.

Lavrakas, P., M. Traugott, P Miller, eds. 1995. *Presidential Polls and the News Media.* Boulder: Westview.

Lazarsfeld, P., B. Berelson, and H. Gaudet. 1944. *The People's Choice.* New York: Columbia University Press.

Lazarsfeld, P. and E. Katz. 1955. *Personal Influence.* Glencoe, IL: Free Press.

Lee, M. and N. Solomon. 1990. *Unreliable Sources.* New York: Lyle Stuart.

Lemert, J. 1981. *Does Mass Communication Change Public Opinion After All?* Chicago: Nelson-Hall.

Lemert, J. 1992. "Effective Public Opinion."In *Public Opinion, the Press, and Public Policy.* Edited by J. Kennamer. Westport, NY: Praeger.

Lenart, S. 1994. *Shaping Political Attitudes: The Impact of Interpersonal Communication and Mass Media.* Thousand Oaks, CA: Sage.

Lewis, J. 1991. *The Ideological Octopus: Explorations Into the Television Audience.* New York: Routledge.

——. 1996. "What Counts in Cultural Studies." *Media, Culture, and Society* (Winter): 83–98.

Lewis, J., M. Morgan, and S. Jhally. 1991. *The Gulf War: A Study of the Media, Public Knowledge, and Public Opinion.* Center for the Study of Communication, University of Massachusetts, Amherst.

Lewis, J. and M. Morgan. 1996. "Images/Issues/Impact: The 1992 Presidential Election." In *The FAIR Reader: An Extra Review of Press and Politics.* Edited by J. Naureckas and J. Jackson. Boulder: Westview.

Lewis, J., M. Morgan, and Jhally. 1998. "Polling Clinton's Appeal." *The Nation*, March 9th, 1998.

Lewis, J., M. Morgan, and A. Ruddock. 1992. *Images/Issues/Impact: The Media and Campaign '92*. Center for the Study of Communication, University of Massachusetts, Amherst.

Lipari, L. 1996. "Rituals and Identification: A Critical Discourse Analysis of Public Opinion Polls." Ph.D dissertation, Stanford University.

Lippmann, W. 1922. *Public Opinion*. New York: Macmillan.

——. 1925. *The Phantom Public*. New York: Harcourt, Brace.

Lodge, M and R. Hamill. 1986. "A Partisan Schema for Political Information Processing." *American Political Science Review* 80 (5): 5–19.

MacKuen, M. 1981. "Social Communication and the Mass Policy Agenda." In *More Than News: Media Power in Public Affairs*. Edited by M. MacKuen and S. L. Coombs. Thousand Oaks, CA: Sage.

Manheim, J. 1994. "Managing Kuwait's Image During the Gulf Conflict." In *Taken by Storm: The Media, Public Opinion and U.S. Foreign Policy in the Gulf War*. Edited by W. Bennett and D. Paletz. Chicago: University of Chicago Press.

Mann, T. E. and G. R. Orren. 1992. *Media Polls in American Politics*. Washington DC: Brookings Institution.

Margolis, M. and G. Mauser. 1989. *Manipulating Public Opinion*. Pacific Grove, CA: Brooks/Cole.

Mayer, W. G. 1992. *The Changing American Mind*. Ann Arbor: University of Michigan Press.

McChesney, R. 1996. "Is There Any Hope For Cultural Studies?" *Monthly Review* 46 (10): 1–18.

——. 1997. *Corporate Media and the Threat to Democracy*. New York: Seven Stories Press.

McCombs, M. 1981. "The Agenda-Setting Approach." In *Handbook of Political Communication*. Edited by Nimmo, D. and Saunders, K. Thousand Oaks, CA: Sage.

McCombs, M., L. Danielian, and W. Wanta. 1995. "Issues in the News and the Public Agenda." In *Public Opinion and the Communication of Consent*. Edited by C. Salmon and T. Glasser. New York: Guilford Press.

McCombs, M. E. and D. Shaw. 1972. "The Agenda-Setting Function of the Mass Media." *Public Opinion Quarterly* 36:137–65.

McKinley, E. G. 1997. *Beverley Hills 90210: Television, Gender, and Identity*. Philadelphia: University of Pennsylvania Press.

McRobbie, A. 1978. "Working Class Girls and the Culture of Femininity." In *Women Take Issue*. Edited by L. Bland et al, 96–108. London: Hutchinson.

Miller, P. 1995. "The Industry of Public Opinion." In *Public Opinion and the Communication of Consent*. Edited by C. Salmon and T. Glasser. New York: Guilford Press.

Miller, T. 1993. *The Well-Tempered Self: Citizenship, Culture, and the Postmodern Subject*. Baltimore: Johns Hopkins University Press.

Monroe, A. 1975. *Public Opinion in America*. New York: Dodd, Mead.

Morgan, M. 1989. "Television and Democracy." In *Cultural Politics in Contemporary America*. Edited by I. Angus and S. Jhally. New York: Routledge.

Morgan, M., J. Lewis, and S. Jhally. 1992. "More Viewing, Less Knowledge." In *Triumph of the Image: The Media's War in the Persian Gulf—A Global Perspective*. Edited by H. Mowlana, G. Gerbner, and H. Schiller. Boulder: Westview.

Morley, D. 1980. *The Nationwide Audience*. London: British Film Institute.

——. 1986. *Family Television*. London: Comedia.

——. 1992. *Television, Audiences, and Cultural Studies*. London: Routledge.

Morris, D. 1997. *Behind the Oval Office—Winning the Presidency in the Nineties*. New York: Random House.

Mowlana, H., G. Gerbner, and H. Schiller. 1992. *Triumph of the Image: The Media's War in the Persian Gulf—A Global Perspective*. Boulder: Westview.

Mueller, J. 1994. *Policy and Opinion in the Gulf War*. Chicago: University of Chicago Press.

Murdock, G. and P. Golding. 1973. "For a Political Economy of Mass Communications." *Socialist Register*. Edited by R. Milliband and J. Saville. London: Merlin.

Nadeau, R. and R. G. Niemi. 1995. "Educated Guesses: The Process of Answering Factual Knowledge Questions in Surveys." *Public Opinion Quarterly* 59 (3): 323–346.

Naureckas, J. 1996a. "Crossfire: Still Missing a Space on the Left." *Extra* (April).

——. 1996b. "Media on the March: Journalism in the Gulf" and "Gulf War Coverage: The Worst Censorship Was at Home." In *The FAIR Reader: An Extra Review of Press and Politics*. Edited by J. Naureckas and J. Jackson. Boulder: Westview.

Naureckas, J. and J. Jackson. 1996. *The FAIR Reader: An Extra Review of Press and Politics*. Boulder: Westview.

Neuman, W. R. 1986. *The Paradox of Mass Politics*. Cambridge: Harvard University Press.

Neuman, W. R., M. R. Just, and A. N. Crigler. 1992. *Common Knowledge*. Chicago: University of Chicago Press.

Nie, N., J. Junn, and K. Stehlik-Barry. 1996. *Education and Democratic Citizenship in America*. Chicago: University of Chicago Press.

Niemi, R.G., J. Mueller, and T. W. Smith. 1989. *Trends in Public Opinion*. New York: Greenwood Press

Noelle-Neumann, E. 1993. *The Spiral of Silence*. Chicago: University of Chicago Press.

Oskamp, S. 1977. *Attitudes and Opinions*. Edglewood Cliffs, NJ: Prentice-Hall.

Ouellette, L. 1998. "A Chance for Better Television—PBS and the Politics of Ideals, 1967–1973." Ph.D disseration, University of Massachusetts, Amherst.

———. 1999. "TV Viewing as Good Citizenship?: Political Rationality, Enlightened Democracy, and PBS." *Cultural Studies* 13 (1): 62–90.

Page, B. 1996. *Who Deliberates? Mass Media in Modern Democracy.* Chicago: University of Chicago Press.

Page, B. and R. Shapiro. 1983. "Effects of Public Opinion on Policy." *American Political Science Review* 77:175–90.

———. 1992. *The Rational Public.* Chicago: University of Chicago Press.

Paletz, D. 1994. "Just Deserts?" In *Taken by Storm: The Media Public Opinion and U.S. Foreign Policy in the Gulf War.* Edited by W. Bennett and D. Paletz. Chicago: University of Chicago Press.

Paletz, D. and R. Entman. 1981. *Media Power Politics.* New York: Free Press.

Parry, R. 1992. *Fooling America.* New York: Morrow.

Patterson, T. 1980. *The Mass Media Election.* New York: Praeger.

Peters, J. D. 1995. "Historical Tensions in the Concept of Public Opinion." In *Public Opinion and the Communication of Consent.* Edited by C. Salmon and T. Glasser. New York: Guilford Press.

Philo, G. 1990. *Seeing and Believing: The Influence of Television.* London: Routledge.

Popkin, S. 1991. *The Reasoning Voter: Communication and Persuasion in Presidential Campaigns.* Chicago: University of Chicago Press.

Press, A. 1991. *Women Watching Television.* Philadelphia: University of Pennsylvania Press

Press, A. and E. Cole. 1991. *Speaking of Abortion: Television and Authority in the Lives of Women.* Chicago: University of Chicago Press.

———. 1999. *Speaking of Abortion: Television and Authority in the Lives of Women.* Chicago: University of Chicago Press.

Price, V. and E. Czilli. 1996. "Modeling Patterns of News Recognition and Recall." *Journal of Communication* 46 (2): 55–78.

Qualter, T. 1989. "The Role of the Mass Media in Limiting the Public Agenda." In *Manipulating Public Opinion.* Edited by M. Margolis and G. Mauser. Pacific Grove, CA: Brooks/Cole.

Radway, J. 1984. *Reading the Romance.* Chapel Hill: University of North Carolina Press.

———. 1986. "Identifying Ideological Seams: Mass Culture, Analytical Method, and Political Practice." *Communication* 9:93–121.

Reeves, J. and R. Campbell. 1994. *Cracked Coverage: Television News, The Anti-Cocaine Crusade, and the Reagan Legacy.* Durham, NC: Duke University Press.

Robinson, J. and M. Levy. 1996. "News Media Use and the Informed Public: A 1990s Update." *Journal of Communication* 46 (2): 129–135.

Rousseau, J-J. 1968. *The Social Contract.* London: Penguin.

Ruddock, A. 1998. "Doing It by Numbers." *Critical Arts* 12 (1–2): 115–37.

Saad, L. 1999. *No Public Outcry For Campaign Finance Reform.* Princeton, NJ: Gallup.

Said, E. 1978. *Orientalism*. New York: Pantheon.

Salmon, C. and T. Glasser. 1995. "The Politics of Polling and the Limits of Consent." In Salmon, C. and T. Glasser, eds. *Public Opinion and the Communication of Consent*. New York: Guilford Press.

Schell, J. 1999. "A Master of All He Surveys." *The Nation*, June 21, 25–30.

Schiller, H. 1989. *Culture, Inc.: The Corporate Takeover of Public Expression*. New York: Oxford University Press.

Schoenbach, K. and L. Becker. 1995. "Origins and Consequences of Mediated Public Opinion." In *Public Opinion and the Communication of Consent*. Edited by C. Salmon and T. Glasser. New York: Guilford Press.

Schulz, W. 1978. "Mass Media and the Image of Political Reality." Paper presented at the IAMCR Congress, Warsaw.

Schuman, H. and S. Presser. 1981. *Questions and Answers in Attitude Surveys*. New York: Wiley.

Shaheen, J. 1984. *The TV Arab*. Bowling Green, KY: Bowling Green University Press.

Shuldiner, A. and T. Raymond. 1998. *Who's in the Lobby? A Profile of Washington's Influence Industry*. Washington, DC: The Center for Responsive Politics.

Signorielli, N. and M. Morgan. 1990. *Cultivation Analysis*. Thousand Oaks, CA: Sage.

Siune, K. and F. G. Kline. 1975. "Communication, Mass Political Behavior, and Mass Society." In *Political Communication: Issues and Strategies for Research*. Edited by S. Chaffee. Thousand Oaks, CA: Sage.

Slack, J. 1996. "The Theory and Method of Articulation in Cultural Studies." In *Stuart Hall: Critical Dialogues in Cultural Studies*. Edited by D. Morley et al, 112–27. London: Routledge.

Smith, T. 1987. "That Which We Call Welfare by Any Other Name Would Smell Sweeter: An Analysis of the Impact of Question Wording on Response Patterns." *Public Opinion Quarterly*. 57 (75–84).

Smith, T. W. 1993. "Is There Real Opinion Change?" *GSS Social Change Report* 36. National Opinion Research Center, University of Chicago.

Sniderman, P., R. Brody, and P. Tetlock. 1991. *Reasoning and Choice: Explorations in Political Psychology*. New York: Cambridge University Press.

Streeter, T. 1996. *Selling the Air*. Chicago: University of Chicago Press.

Stromer-Galley, J. and E. Schiappa. 1998. "The Argumentative Burdens of Audience Conjectures: Audience Research in Popular Culture Criticism." *Communiation Theory* 81:27–62.

Sussman, B. 1986. "Do Blacks Approve of Reagan? It Depends on Who's Asking." *Washington Post* (weekly edition), February 10.

———. 1988. *What Americans Really Think and Why Our Politicians Pay No Attention*. New York: Pantheon.

Taylor, S. and S. Fiske. 1978. "Salience, Attention, and Attribution: Top of the Head Phenomena." In *Advances in Social Psychology*. Edited by L. Berkowitz. New York: Academic Press.

Taylor-Gooby, P. 1995. "Comfortable, Marginal, and Excluded: Who Should Pay Higher Taxes for a Better Welfare State?" In *British Social Attitudes*. Aldershot, Eng.: Dartmouth.

Thompson, E. P. 1968. *The Making of the English Working Classes*. London: Penguin Books.

Tocqueville, A. de 1969. *Democracy in America*. Garden City, NY: Anchor Books.

Traugott, M. and P. Lavrakas. 1995. "The Media's Use of Election Polls: A Synthesis and Recommendations for 1996 and Beyond." In *Presidential Polls and the News Media*. Edited by P. Lavrakas, M. Traugott, and P. Miller. Boulder: Westview.

Traugott, M. and P. Lavrakas. 1996. *The Voter's Guide to Election Polls*. Chatham, NJ: Chatham House.

Tuchman, G. 1978. *Making News*. New York: Free Press.

Tulloch, J. and H. Jenkins. 1995. *Science Fiction Audiences*. London: Routledge.

Verba, S. 1996. "The Citizen as Respondent: Sample Surveys and American Democracy." *American Political Science Review* 90 (1).

Weaver, R. K., R. Shapiro, and L. R. Jacobs. 1995. "Trends: Welfare." *Public Opinion Quarterly* 59 (4).

Wilcox, C., J. Ferrara, and D. Allsop. 1991. "Before the Rally: The Dynamics of Attitudes Toward the Gulf Crisis Before the War." Paper presented at the American Political Science Association, Washington D.C.

Williams, L. and N. Wollman. 1996. "Pundits Had It Wrong: The Voters Did Not Embrace Moderation." *Roll Call*, December 12, 1996.

Williams, R. 1963. *Culture and Society*. New York: Columbia University Press.

Willis, P. 1977. *Learning to Labour*. London: Saxon House, 52–166.

Wilson, T. and S. Hodges. 1991. "Attitudes as Temporary Constructions." In *The Construction of Social Judgement*. Edited by A. Tesser and L. Martin. Hillsdale, NJ: Erlbaum.

Wittkopf, E. 1990. *Faces of Internationalism: Public Opinion and American Foreign Policy*. Durham, NC: Duke University Press.

Zaller, J. R. 1992. *The Nature and Origins of Mass Opinion*. Cambridge: Cambridge University Press.

——. 1994. "Elite Leadership of Mass Opinion." *Taken by Storm: The Media Public Opinion and U.S. Foreign Policy in the Gulf War*. Edited by W. Bennett and D. Paletz. Chicago: University of Chicago Press.

Zhao, X and S. Chaffee. 1995. "Campaign Advertisements Versus Television News as Sources of Political Issue Information." *Public Opinion Quarterly* 59:41–65.

Zhu, J-H. 1991. "Media Agenda-Setting and the Priming Effects in the Midst of the Federal Budget Crisis and the Persian Gulf Crisis." Unpublished paper.

INDEX